Burke

Just Around the Corner

"Come along. We're going to the Trans-Lux to hiss Roosevelt."

Drawing by Peter Arno: copyright © 1936, 1964 The New Yorker Magazine, Inc.

Robert Bendiner

JUST
AROUND
THE CORNER

A Highly Selective History
of the Thirties

E. P. DUTTON / New York

Grateful acknowledgment is extended to the following for permission to reprint material:
Lines from *A Time to Remember*, by Leane Zugsmith, published by Random House, Inc., reprinted by permission of the author. Lines from *My First Days in the White House*, by Huey Long, reprinted by permission of Stackpole Books. Lines from "Café Society," *Fortune*, December 1937, courtesy of *Fortune* magazine. Lines from "Depression Debutante," by Elinor P. R. Ferguson, the *Saturday Evening Post*, November 12, 1932, reprinted by permission of the Curtis Publishing Company. Lines from *The Age of Suspicion*, by James A. Wechsler, copyright 1953 by James A. Wechsler, reprinted by permission of Random House, Inc. Father Divine's speech, quoted by Langston Hughes in the New York *Post*, reprinted by permission of Langston Hughes. Lines from *Treadmill to Oblivion*, copyright 1954 by Fred Allen, reprinted with permission of Atlantic–Little, Brown and Company, Publishers. Lines from the play *Power*, by Arthur Arent, quoted in *Federal Theatre Plays*, edited by Pierre de Rohan, copyright 1938 by Random House, Inc., reprinted by permission of the publisher. Many of the quotations used throughout the cartoon section were taken from *Literary Digest*. And, for the use of cartoons, the following: Baltimore *Sun*, Chicago *Tribune*, Columbus *Dispatch*, Detroit *News*, Kansas City *Star*, Louisville *Courier-Journal*, Memphis *Commercial Appeal*, New York *Daily News*, "New York's Picture Newspaper," New York *World Journal Tribune*, Pittsburgh *Post-Gazette*, Richmond *Times-Dispatch*, St. Louis *Post-Dispatch*, Washington *Daily News*, and *Forbes* magazine.

Published in the United States by E. P. Dutton, a division of NAL Penguin Inc., 2 Park Avenue, New York, N.Y. 10016.

Published simultaneously in Canada by Fitzhenry & Whiteside Limited, Toronto

Library of Congress Catalog Card Number: 86-71611

ISBN: 0-525-48273-3

COBE

10 9 8 7 6 5 4 3 2 1

For Peggy

ABOUT THE AUTHOR

"I spent my twenties in the Thirties," says Robert Bendiner, "moving with and without my family six times in seven years in search of progressively less luxurious quarters." Serving his journalistic apprenticeship as switchboard operator and errand boy at the *World Tomorrow*, "a small but highly literate periodical committed to peace, Christian ethics, and limited circulation," he moved on in fast succession to several writing jobs in Washington, with occasional access to President Roosevelt's press conferences and, at the height of the Popular Front period, a nine months' strange interlude on the editorial staff of the *New Masses*, "embarked on in gullibility and immediately colored by wild doubts and a rising sense of absurdity."

After a short fling at free-lancing, he moved on to the "rational, congenial, and heady atmosphere of *The Nation*," where he wound up the decade as managing editor and political reporter. "It was principally from this elevation that I saw the Thirties—in all their nonsense, idealism, challenge, and disappointment."

Mr. Bendiner remained with *The Nation* in the Forties, except for two years in the Army from which he emerged as a buck sergeant. In 1950 he left *The Nation* "for complex reasons" to embark on a free-lance career and has written extensively for various magazines, among them *Harper's*, *Saturday Evening Post*, *McCall's*, *Life*, *Look*, *Redbook*, and *Horizon*. He has been a contributing editor to the *Reporter* and American correspondent for the *New Statesman* (London), with time out occasionally to work on books (among others, *White House Fever*, *Obstacle Course on Capitol Hill*, and *The Fall of the Wild and the Rise of the Zoo*) and to accept the Franklin Award for distinguished magazine reporting and a Guggenheim Fellowship. From 1969 through 1977 he was a Member of the Editorial Board of *The New York Times*.

Just Around the Corner was first published in 1967.

Contents

Illustrations

Cartoons and other illustrations: Pages 7-14, 61-68, 159-166

PHOTOGRAPHS

Following page 80:

Depression: Bank run; The Bowery; Hooverville
Hunger: "Lady Bountiful"; "Mr. Zero"; Appleseller; Breadline
Drought: Oklahoma dust storm; Tenant farmers
The Corner: President Hoover and President-elect Roosevelt;
    Miniature golf course
Cooperation: Eleanor Roosevelt; General Hugh S. Johnson
Cabinet: Secretary of Labor Frances Perkins; Secretary of the
    Treasury William H. "Wee Willie" Woodin; Secretary of the
    Interior Harold Ickes, Secretary of Agriculture Henry Wal-
    lace with F.D.R.
Personalities: Al Smith; John L. Lewis; Vice President and Mrs.
    John Nance Garner; Jesse Jones, Will Rogers

Following page 112:

Marx: May Day Parade; Harpo, Zeppo, Chico, and Groucho
Relaxation: Harry Hopkins; Mae West

More Personalities: W. C. Fields with Baby Leroy; Fred Allen;
  Fiorello H. La Guardia
Class Structure: Vincent Astor; Norman Thomas
Panaceas: Father Coughlin; Huey Long; William Lemke
Evangelists: Dr. Frank Buchman; Father Divine
Utopias: Technocracy, Inc.'s motor corps; Dr. Francis E. Town-
  send
Radio Stars: *Information Please:* John Kieran, Clifton Fadiman,
  and Franklin P. Adams; F.D.R.'s fireside chat

Following page 208:

Candidate: Alfred M. Landon; Landon with sunflower
Labor at Play: *Pins and Needles;* Sitdown strike
Hits: *Tobacco Road; The Swing Mikado*
Crusaders: Prohibitionists; Veterans of Lincoln Brigade
Race: Joe Louis defeating Max Schmeling; One of the seven
  Scottsboro boys awaiting trial
Left: Workers' Bookshop; May Day Parade
Right: German-American Bund rally
Invaders: Armed citizen after Orson Welles' broadcast; Adolf
  Hitler, Hermann Goering, Benito Mussolini, signing of
  Munich Pact; Joseph Stalin and Joachim Von Ribbentrop
  after Nazi-Soviet treaty

A Necessary Foreword

My father, a man who was clearly ahead of his time, went bankrupt in 1922. The fault was not his but that of a precociously floundering economy in a small town of what was later to flower into Appalachia. To no good purpose we migrated to New York, where he died two years later, leaving a large family and small resources. So it was that while the United States in general was enjoying the reckless boom of the Twenties, we were busily gaining experience in the ways of genteel poverty. When the rest of the country caught up with us, after 1929, we were inured to those ways, and there was, all in all, less about the Depression to depress us than might have been the case if we had come to that watershed in the nation's history still hattening on the middle-class comforts we once knew.

I introduce this brief autobiographical note at the start only to make the possibly simple-minded point that personal circumstances color, if indeed they do not determine, attitudes toward a passing period in history. It has always seemed to me fatuous to fix a single label on a whole decade —as though the Nineties were gay for immigrant ladies in the garment sweatshops of Manhattan or the Twenties stood for hot jazz in the mind of Calvin Coolidge. When I write about the Thirties, then, I write about the decade as at the time it appeared to *me*, brash and in my twenties, and not as it must have seemed, say, to an aging gentleman of Westchester who had suddenly had to switch callings from building contractor to demonstrator of potato parers in an empty Sixth Avenue shop window, or as it seemed to an Iowa farmer moved to take part in pulling a judge off the bench with a halter for persistently foreclosing on local mortgages, or to the judge for that matter, or to one of John Steinbeck's Okies, or even to a millionaire constrained to ride the *Leviathan* first class instead of decently sailing to Europe on his own yacht.

Yet I do not intend to offer autobiography either, feeling that such indulgence should be reserved for strenuously honest people like St. Augustine or strenuously egocentric ones like Rousseau. I intended merely to describe the Thirties as viewed from the particular, even peculiar, vantage points that I held, relegating necessary or illuminating bits of personal history to asides or footnotes, where perspective tells me they belong.

As for the vantage points, let them quickly be stated. The year 1930 found me at twenty, with five years of odd-job work behind me and as many years of education by night, serving my journalistic apprenticeship on the *World Tomorrow*, a small but highly literate periodical committed to the principles of peace, Christian social ethics, and limited circulation. Recently promoted from switchboard operator and errand boy, I doubled at the moment as subscription manager and eager acolyte in the editorial mysteries, innocently unawed to be learning the trade by manhandling the copy of staff writers on the brink of national fame—notably Paul Douglas, then a professor of economics at the University of Chicago, and Reinhold Niebuhr, who had just given up a pastorate of automobile workers in Detroit to adorn the faculty of Union Theological Seminary.

As the decade wore on and jobs, grown scarce, slipped quickly underfoot, I moved on in fast succession to a chain of news periodicals for school use, a Washington editorial background service for newspapers, which allowed me once or twice to attend President Roosevelt's press conferences in the Oval Room of the White House, and, at the height of the Popular Front period, a nine months' stint on the editorial staff of the *New Masses*, a strange interlude embarked on in gullibility and immediately colored by wild doubts and a rising sense of absurdity, yet instructive all the same in the curious ways of the Left.

From this knoll I moved on, after a short fling at freelancing, to the rational, congenial, and heady atmosphere of *The Nation*, where the range of opinion was refreshingly wide. I was lucky enough to wind up the decade as managing editor and political reporter, with the country for my beat—or as much of it as a tight expense budget would allow me to traverse—and easy access to governors, senators, mayors, presidential candidates, and even trade-union leaders, in addition to the cream of Europe's social democracy as it streamed into exile. It was principally from this elevation that I saw the Thirties—in all their nonsense, idealism, challenge, and disappointment.

I did not really see the Thirties, of course, but only aspects of them, and these sketches will accordingly deal only with aspects. They will not attempt to tell you all about the decade, in the manner of a history or a sociologist's treatise, but rather what it looked like to a reasonably alert individual, with a prime but not exclusive interest in politics, who happened to be in a position to cover a fair amount of ground and who had to ask a lot of questions.

Even to me, as a single individual, the decade was a mixed bag. Remarkably like Dickens' paradoxical era, "It was the best of times, it was the worst of times . . . it was the spring of hope, it was the winter of despair, we had everything before us, we had nothing before us, we were all going direct to Heaven, we were all going direct the other way . . ." But—and this is the crux of these introductory remarks—so much has been written of the wintry despair of the Thirties, of lives stunted and people demoralized, that its springtime hopefulness has been underplayed. Admittedly one would be more fatuous than Pollyanna herself to talk about the good old days when fifteen million people were unemployed, but there is no harm—indeed there is some use—in recalling the fact that in those same years much of the dross of American life was stripped away, truths were faced with more candor than is normally in evidence, and America came closer to knowing its aims and its real worth than at any time before or since.

Just Around the Corner

The Gloomy Depression
of Herbert Hoover

1

In December of 1932 Calvin Coolidge observed to
a reporter for the New York *Sun*, which was still wistfully
following his fading career: "We are in a new era to which I
do not belong, and it would not be possible for me to adjust
myself to it. . . . When I read of the newfangled things that
are so popular now I realize that my time in public affairs is
past."

One of the newfangled things the former President may
have had in mind was the Depression, which was popular in
the sense that the common cold is popular—that is to say, it
was widespread. But he must have sensed that the novelty of
the decade had barely come into view, for, departing this
world the following month, he seemed almost willfully to
have timed his exit between the election of Franklin D.
Roosevelt and Inauguration Day. Thus he saw neither Blue
Eagles on parade nor Tobacco Roads lit up by publicly
owned electricity; he could hardly have dreamed of such
innovations as monthly Treasury checks to the old and the
jobless, the doing-in of surplus little pigs, and a Federal
Theatre capable of bringing something called *The Swing
Mikado* to the very hills of his native Vermont.

What he *had* witnessed must have been quite enough,

nevertheless. For in the last months of the Hoover Administration we had come to a time in the history of the Republic
when even solid subscribers to *Business Week* were being
exposed to the view that "there is now no alternative to
chaos save to invoke the ultimate authority of the State,"
and members of the Bond Club could applaud a Republican
speaker's warning that unless the economy righted itself in a
hurry Washington would have to take over private indus-
tries "to an extent that would amaze the most ardent advocates of socialism."

As an ex-President of the United States and President of
the American Antiquarian Society (as far as I know, the
terms were served successively), Coolidge had done his best
to warn the country of the follies that were to come. From
mid-1930 to mid-1931 he had furnished small daily doses of
syndicated wisdom to the morning newspapers—like Will
Rogers' little box in format, though as a rule less quotable at
smart dinner parties. "Our country, our people, our civil and
religious institutions, may not be perfect," went one of his
unarguable reflections, "but they are what we have made
them." Another fresh thought for the day was that "When
Congress passes laws requiring the expenditures of money,
the people will have to pay for it."

Mr. Coolidge thought it would "do no harm" to remember
this sort of thing, but it seemed to do no good either, for
Congress itself had its collective mind elsewhere. Little
more than a month after his death a run-of-the-mill Democrat from Texas could go so far as to ask whether the "ma-
nipulating money barons" had possibly "forgotten the
French Revolution with its guillotine, its Dantons and
Robespierres," adding with a grim flourish that "When the
storm breaks, it will be too late then, and there will be no
cellars in which to hide." And the House, which had no Un-
American Activities Committee at the time, regarded such
talk as perfectly and prosaically American.

Certainly those pre-Roosevelt days of the Thirties, so discouraging to a Coolidge, were far from invigorating for any of us, and the most rampant collector of nostalgia cannot want to see their return. But they did provide the darkness that was to make bright the dawn, when the real story of the Thirties begins. There is hardly a doubt that the brilliance of the Roosevelt day, when it came, was enhanced by the blackness of the Hoover night that preceded it.

For, unlike Coolidge, Herbert Hoover appeared to entertain no notion that *his* time in public affairs might be past. Still in command, he could not have acknowledged such a thought in any case, and if he had, his only recourse would have been to turn over the reins to Vice President Charles Curtis, whose time had indubitably passed some time prior to the Spanish-American War. So it was that an anachronistic air hung low over Washington, accurately, if acidly, caught by H. L. Mencken, himself a receding phenomenon of the Twenties. Mindful of the President's stubborn Toryism and the Vice President's Kaw ancestry, he regularly referred to those heads of state as "Lord Hoover and the Injun."

But even if Hoover had taken bold and creative action in the long years of 1930, '31, and '32, it is doubtful that he would have survived, politically, the catastrophe that had come early in his Presidency and that *Variety* had immortally compressed into the headline "Wall Street Lays an Egg." With his high stiff collar and his higher and stiffer manner, he had no more flair than an assistant funeral usher for putting across radical innovations. (Twenty-five years later I had occasion to interview him for *Collier's* and found him, at eighty-three, acute and rather witty. Either the terrible strain of an unsuccessful Presidency had been too much for him while in office or he was what the educators call a "late bloomer.") As it happened he had no innovations to offer, preferring to persuade the country that it was not badly off, after all, and that if we would just sit tight while certain adjustments were made at the top, things would soon straighten out.

The trouble with this approach was that simply by stepping out of our doorways we could plainly see that the President's minimal view of the crisis was somewhat out of focus. To a New Yorker, as I was by then, the signs of collapse were aggressive. Along the Hudson, below Riverside Drive, I daily passed the tarpaper huts of a Hooverville, where scores of families lived the lives of reluctant gypsies, cooking whatever they had to cook over open fires within sight of passengers on the double-deck Fifth Avenue buses. Dozens of such colonies had sprung up in the city—along the two rivers, in the empty lots of the Bronx, and on the flats of Brooklyn, but not nearly enough to accommodate the swelling army of the jobless and the dispossessed. From time to time people were picked up as vagrants for keeping house, after a fashion, in the shacks abandoned by workmen who had been draining a reservoir in Central Park. Subways were definitely for sleeping, and the papers constantly ran feature stories like the one about the youth who passed three warm, if furtive, days and nights in the bowels of the Roxy Theatre, exposed to four daily shows, starting with an "Early Bird Matinee" and punctuated by crescendos from a blaring pipe organ.

At times it seemed as though half the city was selling objects of token value to the other half. Very bourgeois-looking gentlemen a little gone to seed, some in worn suits that must originally have run to $75, sold well-polished fruit on busy downtown streets, using the crates sometimes as display counters and sometimes, toward the end of the day, as seats, though as such they didn't tilt back like the swivel chairs their owners had known in earlier professional incarnations. After a while people who didn't have to sell fruit on street corners complained of the danger to life and limb from discarded apple cores and tangerine peels, and then business groups like the Fifth Avenue Association got the police to rule the peddlers off the main avenues.

Some of the politically sophisticated jobless peddled copies of the *Unemployed*, a Socialist journal featuring articles by Heywood Broun, Norman Thomas, and other radical stars of the day. Vendors could buy copies for five cents and sell them for ten, thus combining a small assault on the profit system with an equally small profit. In the street windows of vacated shops former lawyers, teachers, and men of business, now become pitchmen, traced with pointer and color charts the beneficent action of patent medicines after leaving the gullet, thus anticipating by several decades this major art of television. Other newcomers to merchandising dealt in toy balloons, candy bars, or sleazy neckties at three for a half dollar. And from time to time I watched a poet hawking his wares in front of the Forty-second Street Library at the special rate of ten verses for fifteen cents. Nobody seemed to buy the product but he usually took in enough in what passed then for literary grants to finance him at the Sixth Avenue Automat.

On another cultural front a common sight was the sidewalk chalk artist. Under some such caption as "Out of Work" he would draw an attractive girl in various hues against a blue or purplish background that merged easily into the grimy pavement. His work done, the artist would sit on a nearby stoop or church step and wait for sympathetic connoisseurs to drop coins on his masterpiece.

Insurance companies, faced with staggering claims resulting from the strains of the business world, drastically reduced the maximum amounts of their policies and suicides were reported at an all-time high. One that occurred in the shaft outside my office window prompted the magazine I then worked for—it was the *World Tomorrow*—to comment on the prevailing need for "an ennobling philosophy" to sus-

tain people "in hours of tragic adversity" and to recommend
for this purpose a combination of socialism and religion. But
the Reverend Norman Vincent Peale disagreed. He did not
think the situation required anything more drastic than one
"good prayer meeting in Wall Street," at which bankers and
corporation executives would freely confess their sins.

Not more than a sixth of those who needed public relief
were getting it because the city, as we were daily informed,
was on the verge of bankrputcy—New York was no exception among the top cities of the country in this respect—and
private charities, the great Hoover hope, naturally found it
harder than ever to raise funds. The President's gracious
wife advised that "If all who just happened not to suffer this
year would just be friendly and neighborly with all those
who just happened to have bad luck, we'll all get along better." But things didn't work out that way.

New York put on a $40-million emergency relief drive,
with the city pledged to give $20 million and the balance to
be raised by private campaigning. Celebrities, led by Al
Smith, kept up a ballyhoo of fund raising, and the newspapers regularly printed the names of individuals and businesses that contributed, along with the respective amounts.
Even speakeasies, illegal and theoretically nonexistent, were
tapped for donations, anonymous of course. Yet, with more
than a million unemployed in the city, some two and a half
million people were in sore trouble. Joining the more tough-
minded experts of the moment, let's say that only a fifth of
these unemployed were reduced to taking direct relief; how
far would the money go? It could give each person in dire
need $20 a month for four months—but in fact it provided
something like $20 a family. Even with the aid of "Poverty
Balls" and other private "benefit" parties—like the greased
pig race arranged by some dear ladies in Newport for the
night before Thanksgiving, winner to take home the pig—it
was soon clear that this was not the way out. As the titanic

VARIETY

PRICE 25¢.

Published Weekly at 154 West 46th St., New York, N. Y., by Variety, Inc. Annual subscription, $10. Single copies, 25 cents.
Entered as second-class matter December 22, 1905, at the Post Office at New York, N. Y., under the act of March 3, 1879.

VOL. XCVII. No. 3   NEW YORK, WEDNESDAY, OCTOBER 30, 1929   88 PAGES

WALL ST. LAYS AN EGG

Going Dumb Is Deadly to Hostess In Her Serious Dance Hall Profesh

A hostess at Roseland has her problems. The paid steppers consider their work a definite profession calling for specialized technique and high-power salesmanship.

Hank on Winchell

Then the Walter Winchells

DROP IN STOCKS ROPES SHOWMEN

Many Weep and Call Off Christmas Orders — Legit Shows Hit

Kidding Kissers in Talkers Burns Up Fans of Screen's Best Lovers

Talker Crashes Olympus

Paris, Oct. 29.

Boys who used to whistle and girls who used to giggle when love scenes were flashed on the screen are in action again. A couple of years ago they began to take the

---

And They Asked for Bread

"It is solely a question of the best method by which hunger and cold shall be prevented. I am willing to pledge myself that, if the time should ever come that the voluntary agencies of the country, together with the local and State governments, are unable to find resources with which to prevent hunger and suffering in my country, I will ask the aid of every resource of the Federal Government, because I would no more see starvation among our countrymen than would any Senator or Congressman."—Herbert Hoover, quoted in *Literary Digest*, Feb. 14, 1931

Macauley, Brooklyn *Eagle*, Feb., 1931

Henry Ford says "the country is far better off to-day than it was a year ago." He may mean that it has fewer dollars and more sense. — Toledo *Blade*, Jan., 1931

[7

"Perhaps what this country needs is a great poem. Something to lift people out of fear and selfishness.

"Every once in a while some one catches words out of the air and gives a nation an inspiration. You remember Kipling's 'Recessional,' and that poem of Markham's, suggested by Millet's painting, 'The Man with the Hoe.' We need something to raise our eyes beyond the immediate horizon.

"A great nation can't go along just watching its feet. The kind of words I imagine needn't be very complicated. I'd like to see something simple enough for a child to put his hand on his chest and spout in school on Fridays.

"I keep looking for it, but I don't see it. Sometimes a great poem can do more than legislation."—Herbert Hoover, quoted in *Saturday Review of Literature*, Oct., 1932

Beggars in cities are said to be making as much as $15,000 a year. Here's another class, we should think, which ought to begin to feel the pinch. — Boston *Herald*, Jan., 1931

What Do You Make of It, Watson

TOO MUCH OIL

TOO MUCH WHEAT

FREE SOUP

TOO MUCH POVERTY

Fitzpatrick, St. Louis *Post-Dispatch*, Jan. 11, 1931

"The *Paris*, on her first Mediterranean Cruises, proposes to take a company of nice people who know best how to defeat winter — who cherish gayety and detest organized whoopee—and who (like most nice people) know how to make each dollar buy its utmost luxury. Old General Depression will not be allowed up the gangplank; these cruises are planned to make Time (which all the economists say is the cure) really *go to work for you!* French Line, 19 State Street, New York, or any authorized agent."—From a French Line ad, *Literary Digest*, Nov. 21, 1931

8]

The Lost Spirit

McCutcheon, May, 1931,
Copyright, 1931 by the Chicago *Tribune*

How's <u>Your</u> Stomach Mr. Brisbane?

Clipped from L. A. Examiner, Oct. 10th—"First meal in 17 days ends Malcom Swenson, 55 years old and jobless, to hospital. Yesterday morning he ate a hearty breakfast of ham and eggs, the first in 17 days, but it proved to be more than his undernourished body could stand, and he collapsed in the restaurant at 4108 S. Alameda St. Swenson worked a short time yesterday, his first job in months, and earned enough money to pay for the breakfast, according to police officers."

Mr. Hearst's newspapers are not in favor of unemployment insurance. If Malcolm Swenson received unemployment insurance his starved body would not collapse. But then where would our patriotic, flag waving Arthur Brisbane get his "hot news" for the Examiner? We don't wish Mr. Brisbane and Mr. Hearst any harm, but if they collapse from starvation before more of us jobless workers do, would THAT be "hot news"?

The Hunger Fighter, Oct. 15, 1932

13 Suicides in 24 Hours In L. A.

Thirteen suicides in 24 hours were reported recently in the newspapers, according to the records of Coroner Frank A. Nance.

Typical of the thousands who are killing themselves in the face of the misery and starvation brought on by the capitalist crisis, the suicides included not only jobless workers but also members of the middle class.

The Hunger Fighter, Oct. 15, 1932

THE
HUNGER FIGHTEI

OFFICIAL ORGAN OF THE UNEMPLOYED COUNCIL
ANGELES COUNTY & THE WORKERS EX-SERVICEMEN'S L

VOL. 1. — No. I.   LOS ANGELES, CAL., OCTOBER 15, 1932   PRICE—FOUR

BREAD! NOT POLICE CLUB

The Voice of 300,000 Jobless

W. R. Hearst's Evening Herald-Express has swell reporters.
They know their stuff. They can smell sensational news, no matter how bad it smells.

And when Mr. Hearst's copy boys find their limited brains overloaded with last night's gin, they begin to see "Red." Those Hearst boys are artists, no kidding. They pick sensational news beats right out of the air. They don't need facts. In fact they ignore them.

Now, for instance. When it comes to news. Another Hearst office boy, "Don't-sell-America-short" Brisbane, tells us that when a dog bites a man, that's not news; but

The Forgotten Man

Sturdy man, strong backed, clean limbed,
    Head carried proudly,
Asking of the Powers that be
    The right to earn an existence
Not gleaming motors, nor yet fine houses
    Bread, shelter, a little coal
And the right to labor a long day in payment thereof,
    A bit of food for hungry babes at home.

—2—

What bent your broad shoulder, slacked your stride,
    Bowed your head?
Was it the horrid spectre of hunger
    Starving slowly your little ones?
Do their piteous prayers for food
    And bony bodies
Haunt your beclouded mind?

HUNGER MARCH FORCES RELIEF

The Hunger March delegation from the Workers' Ex-Servicemen's League and the Unemployed Council appearing before the county supervisors on October 10th, after being refused a hearing on October 3, forced the Sawtelle government authorities to turn over empty barracks that will house over 1457 jobless vets. Before the two hundred workers present at the hearing, the supervisors promised that no unemployed workers in L. A. County would suffer from gas, light and water shutoffs.

When the delegation insisted that the county go on record at once in favor of turning over the empty Sawtelle barracks to us, the county

Nowhere else in th does such a relic of ba exist, as the Los POLICE TERROR. Squad is the pampere the Merchants and M turer's Association, Chamber of Commerce local charity organiza the City Council and County politicians.

We unemployed workers fering conditions that w are completely unknown people of our county. see that the people NEVI of these insufferable cond It is the duty of the Re a specially selected bunch

1. Stay until the bonus is granted
2. No radica! talk
3. No panhandling
4. No booze

Rules for the 1932 Bonus March as quoted by *Literary Digest*, June 25 1932

HENRY FORD
ON UNEMPLOYMENT

I HAVE always had to work, whether any one hired me or not. For the first forty years of my life, I was an employe. When not employed by others, I employed myself. I found very early that being out of hire was not necessarily being out of work. The first means that your employer has not found something for you to do; the second means that you are waiting until he does.

We nowadays think of work as something that others find for us to do, call us to do, and pay us to do. No doubt our industrial growth is largely responsible for that. We have accustomed men to think of work that way.

In my own case, I was able to find work for others as well as myself. Outside my family life, nothing has given me more satisfaction than to see jobs increase in number and in profit to the men who handle them. And beyond question, the jobs of the world today are more numerous and profitable in wages than they were even eighteen years ago.

But something entirely outside the workshops of the nation has affected this hired employment very seriously. The word "unemployment" has become one of the most dreadful words in the language. The condition itself has become the concern of every person in the country.

When this condition arrived, there were just three things to be done. The first, of course, was to maintain employment at the maximum by every means known to management. Employment—hire —was what the people were accustomed to; they preferred it; it was the immediate solution of the difficulty. In our plants we used every expedient to spread as much employment over as many employes as was possible. I don't believe in "make work"— the public pays for all unnecessary work—but there are times when the plight of others compels us to do the human thing even though it be but a makeshift; and I am obliged to admit that, like most manufacturers, we avoided layoffs by continuing work that good business judgment would have halted. All of our non-profit work was continued in full force and much of the shop work. There were always tens of thousands employed—the lowest point at Dearborn was 40,000 —but there were always thousands unemployed or so meagerly employed, that the situation was far from desirable.

When all possible devices for providing employment have been used and fall short, there remains no alternative but self-help or charity.

I do not believe in routine charity. I think it a shameful thing that any man should have to stoop to take it, or give it. I do not include human helpfulness under the name of charity. My quarrel with charity is that it is neither helpful nor human. The charity of our cities is the most barbarous thing in our system, with the possible exception of our prisons. What we call charity is a modern substitute for being personally kind, personally concerned and personally involved in the work of helping others in difficulty. True charity is a much more costly effort than money-giving. Our donations too often purchase exemption from giving the only form of help that will drive the need for charity out of the land.

THE unemployed man is every one's concern, Henry Ford says — most of all the man's own concern. Being unemployed does not need to mean being out of work. There may be work even though one may not be hired to do it. Mr. Ford begins today a discussion of Employment, Charity and Self-Help as the three courses open to us in present conditions. He does not believe in routine charity because, he says, it is neither kind nor helpful. It does not get under the load or tackle the cause. He describes here a method he has followed. In the next issue of this publication he will discuss Self-Help.

Our own theory of helping people has been in operation for some years. We used to discuss it years ago—when no one could be persuaded to listen. Those who asked public attention to these matters were ridiculed by the very people who now call most loudly for some one to do something.

Our own work involves the usual emergency relief, hospitalization, adjustment of debt, with this addition—we help people to alter their affairs in common-sense accordance with changed conditions, and we have an understanding that all help received should be repaid in reasonable amounts in better times. Many families were not so badly off as they thought; they needed guidance in the management of their resources and opportunities. Human nature, of course, presented the usual problems. Relying on human sympathy many develop a spirit of professional indigence. But where co-operation is given, honest and self-respecting persons and families can usually be assisted to a condition which is much less distressing than they feared.

One of our responsibilities, voluntarily assumed—not because it was ours, but because there seemed to be no one else to assume it—was the care of a village of several hundred families whose condition was pretty low. Ordinarily a large welfare fund would have been needed to accomplish anything for these people. In this instance, we set the people at work cleaning up their homes and backyards, and then cleaning up the roads of their town, and then plowing up about 500 acres of vacant land around their houses. We abolished everything that savored of "handout" charity, opening instead a modern commissary where personal I O U's were accepted, and a garment-making school, and setting the cobblers and tailors of the community to work for their neighbors. We found the people heavily burdened with debt, and we acted informally as their agents in apportioning their income to straighten their affairs. Many families are now out of debt for the first time in years. There has appeared in this village not only a new spirit of confidence in life, but also a new sense of economic values, and an appreciation of economic independence which we feel will not soon be lost. None of these things could have been accomplished by paying out welfare funds after the orthodox manner. The only true charity for these people was somehow to get under their burdens with them and lend them the value of our experience to show them what can be done by people in their circumstances.

Our visiting staff in city work has personally handled thousands of cases in the manner above described. And while no one institution can shoulder all the burden, we feel that merely to mitigate present distress is not enough—we feel that thousands of families have been prepared for a better way of life when the wheels of activity begin turning again.

But there is still another way, a third way, so much better than the very best charitable endeavor that it simply forbids us to be satisfied with anything less. That is the way of Self-Help, which I shall discuss in the next issue of this publication.

Prepared and paid for by the Ford Motor Company as a contribution to public welfare.

Bear in mind that automobile tires are wearing out, shoes are wearing out, clothes are wearing out, automobiles are wearing out, steel rails are wearing out ... railroads can not run on the same old rails all the time. What people must have must be replaced in time. That is the basis for a return to normal business conditions.—*Wall Street Journal*, Jan., 1931

Of *course* WE CAN DO IT!

- We dug the Panama Canal, didn't we? And they said we couldn't do that.

- We put an army in France four months after we entered the World War, didn't we? And surprised the world.

- Now we've got a tough one to crack right here in our own back yard.

Men are out of work. Our men. Our neighbors. Our citizens. Honest, hard-working folk.

They want jobs. They're eager to work. But there aren't jobs enough to go 'round. Somebody's got to tide them over.

Who's going to do it? The people who dug that ditch. The people who went to France, or bought Liberty Bonds, or went without sugar—Mr. and Mrs. John K. American.

That means you—and *you*—and Y O U!—every one of us who is lucky enough to have a job.

We're going to share our luck with the folks out of work, aren't we? Remember—there's no National fund they can turn to for relief. It's up to us! And we've got to dig deeper than we did last winter.

But if we all dig deep enough we can keep a roof over every head, food in every pantry, fuel on every fire, and warm clothing on every needy man, woman and child in America.

That will beat Old Man Depression and lead the way to better days. Can we do it? Of course we can do it. Give . . . and give generously.

WHERE TO GIVE: There is no National Agency through which you may contribute. The way for you to give is through your *local* welfare and relief organizations, through your Community Chest or through your emergency unemployment committee if you have one.

THE PRESIDENT'S ORGANIZATION ON UNEMPLOYMENT RELIEF

Walter S. Gifford Director
(WALTER S. GIFFORD)

COMMITTEE ON MOBILIZATION OF RELIEF RESOURCES

Owen D. Young Chairman
(OWEN D. YOUNG)

The President's Organization on Unemployment Relief is non-political, and non-sectarian. Its purpose is to aid local welfare and relief agencies everywhere to provide for local needs. All facilities for the nation-wide program, including this advertisement, have been furnished to the Committee without cost.

If We Had Our Wish

Morris, Jan., 1931,
Copyright, 1931, by the George Matthew Adams Service

If a philosopher is a blind man in
dark room, what is an economist
a depression? — Buffalo *Courier-
press*, May, 1931

Queer Treatment for Nervous Prostration

Darling, May, 1931,
Reprinted from the New York *Herald Tribune*,
May, 1931 by permission of the
World Journal Tribune, New York.

The Hypnotist

Marcus, *Forbes*, June, 1932

It Seems the Patient Desires a Change!

Alley, *The Commercial Appeal*, Memphis, Oct., 1932

"You can't get along without me."
"Well, I haven't gotten along very well with you."

FREE

Let Us Send You Interesting Illustrated Circulars Which Explain How

—to influence people in your favor
—to outgrow your present job
—to master important problems
—to strengthen the memory
—to develop will power
—to banish timidity and self-consciousness
—to make a good impression
—to gain courage in business
—to out-think the average man
—to use the vast power of the subconscious
—to develop the success habit
—to have more time for play

Send This Coupon To-day!

What enables ce tain business m to amass great fe tunes? Psycholog What enables ce tain employees "get the break during business c pressions? Psycho ogy.

From a Funk Wagnalls ad, *Lite ary Digest*, Dec. ? 1932

Batchelor, *Daily News*, Nov. 5, 1932

Literary Digest, Dec. 31, 19

DAILY ☐ NEWS

A PLEDGE TO SUPPORT ROOSEVELT

This newspaper now pledges itself to support the policies of President Franklin D. Roosevelt for a period of at least one year from today; longer, if circumstances warrant.

* * *

Sir, to you !

The News makes this pledge from conscientious motives, believing that the times call for such a pledge.

Our system, normally, is one of checks and balances. The Senate is off-set against the House; the Supreme Court checks both Houses of Congress; the Executive is a kind of governor on the entire engine. And a great part of what we think and get done is accomplished through newspaper publicity and criticism.

It is no small sacrifice for a newspaper to make the pledge that is made above. One of an editor's chief prerogatives in a free-press nation is his right to tell every one, from the President down, how to act, and, on occasion, where to head in. If the Earth should establish communication with the planet Mars, it is a safe bet that American newspapers—including, no doubt, this one—within a week would be telling the Martians how to handle the affairs of their little planet. This right to

14]

Daily News, March 6, 1933

scope of the problem became apparent, all private efforts appeared as preposterous as the attempts of a community to meet an advancing flood with blotting paper.

The breadlines, springing up everywhere, at least saw a great many people through some rough days. These were operated by a dazzling variety of organizations, including the city itself, the Franciscan fathers, Tammany Hall, and the Salvation Army. A major newspaper served sandwiches from three or four trucks plastered with signs trumpeting the paper's great work of charity, and several eccentric individuals seemed to devote all their time to alleviating the Depression personally. One of these was "Mr. Glad," an anonymous friend of the jobless, who could often be seen in the center of Times Square distributing coffee, sandwiches, gloves, nickels, and little cards pointing out that the digits of 1930 added up to 13, which was true of such other depression years as 1903, 1912, and 1921. The reassuring point was that there wouldn't be another such year until 2029.

Another good but whimsical samaritan was Urban Ledoux, who under the name of "Mr. Zero" occasionally led processions of his followers down Broadway in sackcloth and ashes. Using Bryant Park as a base, Mr. Zero regularly passed out wagonloads of doughnuts and crullers to the unemployed, and at one point proposed to auction off jobless New Yorkers to Kansas wheat growers in exchange for grain which he would then bake into bread for the city's poor. Nothing came of it, though some Kansas wheat men were ready to offer $1.50 a day for labor, plus room and board.

At the depth of the Depression something like a hundred thousand meals a day were consumed in New York on breadlines, usually outside, no matter how cold it was, and overwhelmingly by men. Among those who were tapped for contributions to support such good works there was soon an inevitable muttering, which quickly got into print, about shiftless bums gorging themselves on one line after another.

But, since the beneficiaries were obliged to wait hours for each meal they got, I never saw how they could have managed to gorge, even as a full-time occupation.

City welfare handouts provided driblets for the truly destitute, but did nothing for the merely desperate, and evictions began to reach stunning proportions. In the first depression years a dispossess notice was effective in New York after five days, and while some soft-hearted owners allowed back rent to pile up for as much as a year, most landlords were afraid that news of any untoward softness would get around fast and make it difficult for them to collect any rent at all. They tended therefore to stick to the letter of a lease even though eviction might well leave them with an empty apartment to be put on the market at a lower rent and probably with two months' "concession."

Evictions and frequent moves to take advantage of the apartment market were as common in middle-income Washington Heights as in the poor areas of town, and apartment hopping became rather a way of life. My own family moved six times in seven years. In truth we should not have been living in Washington Heights at all, since the combined income of the three wage earners, myself included, rarely exceeded $50 a week. The balance required to keep up a $125 apartment was usually made up by taking in roomers and boarders. Even so, crises occurred monthly, and several times we were saved from eviction by pawning leftover valuables or by my mother's rich talent for cajoling landlords. On one more than routinely desperate occasion she resorted to the extreme device of having one of us enlarge a hole in the bathroom ceiling and then irately demanding repairs before another dollar of rent should be forthcoming.

Through the last two Hoover years evictions proceeded at such a rate that by the time Roosevelt took office seventeen thousand New York families were being put out on the street every month, usually along with their furniture, though

often enough the furniture was left behind to be returned to
the dealer because the installments couldn't be kept up.
Warehouses were filling up with this half-used stuff, but the
furniture dealers continued selling on credit. At our worst
moment, with eviction threatened in twenty-four hours, one
of my brothers came home with the encouraging news that
he had located a pool table available on installment payments. As a matter of course we took it, and for some months
it distracted my venerable grandmother from hearts, whist,
poker, Mah-jongg, and other such buffers against the encir-
cling gloom.

Landlords were not the only villains of course. Tax col-
lectors were worse. Daily newspapers carried tax sale sec-
tions sometimes running to as many as twenty-four pages of
small type, advertising properties to be put up at public
auction for tax arrears. "The march of progress," conceded
President Hoover, "has been retarded."

People took wage cuts without a murmur in those days.
Periodic cuts of 10 percent were common—and most of us
were nervously grateful that we had wages to be cut. Wide-
eyed and very un-Marxian, I volunteered to take a reduction
on one of my several successive jobs rather than let the firm
go under. Snapping up my offer, the company, which dealt
in gum-vending machines, reduced my pay from $16 a week
to $14.50, and so kept its fiscal head above water.

In some industrial plants men were happy to be working
three days a week, at a 10 percent reduction in the hourly
rate. But at least, said *Fortune* magazine, eagerly scanning
the cloud linings for silver, the Depression had "solved the
eternal domestic service problem in America." The supply at
last was so much greater than the demand that maids could
be hired for as low as four dollars a month, plus room and
board, and trained day workers could be had for five dollars
a week. Suburban citizens still solid enough to have gardens
that needed care could have them tended for a dollar a

week. The Women's Trade Union League put out dire case
histories from around the country—of the girl in the Pennsylvania pretzel factory who earned 93 cents one week at a
cost of a dollar in carfare, the woman in a New York establishment who made 23 cents for each 200 trouser pockets she
sewed, and the like. While these may have been extreme
cases, wages in the textile industry, just by way of illustration, had in fact dropped from $19.75 a week in 1929 to
$11.50 three years later.

All in all, the economy had worked itself back to about the
level of 1916. Payrolls were less than half of what they had
been in 1929, and U.S. Steel, which had listed at 185 even a
week after the crash, was down now to 62¼ a share. Contributing his own stock market experiences to the common
pool, Ring Lardner dolefully reported: "I asked Mr. Ny-
meyer, one of the partners, to get me out of Wall Street and
he said he had already moved me as far as Nassau. That is
the kind of friend to have in the stock market."

There were now 15 million people out of work in the
country, with some 37.5 million men, women, and children
directly and painfully affected, confirming Mr. Coolidge's
shrewd assessment that "When more and more people are
thrown out of work, unemployment results." Millions more
in the service professions and occupations were indirectly
but almost as acutely affected. Our family doctor confided
that fully half his patients had become charity cases. Dentists complained that most of their work consisted of pulling
teeth too long neglected to be treated any other way. And so
great was the competition for those who could still afford to
travel that one could go from New York to Boston, by bus,
for $1.50. All forms of public transportation had to com-
pete with private cars willing to take passengers on "share
expense" arrangements from New York to Chicago for
$9.

President Hoover was by no means insensitive to the

chaos around him, and when his face appeared in the news-reels there were in it visible signs of strain. But so far had American capitalism carried him personally, from Iowa farm boy to cosmopolitan millionaire, that he could not bring himself to tamper with it in any serious way, even to save it from its own worst defects. What he regarded as tampering in a serious way included such then far-out proposals as unemployment insurance, a federal public works program large enough to make a real dent in unemployment, a drastic revision in the free and easy ways that bankers were allowed to have with their depositors' money, programs for salvaging the farm economy, and, most urgent, direct federal aid to feed the hungry and shelter the homeless.

His alternative to such programs was not total inaction, but it might just as well have been, for the actions he favored were no more effective than a parasol in a typhoon. He leaned heavily on the psychological approach, and from time to time would call business leaders to the White House so they could tell reporters on the lawn afterward that conditions were "fundamentally sound," a better description of the interviews than it was of conditions. Explaining that the crisis was caused by panic conditions in Europe, the President sensibly declared a moratorium on war debts and reparations, but the move went no further to relieve the Depression than the analysis went to explain it. Whereupon he moved on to create the Reconstruction Finance Corporation, a federal agency designed to apply financial aid at the top in the hope that the benefits would eventually seep down to the luckless and the lowly.

In the *World Tomorrow*, where my opinions were largely formed, Professor Paul Douglas, then seemingly light years away from the Senate of the United States, was scornful of "the spectacle of the President and Congress pouring two billion dollars of public credit into the Reconstruction Finance Corporation in order to help buoy up for the proper-

tied classes the price of securities at the very time when they
are refusing adequate aid to protect the unemployed from
cold and hunger." Douglas then went on to lay down with
prophetic clarity a program for a new deal, including public
works in the field of slum clearance and public housing,
deficit spending, direct unemployment relief, and a carefully
managed inflation. That would all come, but in the mean-
time Hoover's RFC money failed to seep down at all. In the
depths of depression, businessmen were in no mood to bor-
row, or banks to lend, for expansion and new ventures. Instead, the money went largely to make good on doubtful
securities.

For lowlier victims of the Depression who could still invest a dollar or so for kicks there was *Oh Yeah,* a wicked
little opus of the times that spitefully reprinted all the predictions and philosophical reflections put out by the nation's
statesmen. There we could read, for example, the words of
our Secretary of Labor just eight months after the sky had
fallen: "The worst is over without a doubt, and it has been a
disciplinary and in some ways a constructive experience."
We could savor once more Henry Ford's explanation that
"The average man won't really do a day's work unless he is
caught and cannot get out of it. There is plenty of work to
do, if people would do it."* And we could enjoy the broad
view of Arthur Brisbane, who had grown rich from pseudo-
philosophical musings in the Hearst papers: "Sometimes
when things go wrong, it is a comfort to be reminded that
nothing matters very much. If the earth fell toward the sun,
it would melt like a flake of snow falling on a red-hot stove."

Self-hypnosis was, in fact, one of the most widely prescribed forms of relief. Billboards appeared here and there
with the cheery question: "Wasn't the Depression Terrible?"

---

* Five months after this remark Mr. Ford closed down his Detroit
factories almost completely, relieving 75,000 more men from the nagging
annoyance of work.

though signs in New York shop windows more often leaned to the flippantly cynical, like "No Business as Usual During Alterations" or "Opened by Mistake." Henry Ford pointed out that the Depression was "a wholesome thing in general," and Dwight Morrow, running for Governor of New Jersey, spelled out the theory: "There is something about too much prosperity that ruins the fiber of the people. The men and women that built this country, that founded it, were people that were reared in adversity."

Broadway resounded with vocal assurances that everything was for the best in this best of all possible worlds—and, if nothing else, there was always Nature to be enjoyed, free of charge. In *George White's Scandals* Ethel Merman was belting out the deep truths that "Life is just a bowl of cherries" and "you can't take your dough/When you go, go, go," while in *Everybody's Welcome* Frances Williams conveyed Herman Hupfield's message about the reassuring fundamental—"a kiss is still a kiss." Lowbrows in need of philosophical assurance could go to the Roseland Ballroom, where on New Year's Eve of 1931 "Old Man Depression" was tried and found guilty of murdering "Prosperity" and sentenced to death with a good deal of rowdy fanfare.

Probably a record for the merchandising of hypnosis was reached by *True Story* magazine, which at the steepest part of the slide ran institutional advertisements celebrating the way the country had met the "late" Depression. Baffled readers learned that "millions of men and women when they got out of a job went quietly back to their homes and when they got out of food and shelter they quietly went to the organizations that were providing for them." Those who were still employed, not to be outdone in public spirit, "went into their pay envelopes and dug up by far the biggest per centage" of what was needed to carry on, while others maintained "their buying habits to their utmost capacity" in order to preserve the markets of the country. In this way the

Depression was conquered, wrote the ad man, who went on: "It is almost weird for us to realize that we who are living now will go down to posterity as the generation that stood at the turning point of history and turned it right." Two months after this "turning" all the banks in the country were to close their doors for a holiday not listed in any calendar.

True Story's report of Americans patriotically buying their way out of the Depression was pure delirium. It merely reflected the idle hope of industrialists and politicians, though at the same time they were wholly opposed to starting the recovery process with a little government aid to the consumer who was to do the buying. He was somehow to do it on his own. "Men can be put to work and general prosperity will return," said economist Roger Babson, "only by enlisting the unemployed to create under proper leadership the desire to buy." My family, as always, showed this patriotic desire, however little its members were employed, or at what insignificant salaries. Besides the pool table mentioned earlier, my mother rewarded door-to-door salesmen with orders for the complete works of Mark Twain, George Eliot, Charles Dickens, Edgar Allen Poe, and, for some unfathomable reason, a certain Craig Kennedy. But it was all done on credit, probably at 600 percent interest, and the chances are that some of these purchases remain to be paid off to this day. I hope so.

It was not enough to buy, however. One had to be sure to Buy American. At least this was the counsel of groups like the Citizens' Association for America First, Inc., whose purpose was "the organization of citizens in every State under a pledge to buy only goods manufactured in the United States." The Association's solution for the Depression might not have made much of a dent in public opinion if the cry had not been taken up by William Randolph Hearst, who sent the editors of all his newspapers a directive to campaign vigorously for the following solution to the nation's economic difficulties: "Buy American and spend American. See America first. Keep American money in America and provide employment for American citizens." His papers responded, to the point of making exclusively American buying a hallmark of patriotism and a sign of loyalty, but some of the editors may have had trouble squaring the campaign with another Hearst program "to connect our industry with world markets." We were to sell to Frenchmen, Germans, Peruvians, and Mongolians but on no condition to buy from them.*

As if the "Buy American" campaign were not sufficiently flawed as to logic, many states were busily trying to put up commercial walls of their own. Unable to get around the constitutional ban on the direct hampering of interstate commerce, they pushed indirect methods to the same end. By the fall of 1932 half the states in the union had laws requiring compulsory preference for made-in-the-state products, and for exclusive employment of state residents on all public works contracts. And counties carried the isolationist game to its logical absurdity by shipping homeless citizens back and forth across their borders in the hope of avoiding financial responsibility for them. A contemporary article in *Fortune* described the procedure:

Dull mornings last winter, the sheriff of Miami, Florida, used to fill a truck with homeless men and run them up to the county line. Where the sheriff of Fort Lauderdale used to meet them and load them into a second truck and run them up to *his* county line. Where the sheriff of Saint Lucie's would meet them and load them into a third truck and run them up to *his* county line. Where the sheriff of Brevard County would *not* meet them. And whence they would trickle back down the roads to Miami. To repeat.

As an exercise in perpetual motion the scheme was novel, but socially and financially it was altogether in the evasive

* Except for Hearst himself, who went right on importing antiques from all over the world, and Venetian tiles for his indoor swimming pool at San Simeon.

tradition of the last Hoover years, when responsibility flitted
from town to county to state to Washington, and then flitted
back again, without being allowed to alight and be recognized at any point along the way.

Such was the climate of the country when Herbert Clark
Hoover set out in chilled pursuit of a second term and
Franklin Delano Roosevelt in hot pursuit of a first.

For those New Yorkers who looked upon politics as a form
of inexpensive amusement, an important consideration at the
time, 1932 was a bonus year. Besides the opportunity to
retire Mr. Hoover to private life, an outcome considered inevitable from the start, we had the entertainment of a
mayoralty campaign by John Patrick O'Brien, a cheery
windbag whose assaults on his obscure Republican opponent
were minor compared to his assaults on the English language. Running to fill out the term of the dapper James J.
Walker, who at the request of Governor Roosevelt had just
retired from office under eight or nine clouds, Surrogate
O'Brien delighted the town scoffers by his timely warnings:
"I am against pacifists, who are a terrible sedition going
across the country," he said, and "You will *ruin* the day if
you elect that Socialist." On the positive side, Judge O'Brien
favored "a kiddie in every home" and also "teaching students
to love the classics, Latin and Greek, thus enervating them
with the desire for culture." The "Sewergate" himself, as he
pronounced his title, had a few medals at home, he once told
an audience of schoolboys, for his translations of Horace from
the original Greek. And he also made it plain, for some obscure reason, that he did "not believe in placing paramours
on pedestals and ignoring wives."

It was innocent fun in a year that had need of it. For the
Presidential campaign was hardly that. There was about it a
grim edginess fortunately rare in such contests. *Time* was
probably right in its view that "the most potent factor in

keeping the country steady and averting even the threat of an armed uprising has been the certainty that November 8, 1932, would in due constitutional order bring a presidential and congressional election."

The Republican camp was dispirited from the start and plainly showed it. President Hoover knew he couldn't win again, and the convention that picked him knew it, but the party could not dump him without repudiating itself and in effect taking the blame for the Depression. Instead, it adopted a platform that said almost nothing about the country's dolorous state and was just as evasive about repealing Prohibition, the only other issue that anybody cared about, what with bad bootleg Scotch selling at ten or twelve dollars a quart. Even the Chicago *Tribune* called the Republicans' Prohibition plank a "declaration of political bankruptcy— and futile as it is fraudulent." Nevertheless, the convention went about its ritualistic business, including a nominating speech in which Mr. Hoover was found to warrant comparison with Lincoln and St. Francis of Assisi—as a man who in spite of his millions had led a life that "typifies spiritual values and the vanity of mere earthly things."

Hoover accepted the nomination with a defense of pure conservatism and congratulated himself for having beaten the Depression without any sacrifice of American principles. Unfortunately word of this triumph had failed to get through to the apple vendors, breadline diners, bankrupt merchants, foreclosed farmers, evicted tenants, and the like who made up a rather substantial part of the electorate. Moved at the moment to a painful concern with earthly things, they seemed unimpressed with either Mr. Hoover's principles or his chances.

It was hard, in fact, to find anyone who *was* impressed. Nicholas Murray Butler himself sailed for Europe rather than stay around for the wake of the party whose fortunes he had ardently promoted for forty years. At the other end of the Republicans' cultural spectrum, Big Bill Thompson, who as Mayor of Chicago had threatened to punch King George V "on the snoot," loudly wrote off his party's chances: "The history of American politics shows that the people don't vote for continued depression." In between, people reveled in such stories as that of the hitchhiker who got from California to New York in five days simply by carrying a sign that read: "Give me a lift or I'll vote for Hoover."

In the circumstances the President could hardly be blamed for a defensive and lackluster campaign—his tour, he conceded, reminded him of the Harding funeral train— but he need not have gone to the celebrated extreme of predicting that if the Democrats got in, "grass will grow in the streets of a hundred cities, a thousand towns. . . ." For the grass was already showing and the Democrats were reaping it to make hay.

Four years before, in the late-afternoon glow of Coolidge prosperity, Hoover's speeches had been the solemn reports of a board chairman rather than the exhortations of a leader. Now they were the even more solemn tracts of a political philosopher defending the concept of limited national government, from which it followed that relief, welfare, and employment were and must remain problems of state and local governments if indeed they were public problems at all. In defense of this principle Hoover attained to a certain stubborn eloquence, though it hardly came through on the radio, but against a background of desperation and want and the experience of having been rebuffed by bankrupt cities and inept state legislatures, not many people were in a mood for any political theory, least of all Hoover's. The President told Henry Stimson, his Secretary of State, that he could feel the "hatred" for him all through his tour of the West.

The reverse of the coin, naturally, was ebullience on the Democratic side. It is likely that the Democrats in 1932 would have given the electorate a lift no matter what they said or whom they nominated, simply because they were not Republicans. As it did for many another bourgeois family, 1932 rang down the curtain on my family's long record of Republican loyalty. In all the wanderings of my grandparents and parents—family addresses had included Cleveland and Hamilton, Ohio; Fort Wayne, Indiana; Pittsburgh; and, for a few years before we came to New York, the little town of Scottdale in Westmoreland County, Pennsylvania—they had always voted Republican. My maternal grandfather actively promoted the party wherever he happened to find himself, and after President Theodore Roosevelt addressed him by name in the Pittsburgh railroad station we were doomed to read all the Roosevelt travel works, along with biographies of William McKinley and William Howard Taft, enough to make a Democrat of anyone. But now all that was past. My father and grandfather were gone, and my mother swung so ardently to Roosevelt that to the end of her days, at eighty-six, she would not admit that she had ever been anything but a Democrat. In 1932 I voted for the first time, and, being younger, bounced farther. My choice was Norman Thomas.

Before the campaign warmed up, Roosevelt was thought by many to be one of the Democrats' least exciting possibilities, though few went as far as the irrepressible Mencken: "He is one of the most charming of men, but like many another very charming man he leaves on the beholder the impression that he is also somewhat shallow and futile. It is hard to say precisely how that impression is produced: maybe his Christian Science smile is to blame, or the tenor overtones in his voice." Fewer still went so far as Walter Lippmann, whose much-publicized remark probably still haunts him in the dead of night: "Franklin D. Roosevelt is no crusader. He is no tribune of the people. He is no enemy of entrenched privilege. He is a pleasant man who, without any important qualifications for the office, would very much like to be President." My own employers on the *World Tomorrow* found little to praise in his record as Governor and, viewing his mixed bag of supporters—liberal Senators like George Norris and Burton K. Wheeler all in a heap with Hearst, Huey Long, and Frank Hague, the noisome dictator of Jersey City—proclaimed him "a weathervane, beautiful against the sky, shining and resplendent, built of hollow brass." Perhaps most damning of all, the early Republican strategy called for an attack on one member of the Democratic ticket as "unsound" and "radical," but the member, wondrous to relate, was not Roosevelt but John Nance Garner.

Almost as soon as the nomination was safely in Roosevelt's hands, however, he moved to change the atmosphere dramatically. Violating the hoary protocol that a nominee had to wait for a delegation to solemnly apprise him of his selection before he could open his mouth, Roosevelt flew out to the convention in Chicago to symbolize a fresh approach to the country's dire problems: "Let it be from now on the task of our party to break foolish traditions." In his acceptance speech the "forgotten man" was thoroughly remembered, dwelt upon, and courted, and for the first time we heard the promise of a "new deal." The beaming self-confidence that was gradually to warm a shaken people in the campaign, the cigarette holder tilted at an angle that was to convey the verve of the man in countless newspaper photographs and newsreels, the vibrant voice that was to make of radio a first-class political weapon, the gallantry with which he minimized his physical affliction, and, above all, the pledges to deal specifically and from above with all the country's agonies—all these burst on a nation starving for leadership and imagination. It would be months before St. George could be duly vested with power to take on the dragon, and meanwhile things could and would get worse.

But, all the same, bands across the country were playing "Happy Days Are Here Again," and even if they weren't quite here yet, there was a widespread disposition to believe they were on the way.

The Exhilarating Depression
of Franklin Roosevelt

2 ❧

When the banks of the United States closed their doors on March 3, 1933, I had $8.32 in a savings account, the result of an improbable New Year's resolution of 1931 to invest systematically in my future. My family were a little more shocked about this private hoarding than they were by the country's financial collapse, but I felt that the circumstance gave me a balanced view of the historic occasion. I had a stake in the banking system, as it were, and yet not so large a stake as to separate me from those imprudent non-banking types who could now sit back and enjoy the excitement and color of the emergency.

For, in spite of the extreme gravity of the event, there was also a feeling that a great turning point had come, that with a bold new President entering the White House that very week—only a kindly fate could have brought about this happy coincidence—an end had come to the long period of wretched deterioration. What would follow was bound to be better and offered besides all the prickly pleasure of the unknown. The *New Yorker's* Reporter at Large, writing from Washington, found the air "charged with the excitement of action. Things were being done. What things? Nobody bothered much about that, for it would be the wildest guesswork anyway. Just as long as something was being done, anything, that would suffice to keep spirits up."

Actually the closing of the banks was more gradual than it seemed at the time. It had started three weeks before in Michigan, where Detroit bankers had been busily investing their depositors' money in insolvent auto companies, and spread by contagion from state to state, as the more knowing depositors grew eager to get out while the getting was good. Maryland went a week or so later, and individual banks in several other states then limited withdrawals to 5 or 10 percent. Newspapers played the developments with downright British understatement in New York, where reports of closings elsewhere appeared only in the financial section under such classically restrained heads as "Banks Protected in Five More States." But by then the contagion was spreading fast, and people didn't have to look at the financial pages to know what was going on. Long lines wound in and out of the lobbies of neighborhood banks, which proceeded to disgorge currency and gold at a rate to frighten and disgust those who hadn't yet taken out theirs. By March 3, the eve of the Inauguration, thirty states had limited banking operations at best, and the next day, as the new President was asserting his "firm belief that the only thing we have to fear is fear itself—nameless, unreasoning, unjustified terror which paralyzes needed efforts to convert retreat into advance," the American people learned that they would have to start that advance with their moneychangers on forced leave of absence. Each and every bank would have to meet certain standards laid down by the incoming Administration before it could open for business.

The bank holiday united people as they are rarely united except by war or a profoundly juicy scandal. Everybody was in the same boat, and everybody either had stories to tell or passed along those they had heard—of traveling salesmen peddling their samples in hotel lobbies in order to get themselves home; of successful raids on children's piggy banks; and of those who, canny enough to draw their money out on

Friday, had not been canny enough to take it in small currency and now found that their $20 and $50 bills couldn't get them a telephone call, a subway ride, a newspaper, or a pack of cigarettes. Scrip sprang up here and there, and most cities were reported in the press to be preparing brightly colored currency of their own in the event the banks stayed closed any length of time.*

How Fond du Lac currency would have paid off in Miami and vice versa, I cannot say, but the arrangement could hardly have been more complicated than the spreading system of barter. "I see no reason why there should not be a new theatrical season," Robert Benchley wrote in *Harper's Bazaar,* "providing my proposed plan for using pressed figs and dates as money goes into effect fairly soon."

The Benchley plan was not altogether far-fetched. At Madison Square Garden admission tickets for some boxing matches were swapped for shoes, canned goods, frankfurters, and foot ointment, among other items. Passengers in Salt Lake City were reported paying transit fares with toothpaste (two tubes), silk stockings, and the like. An Oklahoma City hotel announced "We will take anything we can use in the coffee shop" in lieu of payment for rooms. As a result the cashier took in eggs, vegetables, several chickens, and a pig, which must have made difficulties for accountants who later went over the books. And a newspaper in the Middle West went to the length of establishing new subscription rates: "One Year, ten bushels of wheat; two years for 18 bushels."**

* The Chicago *Tribune* was already paying off its employees in "certificates of obligation," which came in denominations of 1, 5, 10, and 20 dollars and bore the likeness of Theodore Roosevelt, not Franklin. The explanation lay not in partisanship but in the fact that the notes were frugally run off from plates left over from the panic of 1907.

** Five years later, in the "recession," the *Nation,* where I then worked, was still from time to time entering subscriptions in return for farm produce. I recall, especially, a crate of grapefruit, which was peddled around the office for the sake of the bookkeeping department. Months later, when we moved, water coolers and editors' desk drawers turned up desiccated grapefruit which people had meant to take home but never got around to.

Credit, too, was rampant. Even the stern cash policy of R. H. Macy's melted in the dire need for cash. A Philadelphia department store passed out streetcar tokens to its customers, who were allowed to charge them to their accounts. And Pebeco toothpaste took three-quarters of a page in the *New York Times* to advertise: "Better times are on the way! . . . To show our faith in our government, our banks, our people, We Will Take Your Check Dated Three Months Ahead—For a Three Months' Supply of Pebeco Toothpaste for Yourself and Your Family." The price of this ninety-day credit item was one dollar.

In spite of barter and credit, some employers felt obliged to dig into their personally hoarded funds to give their working staffs enough to keep going. When a Manhattan executive dramatically placed a $3,000 diamond ring on the table of his board room, inviting his colleagues to contribute likewise, the gesture called forth watches, rings, and a pearl necklace, just brought to town for repairs. The pot yielded a few thousand dollars at a nearby pawnbroker's, enough to give all employees, including the executives, ten dollars apiece.

Americans abroad were perhaps hardest hit of all, with the dollar losing as much as a third of its value overnight. But from Paris, via the *New Yorker's* correspondent Gênet, came a touching report. "A few French chauvinists wondered if they would have the privilege . . . of pasting worthless dollar bills on their suitcases as some Americans regrettably pasted the franc in 1926," but on the whole, she wrote, people were remarkably kind to stranded Americans. Waiters staked students to a week of breakfasts, butlers presented their mistresses with potted plants as a sign of sympathy, and sewing women appeared after a weekend in the country with gifts of fresh-laid eggs. A stricken Uncle Sam clearly had more appeal than one armed with a vulgarly healthy dollar, a point not to be appreciated by advocates of foreign aid programs.

On Sunday, March 12, President Roosevelt went on the air with his first fireside chat. "My friends," he began in an opening we would come to recognize as the regular prelude to a sharing of what were once official mysteries,

. . . when you deposit money in a bank, the bank does not put the money into a safe deposit vault. It invests your money, puts it to work. . . . What, then, happened? There was a general rush so great that the soundest banks could not get enough currency to meet the demand. . . . Why are all the banks not to be reopened at the same time? Because your Government does not intend that the history of the past few years shall be repeated. . . . There is no occasion for worry. . . . When people find they can get their money, the phantom of fear will soon be laid. I can assure you it is safer to keep your money in a reopened bank than under the mattress.

Everybody understood, as they had never understood Mr. Hoover, even the bankers, and money and gold immediately began the return trip to the vaults, encouraged a little perhaps by threats to publish the names of all hoarders.

By far the greater number of the nation's banks did reopen on Monday, March 13, nine days after the inaugural, and by the end of that week some 75 percent were back in business. But a few thousand were not, and a few hundred were still going through the wringer as late as the following October.

Socialists and other radicals, including my employers on the *World Tomorrow*, were disappointed at the Administration's failure to grab so unique an opportunity to nationalize the banks. And in view of the popular temper at the moment it is probably true that Roosevelt could have gotten away with almost anything. For even to the Washington press corps, according to a member of that badly shaken body, the day before the bank holiday had looked like the end of the American way. "Gentlemen, it's revolution," a possibly melodramatic newsman proclaimed to his colleagues. "I can see 'em now, howling up Fifth Avenue with blood in their eye, howling up Market Street and Beacon Street and Michigan Avenue!" And who were the howlers? "Why, the birds that get hungry, that's who. And I've already picked my side. I'm going to join me a good Communist club."

E. T. Weir, chairman of the National Steel Corporation, who was to be one of Roosevelt's most savage critics a few months later, when he felt better, was less hysterical than the reporter but just as eager for strong action: "I fear we will sink further without the assurance that the banking situation of this country has the Federal Government behind it in an aggressive way." And Will Rogers gave the new President carte blanche: "If he burned down the capitol, we would cheer and say 'well, we at least got a fire started anyhow.'"

Catching the prevailing winds, the House of Representatives whooped through the President's emergency banking legislation in thirty-eight minutes with a unanimous roar, and the Senate passed it the same day, 73 to 7, with no amendments. In less than eight hours Mr. Roosevelt (some of the papers were now calling him "F.R." and some "F.D.," reviving the fond custom of initials for Presidents which had lapsed with T.R.)* had on his desk the greatest grant of power over the nation's wallets ever given in peacetime. Said Representative Steagall, in charge of the bill in the House: "The people have summoned a leader whose face is lifted toward the skies. We shall follow that leadership until we again stand in the glorious sunlight of prosperity and happiness." Everybody cheered, and Mrs. Roosevelt, in the gallery, looked up from her knitting to smile. Nobody compared her to Madame Defarge until much later, and nobody said a word about a "rubber-stamp Congress."

* Nobody ever spoke of "C.C." or "H.H."

As for socializing the banks, however, Roosevelt had never entertained such a thought or indeed the thought of doing anything except to save the existing order from its grossest follies and its most immediate dangers. If conservatives were in a few years to forget that fact, and indeed to regard its utterance as heresy, they were at least alert to it at the time. "The fact that he acted without shilly-shallying indicates that he knows what it is all about," said the Chicago *Tribune*, which was later in effect to compare Roosevelt with Satan, much to the latter's advantage. From the *Magazine of Wall Street* came the reminder that we were "in a chaotic and revolutionary period," in which "innovation and experiment" were "inevitable" and couldn't be more harmful in any case than what had gone on before. But it was left for William Randolph Hearst's New York *American,* which would soon rival the Chicago *Tribune* for top honors in Roosevelt baiting, to spill over in gushy rhetoric:

The ship of state moves steadily on its way with gathering pace. The wind has caught its sails. There is a rush of waters alongside as it forges forward on its course.

Things are better. The clouds are parting. The light is growing stronger and the courage and the confidence of the people are returning. . . .

Honor to President Roosevelt who, more than any man, is responsible for the wondrous change in the nation's outlook and in its prospects! Let us pour out the thankfulness that is in our hearts. . . .

That is the sort of thing we read in *conservative* journals.

Everywhere, it seemed, newspapers and radio were singing the President's praises. And when he shortly afterward moved to restore beer to the people as well as banks, his popularity was enough to bring tears to the eyes of his bodyguard. The chief of the Secret Service, who had served four years with Herbert Hoover, was so overcome at having his charge greeted everywhere with cheers and applause that he unprofessionally whispered to reporters, "Gosh, but it sounds good to hear that again."

On Broadway the ladies of the cast of Strike Me Pink, which had just opened the week the banks closed, first bemoaned in song the dire effect that the world Depression had been having on their income of diamonds and mink. And then, arms raised high, they burst into a paean of hope and confidence: "We depend on Rose-a-velt! We depend on him!" Covering the show, Robert Benchley was of the opinion that not even the economic fates could withstand such impudence. "It was so staggering, even shocking, in its brashness in the face of a national emergency unequaled since the firing on Fort Sumter that the Forces of Darkness collapsed then and there out of sheer chagrin."

The mingling of relief, admiration, and excitement in that first week was infectious. It set the national tone for the next year or so, even if the plight of a great many individuals was not to be soon or greatly changed. Suddenly, after years of bucolic languor under Coolidge and chilled remoteness under Hoover, Washington had become the swirling, raucous, highly personal center of American life. People who could not possibly have interested themselves in a Secretary of the Treasury like Ogden Mills, to take an extreme case, had to be aware even in that first week of one like "Wee Willie" Woodin, who so wore himself out in the bank crisis that he had to retire in November and died a year later. Something of a biological sport among Pennsylvania industrialists, a Union League Club member, and a lifelong Republican, William H. Woodin was also a heavy contributor to the Roosevelt campaign, a writer of verses for children about "happy bluebirds singing in the rain," a performer on violin and zither, and composer of "The Franklin Delano Roosevelt March," which was played at the Inauguration.

Similarly, no one could for long ignore the new Secretary of the Interior, Harold Ickes, a self-styled "curmudgeon"

with the incorruptibility of a Vestal Virgin and the temper
of a grizzly bear.* Then there was Henry Wallace, creator of
the "ever-normal granary" and the "Century of the Common
Man," who took his daily workout with a boomerang and
carried on a correspondence with a Manhattan mystic in
which he regularly referred to Roosevelt as "The Flaming
One." And Professor Rexford Guy Tugwell, King of the
Brain Trust, whose blunt prescription was to "Take incomes
from where they are . . . and place them where we need
them." There was the genial controller of patronage, Jim
Farley, whose written recommendation for a government job
meant nothing if it wasn't signed in green ink and everything
if it was; and the semi-invalided, saturnine, hard-boiled but
socially sensitive Harry Hopkins, who lived in the White
House after a time and lounged about in an old robe. The
burgeoning trade unions found a crisp champion in Secretary of Labor Frances Perkins, the country's first female
Cabinet officer, who found her sex a handicap, she said,
"only in climbing trees." And among the foremost of this
colorful crew was General Hugh Samuel Johnson, who
under the sign of the Blue Eagle whipped the businessmen
of the country into adopting voluntary codes of fair competition and was known as "Ironpants."

Almost immediately these and other early New Dealers
presented us, meaning everybody, with visible, tangible,

* Interviewing the irascible Mr. Ickes as a *Nation* reporter very late in the
decade and finding him helpful and courteous, I could hardly believe that
only two years earlier, in a passing row, he had written to Freda Kirchwey,
my editor, in the following highly typical vein: "Your editorial in the issue
of October 30, on the appointment of Mr. Nathan Straus as Federal Housing
Administrator shows a vindictiveness that leaves no place for mutual understanding. I prefer to deal with you at arm's length . . . it would be a waste
of time to appeal to your reason. As to your sense of fair play, you haven't
any, so that can be left out of consideration. . . ."
   Since the *Nation* was for the most part a strong supporter of the Administration, and even of Harold Ickes, the reader may imagine the kind of
missives with which he honored his opponents. Still he *was* death on graft,
worked for ten, and added splashes of color to the dispatches coming out
of the capital.

often noisy and colorful, evidence that government was moving, taking action to get the country around the corner where prosperity was reported to be lurking instead of waiting for her to make the turn in our direction.

Very quickly the Hoovervilles and breadlines of pre–New Deal days gave way to the first fruits of Federal relief—sanitary transient centers to which the homeless and jobless were directed by their local relief offices, carfare provided. These Federal Emergency Relief Administration camps offered not only hygienic food and lodging with the inevitable governmental touch of formaldehyde and red tape, but free medical services and such amenities as radio receivers as well. In addition, of course, the recipients, like others in need, drew cash relief in monthly checks, the amounts ranging from $15 to $20—not much but for the first time the money was offered to them as an obligation of government, not as charity.

Eighteen months after Roosevelt took office about twelve million Americans were on direct relief and another five million on work relief, which naturally took longer to set up and was a good deal more costly for the government. While the Public Works Administration was slowly getting into position to give a massive lift to industry, a temporary Civil Works Administration put several million people to work building new airports and improving old ones, patching up secondary roads, teaching adult courses, and keeping rural schools going that would otherwise have had to close down. Naturally charges of waste and graft sprang up and no doubt had substance, but it was all much better than the desperation that had gone before, and to most it seemed better than the direct dole.

PWA, when it got going, operated on the theory that for every man put to work on a massive government project, two other persons would indirectly find employment. Whether or not the expected ratio worked out, the country did not lose, for the PWA's monuments included Boulder Dam, New York's Triborough Bridge, a new sewage system for Chicago, and the aircraft carriers *Yorktown* and *Enterprise,* none of them in the leaf-raking category. Moreover, unemployment did drop—something like three million in the first eighteen months of the New Era—and if that effect was not literally visible, the spirit it generated was much in evidence. It was like war in that even if no one from your immediate family happened to be at the front, everyone you knew was involved somehow or had a relative or a friend who was caught up in some agency or project of the new dispensation —Civil Works Administration, Public Works Administration, Civilian Conservation Corps, or, a little later, the Works Progress Administration.

Producing a gaudy hullabaloo and well-nigh ubiquitous was Hugh Johnson's NRA, which combined the elements of a wartime crusade for homefront support and amateur night at a neighborhood theatre. Businesses that agreed to abide by the proposed voluntary codes were awarded a Blue Eagle emblem, and in short order the bird bobbed up everywhere. In shop windows, in advertisements, stamped on products, in exhortatory movie shorts, wherever you turned, there was the Blue Eagle under the slogan "We Do Our Part," the sign and symbol of participation in a vast popular effort to get the country out of the slough.

My own most unexpected sighting of the New Deal bluebird was on a cardboard poster pathetically worn, as a protection from the cold, under the vest of an unemployed barber, who called now and again at our apartment house to administer private shaves and haircuts at bargain rates. One morning he arrived caroling a Verdi aria that could be heard for several blocks and, on being greeted, tore open his jacket to reveal with pride the sign and symbol of his patriotism. With each succeeding breath he revealed, likewise, a state of alcohol that fitted so poorly with the use of a straight-edged razor that he was suffered to depart, Blue Eagle and all.

Business, at least in the beginning, professed great enthusiasm for the NRA, which did allow a certain relaxing of the antitrust laws. Labor unions were all for it because Section 7-A called for agreement on maximum hours and minimum wages and, more important, gave government's official blessing to the principle of collective bargaining. John L. Lewis compared it to the Emancipation Proclamation. And the public loved it because it held out promise, made an exciting splash, and gave people something to do. Delegations bearing scrolls of pledges arrived daily at NRA offices for ceremonial acknowledgments. A monster parade, bands blaring out "Happy Days Are Here Again," went up Fifth Avenue bearing the Blue Eagle more proudly than its avian counterpart was ever borne through the streets of Rome. With a major general for grand marshal, it met all the requirements for Manhattan pageantry, including a pretty "Miss NRA" in a shell-shaped float, who smiled continuously for three miles; Grover Whalen, the city's permanent master of ceremonies; and successive waves of West Point cadets, Chinese schoolchildren, newspaper editors, film and stage stars headed by Al Jolson and Ruby Keeler, and scores of business, trade, and labor contingents complete with captains of industry and trade-union chiefs—all marching under banners proclaiming themselves "100 percent organized, 100 percent NRA." And over all the national excitement could be heard the raucous voice of the barrel-chested trainer of the Blue Eagle, "Ironpants" Johnson, threatening to "crack down on the chiselers," promising to give code resisters "a sock right on the jaw," and invoking God's mercy on those who attempted to "trifle with this bird."

Even in the first galvanic years of the New Deal there was of course more to life than the activities of government, but very little of it was unaffected by those activities or by the heaving state of the nation. It would take an extreme and willful fatuousness to swallow the observation of Edgar

Guest, the Good Gray Hack of newspaper poetry, that the Depression "sent every member of the family back to the fireside . . . the depression has been a mighty fine thing for the boys and girls." But inevitably hard times did put a premium on the simpler and less expensive forms of amusement. Entertainment, for better or worse, had by 1933 lost much of the brass and elaborateness that characterized it in the Twenties.

Motion picture houses, which did extremely well as havens of escape from the realities of depression, figured to do still better with the aid of homey come-ons. Whereas a family might feel conscience-stricken about going twice a week merely to dance again with Ginger Rogers and Fred Astaire, to follow in Hitchcock's Thirty-Nine Steps, or to take a fantasy bus ride with Clark Gable and Claudette Colbert, they could justify taking a chance on a lucky ticket number that might bring them some new dishes or a few dollars in cash. The result was that even in New York a visit to the movies took on something of the character of a turkey raffle. Tuesday was usually Bank Night, which one could take part in only if he had registered his name and address on a previous visit to the theatre. Shortly before nine o'clock the manager would appear on stage, pick a child from the audience, and have him, blindfolded, draw a coupon from a revolving drum. The number was then checked against the registration list and the name of the winner announced. If he was not on hand, the prize was forfeited and went to sweeten the following week's pot. Occasionally the prize money really mounted up—to a thousand dollars or more— so that one enterprising insurance company found it worthwhile to sell policies against missing Bank Night. The whole thing was directed from a central office in Denver, where the entrepreneurs and copyright owners raked in up to $65,000 a week in fees.

For theatres that did not sign up with Bank Night there

were pale imitations. Some had Dish Night, though I never
understood the attractiveness of this particular bait (why
not cigarettes or aspirin?), and others might offer a session
of bingo. Since admission to neighborhood theatres ran
around 25 or 30 cents, one could make a reasonable investment and at the same time retreat from a still shaky world
—all at the mere sacrifice of having to sit through a double
feature, a painful institution just then coming into vogue.

For those who preferred a dash of reality on the screen,
there were the newsreel houses, which for a time seemed to
be springing up all over Manhattan. Here, as the decade
advanced, you could see for a quarter the appalling dust
storms that compounded the misery and poverty of a dozen
states, but you could likewise see the burgeoning TVA in
construction and hear the promise of better things in Pare
Lorentz's short film, *The River*, with its poetic catalogue of
names:

> We built a hundred cities and a thousand towns:
> St. Paul and Minneapolis,
> Davenport and Keokuk,
> Moline and Quincy,
> Cincinnati and St. Louis,
> Omaha and Kansas City . . .
> Across to the Rockies and down from Minnesota,
> Twenty-five hundred miles to New Orleans
> We built a new continent . . .

You could see the brokendown flivvers of the Okies, loaded
with bedsprings and babies, but you could also hear the
President grow eloquent, in his Second Inaugural, over "one
third of a nation, ill-housed, ill-clad, ill-nourished," and you
could see the "sitdowns" in the auto plants, where aroused
trade unionists, encouraged by the national government,
were starting the education of American industrialists in the
ways of collective bargaining, a course running from apo-
plexy to acceptance.

More ominous, you could see Japanese planes strafing long lines of civilian refugees in Manchuria as part of the "New Order for East Asia"; Emperor Haile Selassie of Ethiopia riding out under an umbrella to fight the forces of Mussolini alongside warriors who seemed to be dressed in nightgowns; Hitler's thugs goosestepping over what they liked to call "the rotten corpse of liberalism and democracy"; and the Spanish Republic writhing in its death throes. The *March of Time* occasionally used staged shots of hired actors to round out a documentary on Huey Long or Adolf Hitler, but these were, in the timeless phrase of W. S. Gilbert, "merely corroborative detail intended to lend verisimilitude to an otherwise bald and unconvincing narrative." Even with such synthetic touches and the voice of doom proclaiming that "Time—Marches—ON!" they were a great deal better than the regular newsreel programs, which up to then had been devoted almost solely to beauty contests, Presidents stiffly posed in fishing outfits or tricked out in Indian head-dress, ship launchings, Florida speedboats just clearing a palm tree in a spray of bad puns, and a Teutonic comedian named Lew Lehr, whose comments on the animal world always wound up with the reflection that "Monkeys iss de cwaziest people." Completing the bill as a rule was a Fitzpatrick travelogue that inevitably ended with a ponderous farewell to something like "Indianapolis, home of charm and mystery" or "Staten Island, that truly hidden Paradise."

Among the scaled-down amusements none was less to be expected or, at least in New York, more ubiquitous than miniature golf, of all things. Along upper Broadway dozens of vacant corner shops were replaced by these Tom Thumb courses, each hole of which called for getting the ball through a Rube Goldberg arrangement of waterpipes to a putting green surfaced with crushed cottonseed hulls. Since the fee for nine holes was rarely more than fifteen cents, an afternoon's or evening's entertainment of sorts for two could be had for less than a dollar. Around the country some thirty thousand of these courses were said to be in operation, and the government was hopeful that the vogue would rescue the depressed cotton industry. That proved a wistful dream, but just planning the hazards must surely have given employment to some—hopefully to architects, who certainly didn't have much else to do in those years, but more likely to surrealist artists in advance of their times.

To build a "date" around a miniature golf game or a movie was no difficult feat. The open upper deck of a Fifth Avenue bus was ideal for air-cooled romance of a summer evening, and the ten-cent ride from Washington Heights to Washington Square, via Broadway, Riverside Drive, and Fifth Avenue, was good for at least an hour each way. On a Sunday afternoon there was always, as there is to this day, the nickel ride across the harbor on the Staten Island Ferry, a much longer boat ride from the Bronx to College Point, free music in a Neo-Gothic hall at City College, free lectures all over the place, and free necking in the public parks, where muggings were still rare and the chief hazards were amorous.

For indoor sport whole families relived the financial excitements of the Twenties by playing Monopoly, and minor forms of gambling were extremely popular. In cigar stores, ice-cream parlors, diners, bars, and the lobbies of office buildings were the new and gaudy pinball games at which someone was always to be found swaying from side to side or rocking back and forth in an automatic but futile effort to guide a little metal ball along high-score paths in the hope of making a quarter on a nickel investment. Newsdealers and cigar stands generally had on hand a few punchboards with a hundred holes that could be punctured for a nickel apiece to release tiny slips of paper. One of these would oblige the board's owner to pay the lucky puncher the magnificent sum of one dollar. The spread of petty gambling was rarely denounced from the pulpit, possibly out of regard for the bingo games which had unexpectedly taken on a budgetary function in many parishes. The bulletin board of one house of worship bore the standing inscription, "Bingo Every Night in the Holy Spirit Room."

Of books, plays, movies, music, and radio there will be occasion to talk in a later chapter, but an aspect or two of the last of these cultural outcroppings should be touched on here. Only occasionally among the arts, radio was nevertheless a pervasive force, coming into its own in the Thirties because, providentially, it could provide just the cheap diversion required by the times. If Edgar Guest was right about the Depression sending "the family back to the fireside," the family went not so much in order to roast chestnuts and tell stories in the coziness of it all, still less to develop the art of conversation. It went rather to munch Indian nuts and enjoy a choice of two dream worlds—one that sold Jell-O and coffee and made people laugh enough to shrug off their troubles and one that sold soap and was so full of woe that their troubles seemed light in comparison.

With rare exceptions radio, in contrast to the decade's literature, was intensely personal, remote alike from the politics and the economics of depression. Controversy entered only as a playful feuding among the stars, something like the prankish mischief that Zeus and his colleagues perpetrated for the entertainment of the ancient Greeks. With the United States barely recuperating from the worst financial smash in its history and Europe reverting to the *Zeitgeist* of Attila the Hun, fans of American radio comedy were lost in the problems of Edgar Bergen's falling hair and Jack Benny's scroungy ways with a dollar. In real life there were savage feuds between Liberty Leaguers and New Dealers and between Stalinists and Trotskyists, but on the air the big battle was between a pitifully domesticated version of the great W. C. Fields and Charlie McCarthy, a celebrated ventrilo-

quist's dummy of the period. Charlie, who was for millions of
Americans at least as real as Secretary Wallace and much
realer than, say, Adolf Hitler, would hail Fields with the
greeting "Well, if it isn't W. C., the original half-man half-
nose," and get back, in a rasping alcoholic voice, such
endearing rejoinders as "Ah, the woodpeckers' pin-up boy."

Typically, the radio program that came closest to raising a
storm in the country had nothing to do with the Depression
or fascism or the threat of war but with Adam and Eve and
Mae West. In a skit on the Edgar Bergen show, Miss West,
whose luxuriant figure and come-up-and-see-me-sometime
manner in the films had won her a national following, in-
jected a good deal of that manner into a broad burlesque of
the Fall of Man. "I want something to happen, a little excitement—a little adventure," went Eve's not too daring lines,
but Miss West milked them for all they were worth: "A girl's
got to have a little fun once in a while. . . . There's no future
under a fig tree." Inevitably the serpent—addressed as "my
palpitatin' python"—was persuaded to swipe the essential
fruit for her, with the result that churchmen cried out at the
"smutty suggestiveness and horrible blasphemy." The chairman of the Federal Communications Commission issued a
drastic warning, and the National Broadcasting Corporation
not only apologized profusely but forbade any of its stations
from henceforth even allowing the mention of Miss West's
name.

But of the arts in the Thirties—from *Murder in the Cathedral* to the Alger books of the Left—more later. For the
moment let it merely be recorded that even in that hungry
decade, perhaps especially in that hungry decade, bread was
by no means enough.

Hardships of the Rich—
The Right and Roosevelt

3

If it was hard in the long run for the well-to-do to forgive President Roosevelt for having saved them from the consequences of their folly, it was next to impossible to forgive him when he tried to make sure they wouldn't repeat it. As he went his merry way preserving the American rich from future revolution, they became first annoyed, then resentful, and at length, though not too great length, hysterical.

In the early stages of mere annoyance, efforts were still made to preserve the amenities. Thus when the American Bankers Association met in Washington toward the end of 1934, the expansive dinner that usually preceded a Presidential speech was omitted because officials of the organization were fearful, as they reluctantly admitted, that liquor might loosen tongues to the point where an exhilarated banker might bawl out his thoughts about the President of the United States. Similarly, when the newly created Securities and Exchange Commission was about to pay its first visit to the New York Stock Exchange, an informal notice was sent to all brokers and employees requesting them kindly to refrain from booing the commissioners, a delicate feeling for the proprieties that was not destined to last.

Admittedly, little of what I learned of the lives of the rich in the 1930's came from personal experience. We had an unspoken agreement whereby I kept my distance from Newport, El Morocco, and the North Shore of Long Island, and they left me the lake in Central Park, the Coney Island boardwalk, and the subways. But, more than at any other time in American history, a powerful spotlight was trained on their activities, so we all got to know quite a bit about their habits and their problems. Then, too, there were always some who insisted on making good copy with public pronouncements in the artless tradition of Marie Antoinette. There was the Du Pont, for example, who, when urged by an advertising agency to have his company sponsor a Sunday-afternoon radio program, rejected the proposal out of hand because, he said, "At three o'clock on Sunday afternoons everybody is playing polo." Then there was Vincent Astor's reassuring contribution to national recovery: "During the present depression I feel that I should spend my money in my own country, and so I will open my Florida home this winter. Later, however, when the states recover, I plan to enjoy the winters in my Bermuda home."

I recall that in the very week when my family confronted one of several dispossess notices, a friend of mine who still had a runner's job on Wall Street showed me an editorial clipped from the *Financial Chronicle* that he rightly thought I might enjoy. "The wealthy and cultured have all suffered and been compelled to make sacrifices," it said. "The simple fact is that the greater the amount of wealth any individual has, the greater has been his loss." Logically sound, it was nevertheless the kind of arithmetic that may well have brought on the new mathematics.

One of my duties at the *World Tomorrow* was to collect material for a two-page feature called "Not in the Headlines," which consisted of short items designed to keep our readers posted on news of the peace movement, inequities

on the social and economic fronts, and other appropriately
solemn matters. One such item I have managed to dig up
throws at least a pale beam on the life of the rich in that
stricken decade:

> The mother of seven-year-old Lucy Cotton Thomas recently
> appeared before the Surrogate in New York City to demand a
> higher allowance from the estate of the girl's father. . . . The
> mother insisted that the existing allowance of $3,000 per month is
> wholly inadequate, since it restricts expenditures to $800 per
> month as the child's share of the rent of a Fifth Avenue apart-
> ment, $350 for chauffeur and maid service, $300 for clothing, $600
> for food, $700 for furnishings and repairs, and $400 for dancing
> lessons, music, flowers, etc. Surrogate Delahanty decided that
> Lucy must get along the best she can on $36,000 per year.

Another mean-spirited bit had to do with the salaries of
railroad presidents in a three-year period when the Railway
Brotherhoods had accepted several cuts in pay. The presidents, it seemed, had managed to get themselves tidy raises,
notably the head of the New Haven, who went from $75,000
a year in 1929 to $90,000. Awesome as such returns ap-
peared to me, on a salary of $21.50 a week (they are impres-
sive to me even now), they were just adequate compared
with the paychecks drawn by the giant salary makers of the
time. Midway in the Depression decade Alfred P. Sloan, Jr.,
was getting $516,311 for a year's toil as president of General
Motors. George W. Hill, president of the American Tobacco
Company, rated $380,976, President Thomas J. Watson was
paid $419,398 by the International Business Machine Cor-
poration, and, as chief of a publishing empire, William Randolph Hearst got a round half-million a year in salary, which
must have been lost at that in his vast over-all income.

Nineteen thirty-three was the year when Roosevelt became President, when some twenty million people depended
on unemployment relief, and when Barbara Hutton, the
Woolworth heiress, received $45,000,000 for becoming

twenty-one years old. Although the five-and-ten-cent store business was booming at the time, with a 20 percent net profit for the year, the pay of Woolworth salesgirls was down to $11 a week. I mention this sort of thing only in the hope that it may help to explain some of the attitudes of those of us in the Thirties who were not Barbara Hutton. Or Doris Duke, who in the same year came into some $30,000,-000 along with homes in four states and a fifth in Antibes, all fully staffed with servants. Or, for that matter, any of the young heirs named Astor, Vanderbilt, Mellon, and the like who in that decade received the greatest rewards of an acquisitive society without even doing anything acquisitive.

Concerning the private lives of the rich, as I have said, I knew only what I read, or what their representatives testified before Congressional committees. But both sources were copious and informative. It cost only a nickel (the price of a Sunday paper in those days) to catch the advertisement of Stern's department store, in which necessities like mink coats were being offered at crash sales for $595, or to note that a Park Avenue duplex that once fetched $35,000 could be had for $10,000. And at no cost at all one could sit in the public library and read in *Fortune* about the truly great contemporary movement—the gradual merging of High Society into Café Society:

In a day of hunger marches and bread lines an elaborate dinner dance for a hundred people (who arrived behind chauffeurs to descend in the shelter of a marquee to the flickering of photographers' flash bulbs) seemed to the owners of most great houses like vulgar if not dangerous ostentation. So most of them preferred to do their entertaining on their Long Island estates beyond the reach of publicity, or to give smaller (if even gayer) dinners in public hotels or cafés. And thus slowly, compounded of many different elements, at the outset unconscious of its own development in the obtrusive presence of noisier events, Café Society was born.

As one obtrusively involved in the noisier events, I would have been scarcely conscious that the Depression was "dealing a blow to the debutante ball that had been the old order's focal point," as *Fortune* put it, had it not been again for my duties as compiler of "Not in the Headlines." For one of the items I came up with, fairly early in the Depression, was devoted to this very subject. Under the head "The High Cost of Society Buds," it cited an authority on such affairs for the estimate that a young lady could be introduced to the smart set in 1931 for about $40,000. The breakdown of this figure may well have had something to do with my gradual drift leftward: evening gowns, $2,000 to $6,000 (my first and incorrect thought was that the hosts were buying evening gowns for all the guests as party favors); ballroom rental, $1,000; orchestra, $4,000; food, $20,000; and flowers, $5,000 to $12,000, which was almost as much as blooms for a gangster's funeral in the Twenties.

It must be said, however, that even a $40,000 debutante's ball was a step down from the days of glorious pre-depression lunacy, when launching a little girl fresh out of prep school might set a man back $75,000 or more. Long Island estates in the Twenties were converted, for a single evening, into tropical islands or Persian gardens, and one fond father had agents beat the bushes of South America, at untold expense, for thousands of gorgeous butterflies to be released in the ballroom at the peak of the evening.

It should likewise be said that, as the Thirties wore on, even $40,000 seemed a bit flashy, and by all accounts in the society pages and the fashion magazines of the time more and more debutantes were either dispensing with formal launchings or turning them into let's-go-proletarian larks. A Helen Hokinson cartoon in the *New Yorker* showed a weeping young heiress, whose father's scowling face is half-buried in the paper, pleading with her mother: "Well, then, can I come out *after* the revolution?"

Society parents who felt that, Depression or no Depression, some gesture had to be made to established ritual often settled for simple garden parties or teas, and the compromise must have been acceptable to the gods who preside over such matters because the girls were held to be as properly processed as if they had entered Society decked out as mistresses of Louis XIV at Long Island replicas of Versailles. In fact, some, enjoying the change, carried things to extremes. A contemporary account by a writer who saw this sort of thing instead of only reading about it, as I occasionally did, described the comedown in the *Saturday Evening Post:*

Costume balls last season took on a new aspect. Instead of the gorgeous get-ups that formed such a kaleidoscopic riot of color when U.S. Steel was selling around 260, overalls and pajamas were almost universally worn. In fact, costume balls positively thrive on depression. And why not? A boy would far rather put on a pair of blue denim overalls and tie a red handkerchief around his neck in preparation for the evening's festivities than accouter himself in his formal evening clothes, which are uncomfortable and a continual expense.

The girls of last season adored having an excuse to bring out their colorful beach pajamas and sandals instead of worrying over satin or chiffon frocks which would have to go to the cleaner's next day and be paid for out of carefully hoarded pocket money. They all sat around supper tables covered with red-and-white checked cotton cloth, the sole decoration being penny candles stuck in empty bottles, and ate scrambled eggs, frankfurters and sandwiches instead of lobster Newburg and chicken a la king. . . .

No doubt the well-to-do young favored the change, but to their well-to-do elders it was traumatic. Some of them began acting in strange ways. According to Cleveland Amory, a student of the species, there was hardly a club in New York in that depression decade that didn't suffer from the petty larceny of its members. One gentleman arrived at the University Club every Sunday morning in a chauffeur-driven car for the ostensible purpose of passing a quiet Sabbath hour but for the real purpose of stealing the Sunday newspaper.

It would be a mistake, no doubt, to ascribe such conduct solely to shock resulting from a decline in the standards of the debutante ball. There was also the dismay some clubmen may have felt at the frequent public revelations of professional wrongdoing by erstwhile pillars of society and models for the young. That is to say, with the rich in bad repute anyway, one might as well be hanged for a sheep as a goat. And in bad repute they surely were.

With investigations and trials of utilities executives and bank presidents constantly in the news, the wicked ways of the financial elite came almost to be taken for granted by a generation just then reaching the age of awareness. We could still recall our orthodox economics texts of the Twenties, in which the thrifty turned their hard-earned surpluses into savings and wise and prudent bankers converted those savings into investment capital to turn the wheels of industry, which in turn provided still more people with jobs and the opportunity to save and invest in an ever-expanding economy. And to expedite investments there was the Stock Exchange, where securities might be bought and sold at their true value through the free and wholesome play of the open market.

We could dimly recall the theory, I say, and we could still hear isolated voices preaching thrift, hard work, and untrammeled business. But both the memory and the voices were growing dim against mounting revelations of holding companies, stock pools, price manipulations, tips to favorite investors, watered stock, and stories for hire in the financial pages of the papers. By such shady means billions of dollars had been piled up by the cream of the financial community with nothing that their Puritan ancestors would recognize as hard work, thrift, or anything resembling Alger-type honesty. The number of former paragons of respectability who kept turning up as defendants in criminal proceedings or wriggling witnesses at Congressional inquiries was admittedly small compared with the number of bankers and brokers in the country, but it was large enough to reveal the accepted practices of the fraternity and in the public mind to associate such words as banker, magnate, tycoon, and titan with such other words as con man and swindler. I was not one to follow easily the manipulations of high finance, but like millions of other Americans I could understand Will Rogers' explanation that "A holding company is a thing where you hand an accomplice the goods while the policeman searches you."

We innocents could understand, too, that there was something very wrong about the scheme of things when Samuel Insull, the prince of holding company operators, felt obliged to hurry off to Greece, which had no extradition treaty with the United States, with a handbag containing ten million dollars in thousand-dollar notes.* We easily understood the indignation of Ferdinand Pecora, counsel to the Senate Banking and Currency Committee, when Albert H. Wiggin, chairman of the Chase National Bank of New York, admitted that he took some million dollars in pay from his institution while he was allowing it to incur losses of over $200 million, that he also drew salaries as a director of corporations to which he loaned Chase depositors' money, and that, when the climate got too warm, he allowed the Chase board to retire him on a pension of $100,000 a year for life.

The simplest-minded victims of the Depression were taken aback by the brazenness of great financiers like Charles E. Mitchell of the National City Bank, who blurted out to the Senators that he had sold nearly $3 million worth

---

* Even when he was ultimately acquitted of embezzlement, having admitted a $10-dollar mistake in accounting, a certain odor of greediness, to say the least, was bound to cling to a man who, on fleeing the country, could resign 85 corporate directorships, 65 chairmanships, and 11 presidencies.

of securities to his wife "frankly for tax purposes." It turned out to be a common practice among the wealthiest Americans to sell enough of their holdings to their wives, relatives, and friends, at a greatly reduced figure, to offset their year's profits and then buy the securities back at the same price. In this way even Morgan partners fended off the revenuers and in a period of dire national need got away with paying no income tax whatever. Mitchell's performance before the Senate was so raw that Assistant United States Attorney Thomas E. Dewey was constrained to put him under arrest. A jury subsequently acquitted him, the letter of the law being what it was, but the government successfully pressed civil claims that yielded some of what he rightfully owed. Those who paid taxes on grubbier sources of income, like wages and salaries, which they had turned over to their wives and families beyond a chance of recovering, naturally cheered every assault by the Administration on "economic royalists" and every threat by the President to drive the moneychangers from the temple.

But for telling drama none of these episodes held a candle to the downfall of Richard Whitney. Even by Wall Street standards here was an economic royalist in the Bourbon tradition. An extreme conservative, brother of a Morgan partner, and president of the Essex Fox Hounds as well as the Stock Exchange at the time Mr. Pecora was enjoying himself at the expense of that institution, he had treated the Senators with regal arrogance. Whatever was wrong, he said, the fault was not in Wall Street but on Pennsylvania Avenue, even in the spring of 1932 when Hoover was still in the White House. If the Senators wanted to do something constructive about the Depression, let them see to it that the budget was balanced, even if it meant cutting the salaries of all government employees, including Senators, who were then getting exactly one-sixth the pay drawn by Mr. Whitney and enjoying nothing like his opportunities for extensive earnings on the side. Away from the Capitol, not to mention Wall Street, he lectured on business morality and especially the need of brokers to be "honest and financially reliable."

And all the time, hard-pressed by his own astonishingly inept ventures, Mr. Whitney was dipping deep into securities entrusted to him by the New York Yacht Club, of which he was treasurer, those of a trust fund established by his father-in-law, and some belonging to customers of his brokerage firm. Again Tom Dewey stepped in, and this time a grand larceny charge stuck. On a spring day in 1938 some 6,000 people waited around the old Tombs prison and at Grand Central Station for a chance to see an economic royalist on his way to Sing Sing, handcuffed and in the company of two extortionists, a holdup man, and a rapist. For his first prison meal, a metropolitan journal solemnly reported to a public eager for detail, the former president of the Stock Exchange had baked lima beans, boiled potatoes, tea, bread, and cornstarch pudding. It was all very impressive and did almost as much to lower bankers in the general esteem as the lady midget who in one of the lighter moments of the Pecora hearings was suffered to sit on the Olympian knee of J. Pierpont Morgan.

For a short time, during the first year and a half of the Roosevelt era, a real feeling of relief had seemed to prevail among the still affluent Americans. There was to be no revolution after all. Those fearful ones who had stocked their country houses with canned goods—some were said to have laid in arms and ammunition as well—relaxed a bit and even took to sneering at the country's Reds for having no more to show after three years of depression than the election of an unsound fellow who had somehow managed to take the wind out of their sails. But it was not a mood that could survive the strikes, taxes, government controls, and sitdown strikes that lay just ahead.

Even by the end of 1933 the Right, still pale and shaky,

was beginning to find its voice and throughout the following year it nurtured hopes that the first fall Congressional election since the Hoover fiasco would put a brake on the ebullient "professors" in Washington. Some of the criticism was perfectly understandable, given the social views of the critics; some was cynically political, which was to be expected; and some was personally malicious to the point of paranoia.

The understandable outcries came from people who were adversely affected by NRA codes, many of them drawn up in haste and repented in leisure, from those who were nervous about the prospective costs of government aid to the economy, and from those who were genuinely shocked by an agricultural policy that attempted to raise farm prices by cultivating scarcity. Church groups in particular suggested that the drought that soon afflicted the Middle West was a divine punishment for this impious approach to agronomy, and others sardonically recalled Roosevelt's scathing campaign attack on Mr. Hoover's Farm Board for "the cruel joke of advising farmers to allow twenty percent of their wheat lands to lie idle, to plow up every third row of cotton and shoot every tenth dairy cow." In truth, these cavalier twists and turns in Mr. Roosevelt's attitudes—he had likewise denounced government spending under Hoover and promised to balance the budget—were in themselves a source of fearful doubt on the part of those whose ways were less airily pragmatic than the President's. To these stolid folk the very ebullience of the New Dealers, their joy in experimentation when there was in truth nothing to do but to experiment, was so unsettling that Bruce Barton, the archbishop of advertising, could prophetically warn that "The day will come when, compared to the word 'professor,' the word 'banker' will be a term of endearment."

Others, readily persuaded by a spate of articles in the *Saturday Evening Post* and elsewhere, were convinced that "natural forces" would have advanced the country much fur-

ther along the road to recovery if Roosevelt hadn't interfered
with the semidivine laws of economics. And still others,
possibly biased by their position in the scheme of things,
shared J. P. Morgan's view that "If you destroy the leisure
class, you destroy civilization."

Under questioning Mr. Morgan defined the leisure class to
include "all those who can afford to hire a servant." Technically that must have admitted my $50-a-week-income family
to this civilizing segment of society because we had a Slo-
vakian maid who had joined the menage in 1915 and stayed
on until she died in 1956. We would have let her go in the
late Twenties, since we could no longer pay her anything,
but by then she considered herself, and was considered by
us, a member of the family, the management of which she
had all but taken over. Besides, she often pitched in financially when the going was rough. She had been the only one
of us who had been able to take a flyer in the stock market
and had made some small winnings on her shares of what
she called "Misery Paficic."

While Republicans as such seemed at first too dispirited,
or perhaps won over, to lash out at the White Knights charging up and down Pennsylvania Avenue, the very rich of both
parties soon found themselves drawn together in desperate
defense. To combat radicalism, fend off the tyrants of the
New Deal, and preserve property rights, a few dozen sym-
bols of alarmed conservatism banded together to form the
American Liberty League. In the founding group were
Jouett Shouse and John J. Raskob, both former chairmen of
the Democratic National Committee Irénée du Pont, who
predicted that if the Administration didn't stop "trying to
sovietize the United States," the country would wind up
with either a civil war or a Russian scale of living; Nathan L.
Miller, former Republican Governor of New York; John W.
Davis, the Wall Street lawyer who had led the Democrats to
defeat in 1924; and, sadly, Al Smith, whose conservatism

represented the distance he had traveled from the Fulton Fish Market to the Empire State Building, not to dwell on his splenetic aversion for Roosevelt as the man who had prevented his continuing right on to the White House.

The Liberty League was more than faintly ridiculous and from the start suffered the fate of the easily caricatured. Reporters' requests for comment on the new force almost invariably drew quips rather than sober reactions. Harry Hopkins thought it "so far to the right that no one will ever find it." Huey Long guffawed and said he wouldn't join because someone else was president. And a prominent Republican leader declined membership, explaining, "I don't mind its being a rich man's lobby, but I do object to its looking like one." But no one had more sport with the group than F.D.R. himself. The League's defense of liberty and private property was unimpeachable, he observed, but it suggested to him an organization to uphold two of the Ten Commandments while ignoring the other eight. Scanning the New York *Times* in bed that morning, he had come across an item that read "Talk in Wall Street yesterday indicated that the announcement of the new American Liberty League was little short of an answer to a prayer." He laughed, he told reporters, for ten minutes. Such was the climate of the times that he could call the Liberty Leaguers "lovers of property" and have it repeated as a telling gibe.

The pomposities of the League were to prove a great deal easier to deflate than the malicious, often obscene, stories about "Franklin and Eleanor" that presently became a kind of social passport in some circles and a downright obsession in others. On the "Assassination Special" (to be found on all the better commuter lines) the President of the United States was referred to by the kindlier passengers as "That Man," a designation useful for those who didn't want to be nasty in front of children and strangers and who couldn't bear to pronounce the dread name. A noted journalist of the

Thomas, Detroit *News*, Nov., 1933

We Are Closing In on
This Kidnaper

Did I Hear a Bell Tolling?

Fitzpatrick, St. Louis *Post-Dispatch*, 1933

Looks as if the New Leadership Was
Really Going to Lead

F. D.'S JOBLESS RELIEF.

Bronx: Roosevelt talks about getting every one a job if he is elected. Why doesn't he start now by giving two of his wife's jobs to an unemployed teacher and an unemployed editor?

DISGUSTED DEMOCRAT.

Daily News, Nov. 6, 1932

Ray, Kansas City *Star*, March, 1933

DEPRESSION TURNS WELLESLEY LIFE

Decrease in Thoughtlessness and Selfishness in 5 Years Noted Among Students.

PRACTICAL RELIGION GAINS

Survey Finds Rise in 'Social Consciousness' With New Alertness to World Needs.

Special to THE NEW YORK TIMES.

WELLESLEY, Mass., Jan. 12.—
Five years of depression have
caused a considerable decrease in
thoughtlessness and selfishness
among the students of Wellesley
College, according to Stella Brewster, '29, general secretary of the
Christian Association.

In a survey of "practical religion," made for the Wellesley Magazine, Miss Brewster states that "social consciousness" has risen in the
student body as a result of the
depression.

"I find that, on the whole, students are far more alive to the
needs of the world than were my
fellow-students in 1929," she writes.

"I think I am safe in saying that
as social and economic problems
have come to the fore in the past
five years the student interest in
solving them has certainly increased. And I believe that the
average girl who graduates from
Wellesley today is better prepared
to enter our complex world than
was the graduate of 1929."

Although relatively fewer girls attend morning chapel, vespers and
Sunday services, Miss Brewster
finds an increase in those interested in social service, doing volunteer work for the Boston Family
Welfare Society, reading for the
blind at the Perkins Institute, settlement work and assisting in
clinics and in hospital and home
libraries.

New York *Times*, Jan. 13, 1935

Batchelor, *Sunday News*, Jan. 7, 19

We Planned It That Way

Chicago *Tribune*, Oct., 1936

Woman's Work Is Never Done

Hungerford, Pittsburgh *Post-Gazette*, Feb., 1937

Today's Boon-doggle

Special Dispatch to THE SUN, New York

The Sun Bureau,
Washington, Sept. 23.

Since the days of the Caesars and the wise politician has known that in times of strife the populace must be amused.

So in Lawton, Okla., the WPA is building $10,000 worth of shelter houses, suspension and foot bridges, and concrete skating rinks in the parks. The Federal Treasury pays more than 75 per cent of the cost.

New York *Sun*, Sept. 25, 1936

Fifty-Fifty

Thomas, Detroit *News*, Dec., 1935

Secretary Ickes on How to Pronounce It

To the Editor of The Literary Digest—Sir:—It is difficult for me to explain in writing how I pronounce my name. However, I believe you have worked it out pretty accurately. The final "s" should not be pronounced as a "z." Henry Adams Ickes is right when he says that the first syllable rhymes with "tick," and I think you come as close as anybody to it when you suggest that the last syllable rhymes with "sickness" with the "s" omitted. It seems to me that the final "e" is half-way between a short "e" and a short "u".

Harold L. Ickes
The Secretary of the Interior.
Washington, D.C. *Literary Digest*

Biting the Hand That Fed Him!

Talburt, Washington *Daily News*, Nov., 1933

Batchelor, *Daily News*, Jan. 8, 1936

Batchelor, *Daily News*, Oct. 1, 1936

Elephants and Donkeys

Sir:—In your issue of July 6 I believe you made a gross error in reproducing the caricature from the Chicago *Herald & Examiner* entitled "You Ain't Seen Nothin' Yet."

Many of your readers carefully preserve each copy for reference and future use for themselves, and for their posterity; and it is posterity that I am thinking about in drawing your attention to "You Ain't Seen Nothing Yet."

Such a caricature is very apt to give the future generations the wrong information. The picture shows an ascending graduation of the tax burden represented by elephants. To millions the elephant in caricature means nothing else but the Republican Party. In this case, in all fairness to the G.O.P., the cartoon should have been represented by the donkey, under whom all the taxing is being auspiced.

O. Henry Lindemann
Brooklyn, New York,
Literary Digest

Thank God for the Supreme Court!

THE Supreme Court of the United States has again upheld the Constitution and Americanism.

By a unanimous decision, the National Recovery Act has been declared unconstitutional.

This decision will be hailed with gratitude throughout the country.

It marks the emergence of sanity—from the welter of nonsense, confusion, crazy bill-drafting and adolescent experimenting, which make up so large a part of the New Deal.

It spells the knell of as greedy and insolent a bureaucracy as ever attempted to spread itself over a country dedicated to freedom and over a people pre-eminent for their sturdy virtues and self-reliant character.

Let us hope that it spells the end also of the pestilent innovator and empty-headed theorist in government.

* * *

THERE IS a way out of the depression; there IS an avenue to recovery; there IS an open return to happiness and prosperity,—but the road is the way of common sense, of respect for the fruits of work and enterprise, of respect for individual rights.

The way is the American way,—vindicated over and over again throughout our history.

It is the way that has made us a great and powerful nation; that has made the conditions of life among our people better than with any other people in the world.

It is the way of respect for our Constitution, the ark of our liberties, the foundation of our greatness, the source of our security, the promise of our future.

THANK GOD FOR THE SUPREME COURT OF THE UNITED STATES!

* * *

THE shifting gusts of short-lived and fleeting opinion cannot sway it. The froth of the strutting little reformers of the day, the shallow-pated innovators of the moment, the litter of a so-called Brain Trust, are powerless to confuse, much less sway, American judges.

Salutary, timely, needed, was this great decision.

It reminds the American people that the foundations of their life are deep-imbedded in justice and freedom; and that reason, self-command and sobriety both of thought and conduct are still American characteristics.

San Francisco *Examiner*, May 28, 1935

The Trojan Horse at Our Gate

Orr, Nov., 1935, © 1935, by the Chicago *Tribune*

Baer, Milwaukee *Leader*, Jan. 28, 1936

For Whatsoever a Man Soweth,
That Shall He Also Reap

Doyle, Philadelphia *Record*, Sept., 1934

"What Terrible Teeth, Grandma!"

Cargill, Milwaukee *Leader*, Jan. 9, 1936

Thomas, Detroit *News*, Jan., 1933

The Cave Gentleman

MONEY!

Questions and Answers

Much of the mystery of money is deliberate. The international bankers and their economists do not want the people to be informed. Father Coughlin's new book of 1,000 questions and simple direct answers places the whole subject within easy mastery of every person Write for your copy direct to the Rev Chas. E. Coughlin, Royal Oak. Mich

Social Justice, March 13, 1936

Social Justice, March 13, 1936

Don't Fail to Attend the
SOCIALIST BAZAAR
◂ ◂ and CARNIVAL ▸ ▸

MILWAUKEE AUDITORIUM
JANUARY 29, 30, 31, FEBRUARY 1, 2
AFTERNOON AND EVENING

PLAY BINGO, SINGO, DINGO AND SKILLO
DOOR PRIZES EVERY EVENING

| Card Parties Every Afternoon Except Jan. 29 Admission 25 Cents | **BARGAINS GALORE** Thousands of Dollars in Merchandise Given Away | FREE ENTERTAINMENT General Admission 10 Cents |

Hear Heinie and His Grenadiers

Milwaukee *Leader*, Jan. 23, 1936

Advertisement.

For Four Long Years!
Rent in ENGLAND

Devon, edge of Dartmoor

Elizabethan manor house; furnished or unfurnished; 8 master bedrooms; library; etc.; beautiful old paneling; lovely gardens; 900 acres shooting; one mile trout fishing; $1500 year. Telephone REgent 4-6600. Pease & Elliman, Inc., 660 Madison Avenue, N. Y.

New York *Sun*, Nov. 4, 1936

period reported a New Englander who kept talking about "Theodore," meaning the first President Roosevelt. He didn't know him personally, he explained, but he loathed Franklin too much ever to use the last name even when he was talking about a member of the good, Oyster Bay branch of the family.

"Traitor to his class" was a favorite epithet of the best people, and in the privacy of a golf club or a Pullman car references to the President's physical infirmity were considered in perfectly acceptable taste. Gene Talmadge, the wool-hat Governor of Georgia, required no privacy at all when he referred to Roosevelt as "that cripple in the White House."

Jokes about the President were unimaginatively dreadful and dreadfully unimaginative. They leaned heavily on old formulas, like "Have you heard the good news? Roosevelt died and Hopkins got killed on the way to the funeral." What gave this particularly wretched specimen resilience was that any Democrat could be substituted for Hopkins— Governor Lehman in New York, Governor Earle in Pennsylvania, and the like. So automatic, in fact, was the "humor" in this area that when Elsa Maxwell put on a "Pet Hates Ball," to which each guest was to come disguised as his bête noire, the invitations specified that no one was to come as the President or his wife, for fear the ballroom would be monotonously jammed with imitation Roosevelts.

It was not the jokes, however, that made one so uncomfortable in the presence of the anti-Roosevelt fanatics. These could be brushed off, or, if circumstances absolutely demanded, given the recognition of a mild snicker. What was really difficult was to be confronted with glassy-eyed haters who really believed the fearful reports they circulated. It was a common experience to be asked in deadly seriousness and with an air of some surprise whether one really didn't know that the President had suffered a mental breakdown. The first few times that I heard this sort of thing I was appalled that people could carry political opposition to such lengths, not believing for an instant that my informants really believed what they were saying. It was not until some years later that I came across a relevant story by Elliott V. Bell, then a financial writer for the New York *Times* and later chairman of the New York State Banking Department under Governor Dewey.

The head of one of New York's leading banks, Bell wrote, remarked to him that he thought Roosevelt was "crazy," and when the writer expressed doubt that he meant the word literally, the banker replied, "Yes, I do. I think the man is absolutely unbalanced." Bell would have paid no further attention to the remark had he not gone immediately to another banker and heard from him exactly the same comment —"a pathological case." Shortly afterwards, he reports, "it came out in the course of a Senate investigation that an obscure and misguided publicity man had conceived the idea of undermining the President by a whispering campaign to the effect that his mind was unbalanced." The Senate revelation naturally failed to come even close to catching up with the story itself, and for the rest of the Roosevelt era one frequently met perfectly sincere individuals who were convinced that the country was being run by a madman.

Others genuinely believed that a dictator had taken over, not a whit different from Stalin, Hitler, or Mussolini, and they predicted just as ardently in 1944 as in 1940 and 1936 that "If That Man wins—this will be our last free election." Still others explained Mrs. Roosevelt's constant travel, speeches, and general hyperactivity on the ground that she was planning to take over the Presidency when Franklin was through and hold it until the young Roosevelts were ready to step in, just as a later generation was to carry on about the Kennedy "dynasty."* And of course there were those who

---

* The President cheerfully joined in the general teasing about his wife's peripatetic ways to the extent of once giving her the wartime code name of "Rover."

maintained that except for state dinners the whole family lived on an exclusive diet of Martinis, incredibly dry.

Far more appalling than these simple "insights" into the lives of the great were the truly elaborate scare stories that were offered by men in public life as timely exposés of dire mischief afoot. Earliest among these hallucinations was that of Senator Thomas D. Schall, a Minnesota Republican who even in the first months of the New Deal regularly referred to the President as "Frankenstein Roosevelt" and to the NRA Blue Eagle as "the Soviet duck." In November of 1934, Senator Schall went on the radio to impart to millions of Americans his secret information that the Administration was about to clamp a permanent censorship on the nation's press and radio. "The Brain Trust is preparing . . . for a national press service," he reported, which was to take the place of the Associated Press, the Hearst news services, and the United Press, and which would serve only those papers loyal to "the dictatorship." All other news services would be suspended. Nobody knows how many people believed that such a plot was in the making and was nipped only by the alertness of Senator Schall, who felt no compulsion then or later to offer a shred of evidence.

At least as bizarre and more highly publicized was the episode of Dr. William Wirt, erstwhile superintendent of schools in Gary, Indiana. To prove to a committee of the House of Representatives that the Administration was taking the country down the "road from democracy to communism," especially through the bill to regulate stock exchanges which was then before the committee, Mr. James H. Rand, of the Remington Rand Corporation, solemnly submitted a memorandum by Dr. Wirt on a dinner party he had attended some months before. At this affair, Dr. Wirt's document stated, several "brain trusters" had leaked the New Deal plot to hamper economic recovery to such a degree that in desperation the country would willingly accept complete government control. In their own good time the Com-

munist plotters would then get rid of Roosevelt, "the Kerensky of their revolution," and install their own Lenin or
Stalin, possibly one of the guests at the dinner party.

Dr. Wirt himself was shortly thereafter brought before the
committee and he proved at once vapory and garrulous. The
only hard information the committee finally elicited from
him and other witnesses was that none of the guests could
remotely be regarded as influential figures in the government; that Wirt himself had done most of the talking, giving
his table companions no chance for anything more than po-
lite nods; and that the person who had mentioned Kerensky
was not in the government at all or anywhere near it. If the
uproar was ludicrous, it nevertheless filled news columns
and airwaves for days and, though a fiasco in its own right,
the Wirt performance set the style for landslides of nonsense
to come.

None of this farrago on the Right, as repeated elections
would show, was taken seriously by those who had been
jobless and were now working, by those who had been
homeless and were now at least on relief, or by those who
were so warmed by the new glow from Washington that
they wouldn't believe a Wirt if he swore on an anthology of
Herbert Hoover's speeches. But those for whom the New
Deal meant higher taxes, more regulation, and a less free
and easy way with other people's money tended naturally to
accept whatever they read that reinforced their growing re-
sentment. Something like 90 percent of the press gladly ac-
commodated them.

In the New York area it was possible for a rider of the
Assassination Special to insulate himself completely from all
pro-Roosevelt sentiment. His fellow passengers swapped the
Franklin-and-Eleanor jokes he wanted to hear, the *Herald
Tribune* provided him with dignified anti-Administration
and anti-union coverage on his way to work and the *Sun* did
likewise on his way home. The *Sun* in particular could be

counted on to deride all works projects as boondoggles, including Boulder Dam, to predict that Social Security would compel all Americans to wear numbered metal tags, to "link C.I.O. with Reds" every afternoon, and to run such perceptive social comment by featured analysts as the following item on the New Deal's pampered poor:

> You and I know from actual experience that nine out of ten of the poor, among whom we were reared in this city, remained so because of their refusal to accept their opportunities and because of their own vices. We know that nine out of every ten rich, middle class or poor who made a go of things have done so because of their initiative and honesty.

For more flamboyant tastes combined with the same prejudices there were Hearst's *American* in the morning, until 1937, and his *Journal* in the evening. Actually Hearst's anti–New Deal policies were a little slow to flower, and naturally enough since he had been influential in swinging the desperately needed California and Texas delegations to Roosevelt at the Democratic Convention of 1932. He took particularly strong exception to the NRA, with its emphasis on higher wages and shorter hours, but for a while the censure was, for Hearst, gentle: "It would appear that whenever business in the present emergency has succeeded in getting its head above water, the National Recovery Act, with the best intentions in the world, has alertly thrown it a millstone or a coil of lead pipe as a life preserver, and has promptly sunk it again."

What was really disturbing Hearst was disturbing most newspaper publishers, who never forgot that they were running a business first and only then, if at all, a public enterprise. This was the effort of the President, by way of the proposed NRA code, to eliminate child labor, of which newsboys constituted one of the largest blocs in the country. The Administration finally accepted a position far short of

eliminating newsboys, but even a modification of the venerable and cheap custom, such as limiting the hours newsboys
could work, was bitterly denounced as an attack on the freedom of the press. Editors wept over the plight of youngsters
kept from emulating those great Americans who had
launched their careers in Horatio Alger fashion by peddling
papers from dawn to dusk. They did not even blush when
Lewis E. Lawes, the Warden of Sing Sing Prison, revealed
that 69 percent of his charges had likewise started out as
newsboys.

What with the Administration's interference with wages
and hours and its encouragement to the Newspaper Guild to
organize their staffs, whatever enthusiasm publishers had
originally shown for Roosevelt soon vanished from the great
majority of their papers. Hearst ultimately went berserk, as
he had long before with Presidents McKinley and Wilson.
The Wagner Act, which supplanted the outlawed NRA as an
incentive to the unions, was branded "un-American to the
core." The Administration's tax programs were, on orders,
characterized in all Hearst papers as a policy of "Soak the
Successful." And the New Deal itself soon became

> The Red New Deal with a Soviet seal
> Endorsed by a Moscow hand;
> The strange result of an alien cult
> In a liberty-loving land.

By the mid-Thirties he was swinging so wildly that union-
sponsored boycotts were organized against his papers, and
the President felt called on to denounce Hearst's attacks on
himself as "conceived in malice and born of political spite."

If Hearst's papers were losing money, and they were, he
was at least getting a rise out of New York liberals, which in
those days was admittedly no great feat. Six thousand of us
whooping enthusiasts gathered in the old Hippodrome for a
mock trial in which Governor Peterson of Minnesota and

Arthur Garfield Hays prosecuted the great yellow journalist on a charge of "attempting to destroy democracy." Thanks to testimony by such expert, if carefully chosen, witnesses as Oswald Garrison Villard, editor of the *Nation*, he was convicted in the first degree by vote of the entire audience and sentenced to a boycott. Since none of us six thousand jurymen would have used a Hearst paper to wrap fish and not more than a hundred, probably, had cars on which to post the "Don't Read Hearst" stickers which were distributed, the sentence may not have hurt the defendant's pocket as much as his feelings.

In a class with the Hearst press for vitriol, and much sooner to use it against Mr. Roosevelt and all his works, was Colonel McCormick's Chicago *Tribune.** Just as it was later to find that in spite of the attack on Pearl Harbor it could still blame Roosevelt for getting us into the war by suggesting that he had somehow put the Japanese up to it, so in the Thirties the *Tribune* managed to contend that he "saved" us from the Depression only by conspiring to produce it in the first place:

When everything has been revealed of that period it is probable that proof will be found supporting the charge that Mr. Roosevelt himself avoided doing anything helpful and that his supporters did everything harmful they could. The country weaved its way blindly to the crash, which was nicely timed to coincide with the inauguration. The revolutionaries had not only preserved their depression but they had brought it to its full paralyzing effect just when they could take over and assert that only their methods would save what was left.

If the news columns and editorials were not consolation enough for the frightened commuter, there were always the columnists. At the outer edge of respectability, addressing

---

* Throughout the 1936 presidential campaign the *Tribune*'s switchboard operators greeted all callers with: "Good morning. Chicago Tribune. There are only —— days left in which to save the American way of life."

themselves to the passions, were George Sokolsky, who wrote fiercely anti-labor diatribes for the *Herald Tribune* while drawing regular checks as a consultant to the National Association of Manufacturers, and Westbrook Pegler, a free-swinging maverick. Pegler for a time delighted liberals when he wrote that he would rather see Generalissimo Franco in hell than in church, only to embark on a matchless career of Roosevelt baiting that was not in the least slowed down by the eventual death of his targets. Just as comforting to the commuter mind and probably easier on the bile were such equally conservative but less inflammatory columnists as Frank Kent, Mark Sullivan, David Lawrence, and, to some degree in those days, Walter Lippmann. Even Dorothy Thompson, when she wrote on domestic matters, was a defender of traditional economics against the wild men of the New Deal. Among the columnists the only giant the New Deal could claim was Heywood Broun, and he was for Roosevelt intermittently and only as preferable to his enemies.

But editors and columnists have only one vote apiece, as we learned in the 1936 elections, which will be dealt with by and by. Hundreds of commuters greeted each other morning after morning with "Say, did you see what this fellow Sokolsky said about That Lunatic in last night's paper?" Or "By God, Pegler really gives it to Eleanor today!" And, soothed further by *Time* and the *Literary Digest* and the *Wall Street Journal,* they really thought they were hearing the voice of the people. They were surprised by the heavy tremors of the 1934 Congressional elections, terrified by the eruption of 1936, dazed by the third-term shock of 1940, and left numb by 1944. That Man didn't even need a dynasty—he was one.

The Politics of the Absurd—
The Left and Roosevelt

4

Except in a small circle of eccentrics, it is generally conceded now that the American Communist Party, even in that high tide of its history known as the Red Decade, failed to take over the government of the United States. Nationally its vote progressed from 103,000 votes in 1932, to 80,000 in 1936, to 46,000 by the end of the decade, well below the total for the dying Prohibition Party. In all that time of troubles the Communists put nobody in office by *coup d'état* and, except for electing the mayor of Crosby, Minnesota (population 2,500), they enjoyed no single voting triumph in their own right, though they no doubt contributed to seating the late Michael Quill in the New York City Council by the grace of proportional representation.

But if the Communists did not fool most of the people even some of the time, they did make an imprint on the decade somewhat out of proportion to their numbers, their skill, or their native power to inspire. And for this there were reasons that had nothing to do with Karl Marx. If the momentary needs of the Soviet Union had not for four short years happened to coincide, in part, with the longings of a good many decent Americans, there would have been no Popular Front. And without the Popular Front the Commu-

[77

nist Party would have seemed to the thousands of innocents who went in and out of its revolving doors from 1936 through most of 1939 as improbable an instrument for good as it had seemed before that time and has seemed since.

Certainly before 1936 life with the Communists must have required unusual strength of purpose, not to say palate. Little as my circle of friends, attending night sessions at City College, relished our financial prospects in the first few years of the decade, we rarely read the *Daily Worker*, and when we did it was solely for laughs. In free periods we would occasionally spread it out on the great oak tables of the basement dining hall, which looked like a Grade B movie version of Alt Heidelberg, and marvel at the caricatures of journalism that it offered. "Hoover smirks at all the mass suffering," ran a typical report from Washington. "Let the workers die! What does he care, so long as they die quietly, without demonstrating, making a noise about it, threatening to storm the gates of power!" Judging from the *Worker*, the Communists had sold themselves on the idea that nobody else was right about anything or even wanted to be. To convey their sense of a pervasively wicked world, as well as the bouquet of party prose in that period, I cite a few further passages culled at random from that journal:

That the Socialist Party is the third capitalist party and is allied with the gangsters and bosses and is the most ruthless tool in the hands of the capitalists against the workers, was apparent at the Socialists' open-air meeting on Mathon Street, Brighton Beach on June 26. [A news lead never dreamed of in your schools of journalism.—R.B.]

The great danger in the developing struggles against the capitalist offensive is the demagogy and treachery of the leaders of the American Federation of Labor. . . . These must be especially watched and fought against as the enemies and traitors within our midst.

It is obvious that the "pacifism" of the Church is just a fake and a swindle. . . . Especially vicious are the so-called liberal churchmen, who are trying to cover up the reactionary essence of the Church with humanitarian and pacifist phrases.

That is enough, no doubt, to convey the general flavor, though it should be said that party journalism was occasionally capable of stark simplicity. Reporting an atheistic speech in Boston by one Comrade Anthony Bimba, the *Worker* ran the unadorned headline: "There is No God— Bimba."

It would not have occurred to me to take the Communists in those days as anything but a joke, sometimes pathetic but more often preposterous, and the little I saw of them unfailingly reinforced this view. In my nocturnal school life I encountered them chiefly in the form of pickets solemnly parading up and down Convent Avenue with placards reading "Oust Robinson." To which the Robinson in question, in his capacity as president of the college, responded on one occasion by whacking a demonstrator on the head with his umbrella. In the campus hilarity that followed, Dr. Robinson and his umbrella became symbolically linked long before the same sort of thing happened to Neville Chamberlain.

In my working hours I saw the comrades from time to time in skirmishes with the police, who were always called "Cossacks," in Union Square and City Hall Park. Their demands on those occasions were chanted rhythmically and repeatedly, every word receiving the same stress, until they had a hypnotic effect—"We-want-jobs, We-want-jobs," "Free-Tom-Mooney, Free-Tom-Mooney." Against the background of this chorus went a brand of oratory new to me, featuring figures of speech exotic to my Western Pennsylvanian ear. The speakers, usually mounted on soft-drink boxes, seemed to live in a world of outlandish creatures, where "petty bourgeois degenerates" walked by day and

"Social Fascist reptiles" crawled by night. Observing even this much of the Communists, I had no trouble believing tales of their total divorce from reality, like the story—there were several versions—of the *Daily Worker* reporter who burst into his office one day yelling, "Hold everything, it's begun! The masses are storming the Amalgamated Bank!"

But if the Communists alone were too odd to move me, even in mass renditions of "The International," the police could sometimes be counted on to move me for them. The thud of a night stick on a human body was enough to send my temperature soaring and the sight of a mounted cop charging into a packed sidewalk made me, at least for the moment, a silent but seething defender of the masses.

Such flashes of empathy were soon gone, however. Another taste of Communist rhetoric and I was back to my old bourgeois self. Like the "economic royalists" denounced by Roosevelt, the Communists saw the New Deal only as a public "trough," but instead of its being at the disposal of the shiftless, as the rich complained, it was there for "the big capitalists to eat their fill." The NRA was designed to "forge new chains for labor." Roosevelt and Mussolini were "blood brothers," and the devious goal of the Administration, as a party leaflet had it, was to preserve profits, to establish fascism, and to wage imperialist war abroad." "*Why* does Lindbergh fly all over?" asked a Communist street orator of the moment. "*Why* did Post and Gatty go around the world? *Why* does Amelia Earhart, a woman, fly to Ireland? I'll tell you why, my friends: To divert the minds of the masses from the crisis, that's why!"*

* A couple of years later the Chicago *Tribune* showed the same suspicious mentality in dealing with a Soviet aviation feat. In sending a plane from Moscow to the U.S. by way of the North Pole, the *Tribune* explained, the Russians "timed their flight to land in America when Lewis and his C.I.O. needed something to distract the public attention from their violent activities . . ." Possibly the *Tribune* and the Communists were served by the same public-relations firm.

Bank run, New York City, 1930. *(UPI)*

DEPRESSION

The Bowery, 1933.
(Culver Pictures, Inc.)

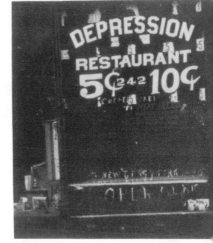

Hooverville, Hudson River and Seventy-fifth Street. *(Culver Pictures, Inc.)*

HUNGER

"Lady Bountiful," who fed 2,000 to 3,500 men daily on the Bowery. (*Literary Digest, Feb. 14, 1931*)

"Mr. Zero" serving food on Thanksgiving Day, 1931. *(UPI)*

Appleseller, 1930. *(UP*

Breadline, New York, 1930. *(UPI)*

Oklahoma dust storm. *(Photo by Margaret Bourke-White, The Bettmann Archive)*

DROUGHT

Tenant farmers near Warner, Oklahoma, 1939. *(The Bettmann Archive)*

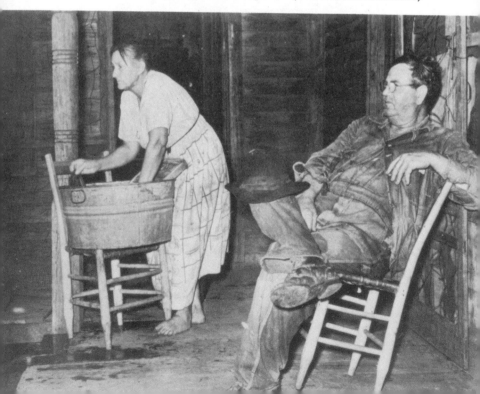

President Hoover and President-elect Roosevelt on inauguration day, 1933. *(UPI)*

THE CORNER

Fun after gloom: miniature golf course. *(Culver Pictures, Inc.)*

COOPERATION

Eleanor Roosevelt,
Poughkeepsie, New York,
1933. *(UPI)*

General Hugh S. Johnson,
NRA administrator, 1933. (

retary of Labor Frances Perkins,
38. *(UPI)*

Secretary of the Treasury William
H. "Wee Willie" Woodin,
1933. *(UPI)*

retary of the Interior Harold
es and Secretary of Agriculture
ary Wallace with F.D.R., 1933.
PI)

Al Smith and his famous brown derby, 1931.
(UPI)

PERSONALITIES

Vice President and Mrs. John Nance Garner;
Jesse Jones, in rear; and Will Rogers, 1935.
(UPI)

John L. Lewis, President, C.I.O.
1937. *(UPI)*

THE POLITICS OF THE ABSURD

In 1934 there was a change, or at least the advance rumble of a change. From the terrible triumph of Adolf Hitler the Communist high command must have concluded that its policies in Germany had been at least questionable, that without some degree of cooperation among the Marxist parties at the very least, fascism would quickly spread, with possibly fatal consequences not only for Communist parties abroad but, eventually, for the Soviet Union itself. The result was the first faint, tentative, and bearlike move toward some sort of common front—not with the bourgeois liberals and reformers, Marx forbid, but only with Socialists; and not with any notion of equals banding together, but only of Communists showing the Socialists the error of their ways and leading them into the light.

As always, what was at least understandable in Moscow lost something in the translation, becoming downright ludicrous by the time it was converted into action in New York. My Socialist colleagues on the *World Tomorrow*, as horrified as any by the bloodthirstiness of the Nazis, might have given a sympathetic ear to the siren call of unity if the American Communists had not incredibly accompanied the call with reminders of the Socialists' "complete bankruptcy," their "traitorous betrayals of the German masses."

When the Socialists showed a certain reluctance to shoulder all the blame for Hitler or to buy unity through total surrender to the Communists, the latter proceeded to bull ahead with what they called—they had an inimitable way with a phrase—the "united front from below." What this meant was that if the rival party would not come over en masse, the Communists would, in the name of anti-Fascist unity, try to turn the rank-and-file Socialists against their own leaders.

The occasion selected for a supreme effort at this type of diplomacy was a rally at Madison Square Garden which the Socialists and a number of trade unions had called as a protest against the murderous bombardment of the Vienna workers' apartments by the Austrian government of Chancellor Dollfuss. Uninvited, the Communists turned out in strength for the meeting, harangued and howled down speakers they disapproved of, like the "wage-cutting, strike-breaking Mayor La Guardia," and sought to woo the Socialists to unity by abusing their "saboteur leaders." Inevitably punches were traded, chairs went flying through the air, and scores left the Garden with contusions, abrasions, and lasting indignation. Enthusiasm for a "United Front" cooled noticeably.

This was the first occasion I knew of—there were to be many more—when intellectuals who had been drawn toward the party recoiled in shock and became in consequence not merely worthless, personally and professionally, in the swift and merciless judgment of the Communist hierarchy, but retroactively so. Among those who signed an open letter criticizing the Communists' sudden and unseemly public lust for unity were such luminaries as John Dos Passos, Clifton Fadiman, Edmund Wilson, John Chamberlain, and Robert Morss Lovett. Except for Dos Passos, whom the party evidently thought worth granting a second chance, the protestors were immediately scorned for their "gratuitous criticism" and put down as "revolutionary butterflies" fresh out of their academic cocoons, "minus political knowledge" —and "minus integrity" as well. They were condemned forthwith to be stripped of their honorary appellation of "comrade."

The Communists did have a talent for latching onto good and appealing causes, however, and an equal talent for exploiting them both politically and financially. Easily the best of these, from both points of view, was the Scottsboro case, which dragged on throughout the decade. For allegedly raping two white Southern ladies who happened to be riding a freight train with them, as ladies will, nine Negro youths spent the Thirties, and considerably more, in Alabama prisons. Long stretches of solitary confinement were included in a nightmare round of convictions, appeals, and reconvictions, with several of the defendants repeatedly under sentence of death in the electric chair. Ruby Bates, one of the belles involved, recanted her testimony after the first trial, but this served only to annoy successive judges and juries, and so did the choice of defense lawyers, notably Samuel S. Leibowitz, who were retained by the Communist International Labor Defense. Summing up in one of the trials, at which the courtroom audience had been encouraged from time to time to cheer the prosecution and jeer the defense, the state's attorney asked the death penalty not only to teach "other rapists" a lesson but to demonstrate that "Alabama justice cannot be bought with Jew money from New York."

With the worldwide revulsion that set in, the Communists, who did in fact initiate the defense and keep it going through the early trials, were able to make considerable hay. Estimates of what was raised in benefits and drives ran as high as a million dollars, and Mrs. Wright, the mother of two of the boys, was sent on a European tour to raise more funds and fever. She was so successful that at one time nine road company "Mrs. Wrights" were working the more remote corners of the world. A reasonable guess of what was actually spent on the boys' defense was closer to $60,000 than a million. But even if these figures are considerably off target, there is no doubt that each legal setback made more friends for the boys and more friends and money for the party, a contribution for which the State of Alabama has yet to claim the recognition that is its due.

Considering the political complexion of the current organization known as the W. E. B. DuBois Clubs, there is a measure of irony in the comment of the late Dr. DuBois in the early days of the Scottsboro affair. "If the Communists want these lads murdered, then their tactics of threatening judges and yelling for mass action on the part of white Southern workers is calculated to insure this," the Negro leader wrote in the *Crisis*. "The ultimate object of the Communists was naturally not merely nor chiefly to save the boys accused at Scottsboro; it was to make this case a center of agitation. . . ."

The Communists had a few other good causes going for them at the time, especially the case of Angelo Herndon, a young Negro whose single speech on Communism got him a twenty-year prison sentence in Georgia under an anti-insurrection statute left over from carpetbagger days. But in spite of these boosts, the comrades, in the doctrinaire spirit of the times, were still more adept at repelling than attracting. With some fifteen million Americans out of work in the early days of the New Deal, they had managed to herd no more than thirteen thousand into the party corral, or less than one-tenth of one percent even of the country's most desperate segment. Somehow the party's propaganda buckshot seemed to pass harmlessly over the heads of the proletariat, lodging instead in the hides of a few New York intellectuals, artists, and actors, and some guilt-ridden or novelty-seeking sons of "economic royalists," all collectively described by a contemporary Wobbly as the "Workers and Peasants of Greater New York." It was this same capacity for misfiring that was to help give the Left side of American politics in the second half of the decade a flavor of eccentricity not contemplated in the works of Marx and Engels.

Late in the summer of 1935 the Seventh Congress of the Communist International convened in Moscow. At the time this was an event of interest in the United States only to *aficionados*, of whom I was not one. But it was soon to have a retroactive interest for scores of thousands who had not previously troubled to distinguish between a kopek and a kulak.

After several years of hopefully watching for signs that the villainous Hitler might either evaporate or become his ally, Stalin had concluded that for his own safety the Nazis had to be roped off. Henceforth the overriding task of Communist parties in every land would be to build a Popular Front against this brute regime. To many Americans the thought of an international movement to "contain" the likes of Hitler, Goering, and Goebbels (though the word containment was not in diplomatic vogue at the time) was in itself almost irresistible. But that was only the beginning in a coinciding of interests that was to give the Popular Front a genuine and powerful appeal—for me, among thousands of others.

Less than a year after the launching of the new Communist line a few Spanish army garrisons stationed in Spanish Morocco rose against the duly elected republican government in Madrid. The attempt would have come to nothing except the imprisonment or possibly the shooting of three or four reactionary generals, who would not likely have been missed, had not Mussolini and Hitler quickly seized on the rising for their own purposes, which included staging a dry run for World War II. As Hermann Goering was to testify years later, it was a chance to try out "my young Luftwaffe . . . under combat conditions." At the end of a few weeks the Spanish government was in control of all but a few cities, having crushed the army rebels in Madrid, Barcelona, Valencia, and elsewhere, but at this point Generalissimo Franco elected to save Christian Spain from its infidel government with Moorish mercenaries, Italian cynics, and German worshipers of Wotan, Thor, and Adolf Hitler. Numerically, by far the greater part of Christian Spain resisted, but 90 percent of the army's top officers went over to Franco, taking their military hardware with them.

The Moors were landed from North Africa and were soon fighting alongside Mussolini's men under skies flecked with Messerschmitts getting their first workout. On the other side, Russian officers, commissars, agents, guns, and equipment soon showed up, and so did volunteers from fifty countries, come to fight for Spanish democracy in an International Brigade. It was the first such unofficial military commingling since Lafayette, Rochambeau, von Steuben, and Pulaski had given a collective hand to the American Continental Army.

A Front centering on support for the Loyalists was bound to be Popular. Exactly what people feared that Hitler and Mussolini planned to do to the rest of Europe, if they could, General Franco, aided and abetted by those two monuments of the New Order, was already doing to the high-spirited people of Spain. There it was, spread out for all to read in the newspapers and magazines, or to hear at lectures given by journalists returned from the front, or to see in the newsreels: women dragging children by the hand across the streets of a bombarded Madrid; the machine-gunning of civilians and militiamen in the bullring at Badajoz, the senseless destruction of Guernica, which Senator Borah, in the innocence of those pre-Coventry, pre-Lidice, pre-Auschwitz days, thought "the most revolting instance of mass murder in all history." When the *New Republic* asked an exhaustive list of writers for their views on the struggle, 410 of the 418 who sent in comments took their stand with the Loyalists. Seven were on the fence, and exactly one, Gertrude Atherton, spoke up for Franco. Respondents were by no means limited to the Left, moreover, and their answers were emphatic. Was Republican William Allen White opposed to Franco? "Sure, multiplied by six." Thornton Wilder was "unreservedly" for the "legal government" of Spain. John Steinbeck indignantly posed the counter-question: "Have you seen anybody not actuated by greed who was for Franco?" And Edgar Lee Masters was "for republican Spain, *of course.*"

In addition a large body of politically disinterested Protestants sympathized with the Spanish Loyalists simply because the Franco side leaned heavily on the most conservative segment of the clergy, socially and religiously, then to be found in the Catholic world. There were some Protestants, too, especially in the South, who were pro-Loyalist out of plain anti-Catholic bias. Needless to say, these were an embarrassment to the flaming liberals of the North, who had up to then enjoyed no common ground with Dixie Fundamentalists except to vote every four years for the same Presidential candidate.

Except for the three thousand or so Americans who joined the International Brigades—these were Communists, Socialists, and some non-Marxist idealists who were later to be branded as "premature anti-Fascists"—opportunities for helping the Loyalists were seriously, though not gravely, limited. People "ate lunch against Franco," as Elmer Davis put it, they drank for the Loyalists at innumerable parties, and at gatherings, on street corners, at theater benefits, and even at private dinners they seemed always to be passing the plate for Spain. Sheet music for "The Song of the Abraham Lincoln Battalion" was sold at ten cents a copy, receipts to be used, it said on the cover, "to send comforts to the Americans in Spain." Even the song itself, which I can't recall ever having heard performed, was stronger in material appeal than inspirational. The final verse, somewhat sacrificing rhythm, rhyme, and spirit to concrete message, went:

The Lincoln Battalion boys in Spain need books and cigarettes,
Let's send them the things they need to carry on,
       you'll have no regrets,
A penny or two, or a buck would do,
You'd be surprised how a few cents help.
Don't forget! Don't neglect, send them books and cigarettes.

Fortunately for the Battalion, it enjoyed more professionally artistic help than that. It was nothing for its supporters to pack the biggest theatre in New York to enjoy the donated performances of top stars. "In Person," proclaimed the ads for a typical Loyalist benefit, "Ed Wynn, Paul Lukas, Al Shean, Duke Ellington, and Juanita Hall Choir, among others."

When people weren't eating, drinking, or collecting for Spain, they might be writing irate letters to the New York *Times* in the running war between the devotees of Correspondent William P. Carney, who idolized Generalissimo Franco, and Correspondent Herbert L. Matthews, who did not. Looking back thirty years later, I find myself still shocked that the *Times* should have been taken in by a propagandist as blatant as Carney, who, contradicting Franco himself, wrote in one defensive dispatch that "Madrid cannot be considered an open city." Even so, the *Times* was far above the *Sun* and the Hearst papers, which always referred to the Loyalists as "Reds" and slyly lumped Mussolini's troops in with the Franco forces, even when the Italians were fighting an action by themselves, under the general term of "insurgents." Pro-Loyalist cartoonists had a field day, of course, depicting the Fascisti and the *Luftwaffe* airmen over such captions as "Nobody here but us insurgents."

The other focus of action was the United States embargo against sending arms to Spain. At President Roosevelt's request the Neutrality Act had been modified to include civil wars, with the result that in the name of non-intervention we allowed the rebels to get all the help they wanted from Germany and Italy, while the elected government of Spain was deprived of help from the democracies, since France and England "non-intervened" even more drastically than we did. Accordingly, a great deal of energy went into bombarding the President, the State Department, and Congress with petitions, demands, denunciations, and occasionally sweet reasonableness. But all in vain. Pressure from pro-Franco groups may have been a factor, but it was a minor one compared with the pressure for "appeasement," the fear that if the struggle was allowed to drag out, with the major powers pouring in arms, civil war would turn into general war. President Roosevelt tried to persuade a press conference, off the record, that if the embargo had been lifted the Franco forces would have gained much more than the Loyalists:

. . . Franco, controlling the sea, could send his ships directly to the United States and load them up with bombs and airplanes and anything else that he could buy and take them over right to his own army.

The Spanish Government, the Barcelona Government, because it did not control the sea, would not be able to buy anything by direct shipment to Barcelona or Valencia. Therefore [we] would have been definitely aiding and abetting the Franco Government.
. . .

The flaw in this argument was that there was no need to be even-handed about it at all. By treaty and by international law we had every obligation to maintain full economic relations with the legal government of Spain, which we had long recognized, and none whatever to sell to a claque of generals with no diplomatic standing at all. A good part of the Front's time and energy went into pointing this out to the Administration, but without success. It was not one of the President's nobler attitudes.

If Spain and anti-fascism in general were not enough to draw fresh thousands to the Popular Front, and so into the Communist orbit, other and even stronger forces were working to that end. Driven leftward for support, as the bankers and brokers got back their wind, the Administration stopped far short of wooing such extreme segments as the Communists, who were numerically insignificant anyway, but the Communists did not have to be wooed. When they themselves took to ogling the Administration and identifying themselves with its aims, they could not help but take on, simply by association, a certain respectability hitherto lack-

ing. Veteran comrades may have thought no more of the
New Deal than they had before, but Soviet policy required a
Popular Front, and in their newfound amiability the Communists no longer seemed queer to the naïve and the innocent, just more vigorous than most—and right on a whole
batch of political issues.

Besides fascism, Spain, the Scottsboro boys, and the New
Deal, they seemed right in those months about the needless
self-paralysis of the League of Nations, about our sending
scrap metal to Japan that would one day be dropped on our
heads at Pearl Harbor, about the necessity to repel industry's last-ditch efforts to stave off collective bargaining as a
fact of life, and about the international risk in passively allowing Mussolini to drop bombs on Ethiopia, a sport that his
pilot son Vittorio had personally found *"molto divertente."*

While none of these historic issues were of interest exclusively to the Communists, the party latched on to all of them
and they combined to create a climate in which a Popular
Front, even one fostered by Communists, came easily to
flower. The spirit was pervasive, and you did not have to be
overwhelmingly political to be attracted. Indeed, if you had
but the stomach, the liver, and the vitality in those sacrificial
days, you could eat, drink, and be otherwise active straight
through the week in the cause of humanity.

On Monday, to make out a hypothetical schedule, a New
Yorker might leave his office at five for a cocktail party given
by a penthouse dowager to raise funds for the Scottsboro
boys, with olives omitted from the Martinis to avoid giving
aid and comfort to Mussolini (which may be how the Gib-
son came into vogue). Tuesday evening features an inter-
organizational rally to protest the sabotaging of the New
Deal by the "Nine Old Men," as the Supreme Court was
then irreverently known in liberal circles. It was not the
Justices' chronological years that were the subject of concern, of course, but their propensity for weighing social

legislation against the judicial standards of the Gilded Age.

Wednesday evening our man might show up at a benefit dance for Georgia sharecroppers put on by the Greenwich Village branch of the Southern Tenant Farmers Union. Thursday he lunches on cold beef and potato salad in the Versailles Room of a sixth-rate hotel off Times Square, where Ralph Bates, an engagingly voluble English novelist doubling as political adviser to the Loyalists, reports on the desperate need for supplies at Guadalajara.

Friday evening is given over to our man's newly formed white-collar union—CIO of course. As an alternate from his "shop," he attends the local's monthly meeting, which will get down to four or five hours of local business only after members have heard a dramatic report from Detroit on the triumphant "sitdowns." Spreading from the great auto plants, where for years men had worked the twelve-hour day and the thirty-five-cent-hour, the new technique of digging in and doing nothing on the boss's property and on the boss's time had swept into department stores, five-and-tens, and even the plush hotels. Denied the state's armed support by Governor Frank Murphy, the moguls of Detroit had yielded inch by inch, and when the revolution ended in a meeting between Walter P. Chrysler and John L. Lewis, the working population went pouring into Cadillac Square, flags flying and bands playing. While many Detroiters still believed, with Congressman Clare Hoffman, that "certain events could only be settled with bloodshed," Murphy had managed to avoid it, and soon all over the country Americans whose only previous notion of proletarian music was "I've Been Workin' on de Railroad" would become familiar with more specialized labor songs, such as:

When they tie a can to a union man,
Sit down! Sit down!
When they give him the sack, they'll take him back,

Sit down! Sit down!
When the speed-up comes, just twiddle your thumbs,
Sit down! Sit down!
When the boss won't talk, don't take a walk,
Sit down! Sit down!

So the calendar went, with even the weekend available for
good works. On Saturday our staggering activist might
picket a Hearst paper or the German consulate, just on principle. And on Sunday, dropping in on an informal gathering
of friends, he would likely find himself charged fifty cents at
the door and subjected to an impost of an additional dime
per drink, proceeds to go to the relief of fugitives from Ethiopia, Manchuria, or a Georgia chain gang. If his friends
were Trotskyists or Socialists, the fugitives might even be
from Russia, but these were scarcer.

While nobody I knew actually adhered, or could adhere,
to a schedule of this sort, the truth is that this feverish atmosphere existed, generated by interest in affairs beyond the
narrow and personal, and it was hugely stimulating. Besides
the interminable meetings, rallies, cocktail parties, and benefits, there were more plodding duties. You might address
envelopes for a committee for this or against that, take part
in a union factional row, or make speeches to small gatherings of the already convinced. On May Day you would
march along with what the *Times* estimated as forty thousand others and the *Daily Worker* as two *hundred* thousand.
In my one and only participation in this spring labor rite, I
am mildly chagrined to recall that I dropped out midway,
lured by the combination of an afternoon off and the sudden
vision of a movie house featuring the Four Marx Brothers in
Animal Crackers. This triumph of Harpo over Karl was a
foretaste of what was to prove my proletarian undoing.

In a negative way one could always advance the good, the
true, and the forces of history by rejecting not only Italian
olives, Hearst newspapers, and all things German, but,

above all, Japanese silk. For the girls, stockings of cotton or lisle were no doubt a trial, especially now that the Popular Front had made attractive clothes, cosmetics, and other bourgeois items of allure not only fashionable for ladies of the Left, but almost mandatory. What saved the day for the hard-pressed Chinese, no doubt, was the occasional news pictures of Hollywood queens proudly displaying cotton legwear as an inspiration to their less glamorous sisters to stand firm and lumpy for peace in Asia.

As a matter of fact, Hollywood had, several years before, undergone a workers' uprising in the classic mold. Taking advantage of the Depression, the studios had cut actors' salaries in half in order, they said, to avert layoffs, after which they made the layoffs anyway and then paid bonuses to their top officers. When the studios then went on to draw up a proposed NRA code that would have dented the actors' wallets still further, such rebels as Frank Morgan, the Marx Brothers, Charles Butterworth, and Eddie Cantor, taking council like Sam Adams and the Sons of Liberty, fired off a two-thousand word telegram to President Roosevelt and overnight blew the tiny screen Actors Guild into a trade union as tough as the plumbers'.

In a few years the Guild included 99 percent of all the actors in Hollywood and put on some good performances. In its finest moment a delegation including President Robert Montgomery and Franchot Tone called at Louis B. Mayer's on a Sunday morning, interrupted a bridge game, and demanded a Guild shop in all studios on pain of a strike vote that very evening. Mayer objected that he couldn't get stenographic help on Sunday, that he had two hundred guests for lunch, and besides some of his fellow producers were at Agua Caliente playing the races. But the revolutionists were adamant, and they came away with a handwritten surrender as painfully yielded as John's at Runnymede. The actors whooped it up at a mass meeting and for some years afterward identified themselves ardently with the underdog. It was in the most humble proletarian spirit that some top star or other could be counted on to rise in the inevitable collection period of most big-cause rallies and declare with downcast eye, "I pledge a week's pay—one thousand dollars." The only thing to touch it was that ritual moment at Communist collections when the chairman, fairly bawling with the pathos of it all, would announce: "From a policeman in the crowd—two dollars!"—and the house would rock with appreciation.

Robert Montgomery, it might be said in passing, was not the only labor hero to emerge on the Hollywood front. Among those whom the *Nation* found worthy of nomination to "a labor Hall of Fame in Hollywood" were also Joan Crawford, James Cagney, Boris Karloff, and, not least, Adolphe Menjou and George Murphy, both destined decades later for strong supporting roles in the political drama of Barry Goldwater.

Many who were not drawn to the Popular Front for political reasons or by way of a trade union came to it for the cultural and social atmosphere it provided—the "Theatres of Action," the "Workers' Film and Dance Groups," the literary associations, the foreign-language societies, the fraternal orders, the swirling social life—all vaguely infused with a comfortable self-righteousness, the assurance that while having a good time one was aligned with the forces of light against the forces of darkness. For some the beauty of the involvement must have been that it allowed one to be a radical without forfeiting respectability, to gibe at one's own bourgeois background and relatives without seriously giving up any of the bourgeois comforts, and with it all, to be a patriotic American in the best sense. For in this period the Communists—and, though small in number, they were the governing part of the Popular Front—carried on under the slogan "Communism Is Twentieth Century Americanism."

Actually they soon carried their new policy to D.A.R. lengths, as we shall observe later, but the newcomer who had heard so much of Communist conspiracy could not help being impressed at first with the fact that only the American flag flew at their public rallies and that "The Star-Spangled Banner" was sung and not "The International," with its ominous invitation to "prisoners of starvation" and the "wretched of the earth" to arise and awake, respectively.

The remarkable thing in the circumstances is not that the Communists attracted some seventy-five thousand people at the peak of their Popular Front period, with possibly two or three times as many sympathizers, but that they failed to do much better than that. There must have been hundreds of thousands in the country, perhaps millions, who, while not inordinately admiring the Communists themselves, anticipated by four or five years the sentiment expressed by Winston Churchill when he suddenly found himself allied with Joseph Stalin: "I have only one purpose, the destruction of Hitler. . . . If Hitler invaded Hell I would make at least a favorable reference to the Devil in the House of Commons."

The new recruits included lawyers, doctors, dentists, painters, accountants (Earl Browder himself was a Kansas bookkeeper), musicians, actors, and a good leavening of businessmen who evidently did not believe that they would be the first victims of any awakening by the wretched of the earth. But no one in the Popular Front talked of revolution at all—that was for the "infantile leftists" of the rival and discredited Marxist parties. Pursuers of profit were as welcome as anyone, more welcome if they brought their profits with them, as long as they were enemies of the enemies of the Soviet Union. Gilbert Seldes, the critic, found himself on one occasion asking a Rotary Club what the members had made of John Strachey, their recent guest speaker and then probably the most brilliant defender of the Stalin way in the entire Communist stable of traveling propagandists. The chairman's reply would be thought extraordinarily mild today: "We did not mind his saying that the Republican Party was done for and we didn't care what he said about the Democratic Party, but some of the boys got sore when he said that we all had to be Communists." Even at that, the "some," he admitted, was only about 10 percent of the group, and when Seldes asked what would have happened if the same episode had occurred in 1930 the answer was that the club would have risen as one man and run Mr. Strachey out of town.

Given the times, then, and the powerful appeal inherent in an anti-Fascist Popular Front, it should have been hard for its Communist initiators to make a botch of it. But it turned out to be relatively easy, even inevitable. For the Front lacked the one and only thing that can hold together an ideological alliance for long, which is a genuine and abiding purpose common to all the participants.

On the face of things the Popular Front had just that purpose in anti-fascism, which is what in the first place attracted the liberals, the humanists, the artists, the trade unionists, democratic conservatives, decent people of all sorts; and the less knowing they were in the ways of leftish politics, the more they were attracted. But one element in the combination was *not* motivated strictly by anti-fascism, and that was the Communist Party itself, which, as it happened, ran the whole show. Its only unchanging concern, it turned out, was the security and advantage of the Soviet Union. Inevitably, then, as international affairs go, the day would ultimately come when that security seemed to lie in an alliance *with* fascism rather than against it, and then Soviet Foreign Minister Molotov would unblushingly declare one's attitude toward that movement to be merely "a matter of taste." But in the mid-Thirties such an idea was grotesque, the stuff of nightmares.

Nevertheless, to those who went into the Front without yielding up their native quota of skepticism, it gradually became apparent that the tactics of the Communists were *just* tactics, after all, and not to be measured, as hard-bitten comrades were fond of saying, by a "sincerometer." To some, especially those on the fringes of Front activity, the realization was slow in coming, while to others the essential phoniness of the new line was soon undeniable.

Remarkably, on my first expression of interest, in the summer of 1936, I was invited to join the staff of the *New Masses*. It was the only activity I was to know in those months of association with the far left, but it afforded me a vantage point of sorts. While the magazine was not officially an organ of the party, or even financed by it, it was such for all practical purposes, and it deferred slavishly to party policy. At the same time its staff, except at the top, was for the most part ignorant of what went on in the inner circles of the party, and any suggestion of the conspiratorial, still more the illegal, would have seemed to us a grotesque canard. As far as we were concerned, it *was* a canard, for, as I later discovered, the *New Masses* was looked upon by the party leaders on Thirteenth Street as a necessary nuisance, a harmless outlet for unreliable intellectuals who were likely at any time to come up with annoying ideas of their own.

It has since been calculated, quite believably, that of twenty-one staff members and frequent contributors to the magazine when I was there, eleven have become "enemies of the people," or the equivalent in party invective; one was killed in Spain, a gentle and dedicated youth named Arnold Reid; and seven couldn't be tracked down. Only two were still faithful, or hooked, in the postwar era. I started to turn "enemy of the people" in my second or third month on the *New Masses*, for reasons I will come to in a moment, achieved the distinction of being attacked by name in the *Daily Worker* while still on the magazine, and was out in the bourgeois cold ten months later, in the spring of 1937.

By and large, I do not regret the experience, looking upon it as a quick vaccination which made me ill for a very short time but left me happily immune to a severe and prolonged attack. At the same time, I can sympathize with those who, at least as idealistic and intelligent as myself, were even farther from the center of activity and accordingly took longer to see the synthetic nature of the thing and its palpable absurdity, which is what I did see rather than anything sinister.

For the spirit pervading the Popular Front, as I have said, was the Spirit of '76, only more so. Suddenly acquired, the new nationalism lacked something in perspective and its promoters lacked the humor to realize what was missing. Red, white, and blue were laid on the canvas with a housepainter's brush and appreciably less subtlety than was to be found on a Fourth of July cover of the *Saturday Evening Post*. The results were rich in entertainment for those who allowed themselves the old American luxury of political irreverence.

"By continuing the traditions of 1776 and 1861," said Earl Browder, the party was entitled "to designate itself as 'Sons and Daughters of the American Revolution.'" And like the other self-appointed sons and daughters, the patriots went big for ancestry. Anyone who went through the period may recall the sudden rise to prominence, at Communist-dominated affairs, of Jefferson, Jackson, Lincoln, and the fife-and-drum trio of '76, but I am indebted to Irving Howe and Lewis Coser, authors of *The American Communist Party*, for dredging up two especially fine expressions of this feeling. One, from the pen of Robert Minor, a top party official, discourses on the family background of Comrade Browder:

It was in the springtime of 1776 and Thomas Jefferson may well have been driving his one-horse shay . . . with a draft of the

Declaration of Independence in his pocket, when a certain boy, just turned 21, stepped into a recruiting station in Dinwiddie County, Virginia. He gave his name as Littleberry Browder and was sworn in as a soldier of the Continental Army of General George Washington.

The other bit concerns the failure of the Daughters of the American Revolution, in the spring of 1937, to commemorate the 162nd anniversay of Paul Revere's ride. Scandalized by the omission, the Young Communist League sent an appropriately costumed horseman prancing up Broadway with a sign reading: "The DAR Forgets But the YCL Remembers."

Even writers of proletarian literature sometimes felt a little genealogy helpful in making a case for the downtrodden. Thus Clara Weatherwax, author of *Marching! Marching!*, although unable to claim an ancestor named Littleberry Weatherwax, did benefit from an introductory note explaining that she "stems from pre-Mayflower New England stock, which has pioneered across the American continent. . . . One of her outstanding forebears was Roger Williams. Fourteen of her direct ancestors fought in the first American revolution. . . ." etc.

Roosevelt's birthday was listed along with Lenin's in the year's calendar of events, the *New Masses* ran contests on "Why I Like America," and the *Daily Worker* solemnly backed Joe DiMaggio's demand that the Yankees raise him from $25,000 to $40,000 a year. The only trouble with this rush of Americanism to the head was that the suddenness of the passion left too many of its practitioners without adequate preparation. "We are legal and defend our legality" was one of the slogans of the day, but I distinctly remember the odd effect it produced when uttered by a veteran comrade out of the corner of his mouth. It was much the same sort of impression I got when I attended what was advertised as an "open meeting" of the party for the benefit of outsiders, where any question might be asked and all questions answered—similar to those meetings the John Birch Society occasionally puts on in this decade, likewise to show that it is not conspiratorial. A young lady new to the Left, and decked out in appropriately simple furs, put the query: "Is it true that there is some danger of Bonapartism in the Soviet Union?" To which the chairman candidly and instantly replied, "Nonsense, comrade. Next question?"

The solemnity with which the affairs of the Left were conducted was enough in itself to separate it from the mainstream of American politics, which, whatever its weaknesses, has always had the redeeming attribute of self-ridicule. It was a jolt to me to discover that, coming to the *New Masses*, I had come to a synod of Calvinists, for whom joking about any aspect of the party line seemed as wicked as joking about original sin would have seemed to Cotton Mather.

In the second or third month of my tenure the Moscow Trials took their initial toll, leaving me, among millions of others, aghast and bewildered. Unable to understand how men like Zinoviev and Kamenev, who I had just gotten around to learn were heroes of the Russian Revolution, were really "cannibals" and "mad dog assassins" in ideological disguise, I went to Joe Freeman, the editor who had hired me and a warm, sympathetic, and eloquent man if ever there was one.* I could understand, I said, how a few of the dozens of accused heroes might be "cannibals" of sorts, but I couldn't begin to see why at least one or two of them didn't

---

* Too sensitive and idealistic to be thoroughly trusted by the party chiefs, the late Joseph Freeman was ousted a year or so after I left the magazine. Re-establishing social contact then, for the first time since my departure, he came around to my rooms on Barrow Street, and as gently as possible I asked him if he had really believed the arguments with which he once sought to persuade me. Only in part, he said, but as long as he was in the party he accepted discipline, which meant putting the line above his personal beliefs. But how could he have done it with such conviction? "It was hard," I remember his answering. "To relieve my feelings I would secretly write poems of protest and disappointment." He produced close to a deskful.

stand up and say, "It's a lie, I didn't do it" even if they had, or "Yes, I did it because I thought it was the right thing to do." Why did they all grovel and damn themselves and beg to be shot as a service to the Socialist Fatherland and a boon beyond their poor deserts? "You have to read Dostoevsky," Joe advised me, "to understand the Russian soul." So when word came from Moscow a month or so later of a second batch of trials, at which Piatakov, Radek, and others were to be charged with operating an "Anti-Soviet Trotskyite Terrorist Centre," I impiously captioned our editorial comment "Dostoevsky Rides Again," knowing I could change it when the proof came back from the printer.

A special editorial meeting followed, at which it was made plain to me that such frivolity was roughly equivalent to tripping up a bishop at High Mass. Nor was my status improved when I pinned up over my desk a cartoon from the *Daily Worker* which depicted Trotsky as the usual mad dog, with bulging eyes and dripping fangs, crouched and ready to spring at his innocent victim. The caption over this horror merely said, "Thoroughly Discredited," an understatement that struck me as so droll that I had to be warned again about the consequences of misplaced levity.

One did not have to be a Stalinist, of course, to be a leftist in the Thirties. There were almost as many sects, creeds, cults, factions, and fractions among the reformers and revolutionaries as the Christian community had endured in the most schismatic years of the Reformation, each with its freight of heresies, finespun interpretations of Marxist gospel, scorn for its rivals, and above all mimeograph equipment.

First, in the order of sober reputation, were the Socialist followers of Norman Thomas. Already reduced greatly from the days of their glory—Debs polled 917,800 in 1920 to Thomas's 188,000 in 1936—they were destined to lose much more ground to New Deal raids on their program and per-

sonnel, though their sophisticates jeered at the flight of radicals to Washington as "the children's crusade." From the
opposite direction they felt the pull of the Communists, who
attracted some of their youthful militants. But it was their
Center that collapsed altogether when those who felt more
strongly anti-Fascist than anti-war walked out to form the
Social Democratic Federation. By the time Roosevelt made
his fourth run, the Socialists were down to 80,000, about 91
percent below the peak they had reached a quarter-century
before, although the number of voters in the country was
some 70 percent higher.

On hand, as they still are, were the remnants of Daniel De
Leon's Socialist Labor Party sect, which went through the
motions of a Presidential election campaign every four years
but otherwise seemed to exist silently in a state of socialist
purity so antiseptic that even trade unions were condemned
by them as capitalist trickery for beguiling the toiling
masses.

Proceeding leftward, we had next the Lovestoneites, who
had broken away from the Communists when the canny Jay
Lovestone was expelled in 1929 for advancing the theory of
"American exceptionalism." What this formidable-sounding
doctrine got down to was the proposition that perhaps the
New Deal and the dying stages of Tsarism were not quite
parallel. But it passed for a pretty bold deviation. And on
the other side of the Communists there was the Socialist
Workers Party, which was formed when Leon Trotsky was
sent into exile by Stalin for being committed, at least in
theory, to world revolution. Sympathizers called its members Trotskyists, but enemies, especially the Stalinists, called
them Trotsky*ites,* a suffix which for some reason was considered pejorative. In retaliation the Communists were sometimes called Stalin*oids,* which was worse. But these were
among the fine points of the business.

The Trotskyists were led throughout the Thirties by

James P. Cannon and Max Schachtman, who split at the end of the decade on the anguishing question of whether even a perverted workers' regime like the one in Moscow rated support when "threatened" by a bourgeois power like mighty Finland. Trotsky himself let it be known from his Mexican exile that he thought it did, but Stalin wasn't for forgiving him that easily and the GPU went right ahead with its plans to do him in.

Schachtman and his supporters broke away on the Finnish question, but by this time the Trotsky followers had already suffered the numerous divisions that come inevitably to amoebas and minority political parties alike. First a faction headed by Comrades Ohler and Stamm went its way, soon to separate again into Ohlerites and Stammites. Somewhere along the way the immediate family of one George Marlen (a name derived by combining Marx and Lenin) left to become Marlenites, and a Mr. and Mrs. Weisbord had a League for the Class Struggle all to themselves until divorce separated their rank from their file. The Fieldites, another group of limited range, were said to have come a cropper when picket signs were borne past their headquarters proclaiming: "Mr. and Mrs. Field are No Longer Fieldites." The deadly seriousness with which all this fantasy could be taken by its dreamers was illustrated at the stormy meeting that split the main body of Trotskyists. At the climax of the evening, so the story goes, Cannon stepped to the rostrum, leveled a finger at his rival, and issued the memorable warning: "Very well, Comrade Schachtman, we will seize power without you!"

Had there ever been a real danger to the established order from any of these sources, it would surely have been dissipated by the enormous quantities of time, energy, verbiage, and talent that they put into bombarding each other, all sects preferring by far to harry the heretic rather than to convert the infidel. To the Stalinists, all other leftists were anti-working-class "wreckers," "bandits," and "social Fascists," and if the calling of these class enemies happened to involve use of the written word, as it almost always did, they were also "gangsters of the pen." To other Marxists, the Stalinists were "counter-revolutionaries," "betrayers of the working class," and "police state murderers." About the scorned Socialists, the Communist ditty went:

> They preach Social*ism*
> But they practice Fasc*ism*
> To preserve capital*ism*
> For the bosses.

The Socialists retaliated with jeers for the sudden changes that were so cruelly and repeatedly inflicted from abroad on their competitors:

> United fronts are what we love,
> Our line's been changed again—
> From below and from above,
> Our line's been changed again.*

And among sophisticated Trotskyists, generally to be found in the colleges, anti-Stalinist parodies were always in order. An example of the genre, this one celebrating Stalin's purge of old revolutionaries, was the following, with profound apologies to Gilbert and Sullivan:

> When I was a lad in Nineteen-six,
> I joined a group of Bolsheviks.
> I read the Manifesto and Das Kapital,
> I even learned to sing the Internationale.
> I sang that song with a spirit so true
> That now I'm in a dungeon of the Gay-Pay-OO.

Of all the sects, the Communists made the most noise, put on the most spectacular shows, saddled themselves with the

---

* "Why is the American Communist Party like the Brooklyn Bridge?" ran a current riddle directed to the same point. And the answer was, of course, "Because it is suspended on cables."

greatest handicaps, and suffered the most dramatic, if ludicrous, reverses, for which they almost always had themselves to blame. Even the language they used was enough to preclude any real chance of penetrating to the core of American political life. It was like grand opera libretto, silly enough in the original and worse when performed in translation. What was the native radical, so desperately wooed, to make of the ideological diseases that so constantly raged through the ranks? He might prime himself against *infantile leftism* only to fall victim to the dread opposite of *rightist deviationism*. How was he to know where a healthy Popular Frontism merged into *petty-bourgeois romanticism* or even *capitalist degeneracy?* Intellectually he had to watch out for *dilettantism* but with too much theorizing he might contract some terrible disorder like *neo-Kantian banditism*. Similarly, to avoid *sectarian super-simplicity* (the state of not knowing your friends from your enemies) one might make a poor guess and come down with *incipient Trotskyism*, for which there was no known cure. Even the titles of party literature had an exotic ring, like the famous pamphlet "What Means the Strike in Steel?" When I frivolously asked a colleague whether it shouldn't be "What Means in Steel the Strike?" some detected signs of *liberal depravity*, which was mild at that. I might have been diagnosed as a chronic case of *White Guardism*.

For those who have long since departed from the circumambience of the Communist Party, including its various fronts, or even from the vague status of fellow traveler, the order of their going conveys a relative standing not unlike the pecking order laid down for descendants of early American settlers. Those disillusioned before 1935 are the Mayflower element, as it were, with those who followed in the next couple of years, when the Popular Front was still in vogue, comparable to slightly later colonials, and so on all the way down to the greenhorn immigrants of the Fifties.

Not to press the comparison further, the first real flight from the Communists came in what promised to be the era of their greatest success, with the outbreak of the sensational Moscow Trials. The local party's ardent defense of these people's inquisitions persuaded thousands that "Twentieth Century Americanism" had little to do with Americanism and not much with the twentieth century. It was much more a throwback to the seventeenth, with only the witchcraft brought up to date. Where the criminals of Salem had freely confessed to riding broomsticks, passing through keyholes, and teaming up with Satan to ruin the crops with hailstorms, the leaders of the Russian Revolution one after the other confessed to undermining the ruble, infecting Maxim Gorky with cold germs and pigs with the plague, and causing glass and nails to be slipped into the butter of consumers' cooperatives. Only then did they move on to reveal how they plotted with Satan-Trotsky to murder Stalin and turn the Soviet Fatherland over to Adolf Hitler and Emperor Hirohito.*

As these Kafka-like proceedings developed, the impossible was added to the incredible. A defendant named Holzman, for example, confessed he had met Trotsky's son Sedov in the lounge of the Bristol Hotel in Copenhagen in 1932, and was taken thence to Trotsky's apartment, where the old Bolshevik warlord told him that "the fundamental task now was to assassinate Comrade Stalin." As soon as the text of this particular confession appeared abroad, which was not soon enough to save Holzman from being shot in the head, some embarrassing facts came to light. The Hotel Bristol, it appeared, had been torn down brick by brick in 1917 and only rebuilt in 1936, the year of the trial, just in time for a careless GPU agent to know of its existence as he sat down to com-

---

* Concerning all this plotting with the enemy, not a shred of evidence was turned up in the tons of German and Japanese documents seized by Allied occupation authorities after the war.

pose ex-Comrade Holzman's confession. What is more, Sedov was proved to have been in Paris at the time of the alleged meeting and, as it turned out, had never been in Copenhagen in his life.

For many who had come into the Popular Front an initially dazed bewilderment soon settled into a deep skepticism, of which my own little difficulty over Dostoevsky and the Russian soul was merely a surface indication. Bound to recur again and again was the question, unutterable for a Soviet sympathizer in those days but to be answered in the Kremlin itself twenty years later by none other than Nikita S. Khrushchev:

And how is it possible that a person confesses to crimes which he has not committed? Only in one way—because of application of physical methods of pressuring him, tortures, bringing him to a state of unconsciousness, deprivation of his judgment, taking away of his human dignity. In this manner were "confessions" acquired.

In his political "Testament" Lenin had mentioned six men as possible successors. Of these he ruled out only one—Stalin, whom he thought to lack the necessary attributes of character. Of the others, this same Stalin was to put four on trial —Zinoviev, Kamenev, Bukharin, and Piatakov—and have them all shot to death in the cellars of the Lubianka Prison. The fifth, Leon Trotsky, would be hounded down in exile until at last his pursuers sank an axe into his skull in the Mexican suburb of Coyoacán. The motive for all these executions may not have been established but a certain predisposition was clear.

Quickly recovering from the initial shock, Stalinist followers soon had a battery of arguments in circulation: If Kamenev and Zinoviev had confessed falsely in return for advance pledges of freedom and were then double-crossed, why should defendants in later trials make the same fatal mistake? If these men had really been brave revolutionaries in the past, instead of secret Fascist conspirators, how could they now be so cowardly as to admit to uncommitted crimes? It was a myth that Trotsky and the others had really been "Old Bolsheviks"; most of them had been at odds with the sainted Lenin at one time or another and only joined with him when victory was in sight. And anyway the Russian system of jurisprudence was different from ours and should not be judged by the same standards.

But such arguments paled beside the vast implausibility that the thousands of Russians, tried and untried, who went down in the great purges of the Thirties, were really the secret agents of Hitler and Hirohito and not the victims of mass hysteria and Stalin's paranoia. Few were the cynics who were then ready to believe that Stalin was holding others guilty of what he himself was preparing to do in the way of accommodating the Fascist enemy, but one did not have to go nearly that far to be thoroughly disillusioned with the Communists and their Front, now grown considerably less popular. While the *Nation* was by no means as emphatic as some in denouncing the trials, it did criticize them enough to be attacked by the *New Masses* as either stupid or Trotskyite, while at the same time the Trotskyists spurned the *Nation* as "bourgeois." All in all, that magazine began to look extremely good to me, and I went there in the summer of 1937.

The next migratory wave from the Front was set in motion by what happened in Spain and was far less extensive than the movement produced by the trials. Few knew of the appalling battles that went on within the Loyalist ranks, and even today the record on certain episodes is too obscure to allow absolute judgments, at least on my part. But what did emerge even then was that Communist objectives in Spain were not limited to the defeat of Franco. Again it was the requirements of Russian foreign policy that motivated the

Stalinists, and if these called for the suppression of Trotsky-ists, Socialists, and Anarchists, then they would be sup-pressed—to the point of liquidation. Stories trickled back of Russian arms and equipment deliberately withheld to com-pel changes in government personnel and in army com-mands that favored "reliable," that is, pro-Soviet, elements. Then came even grimmer stories of executions and murders, of wholesale purging and imprisonment of alleged "Fascist spies" and "wreckers," many of whom had almost literally crawled across mountains on their bellies and smuggled themselves across the border to do battle against Franco. But none of this was provable at the time, and only those who knew someone who had been through it and returned to tell the tale were affected. Yet there is no doubt that even the rumors further soured a Popular Front atmosphere al-ready poisoned by the judicial reports out of Moscow.

While the Spanish Civil War had always about it the dig-nity of high tragedy, the next and fatal blow to the Popular Front was rich in malevolent comedy. Throughout the sum-mer of 1939 there had been faint premonitory rumblings of a Russian-German rapprochement but nobody took them to be more than the wishful prophecies of Trotskyist Cassandras —least of all those still left in the withering ranks of the Popular Front. Had they not read Earl Browder's contemp-tuous retort to such calumnies: "The reactionaries openly speculate that the Soviet Union may try to beat Chamber-lain at his own game by joining hands with Hitler. But even those who hate the land of socialism cannot believe it, when they see that the Soviet Union alone rounds up the traitor-ous agents of Hitler within its own land and puts them be-yond the possibility of doing any more of their wrecking, spying and diversions for fascism."

The first intimation I had of the shape of things to come I naturally took for the sheerest propaganda, since it came directly from a Baron von Münchhausen, supposedly a lineal descendant of the accomplished German liar of that name. A man of ingratiating manners and more Old World charm than was usually to be found in my social circle, the Baron was an extremely indirect guest at one of the Saturday-evening gatherings my wife and I occasionally had in our small apartment on the Manhattan upper West Side. He had come along with a Baltimore newspaperman who, in turn, had been brought along by a friend of mine, the only one of the three who had been invited. From some Teutonically arrogant remarks the Baron had made early in the evening concerning the Czechs, whose country had just been forcibly admitted to the glories of his Third Reich, I was reasonably sure of his Nazi leanings. I was wondering whether to ease him out or break up the party when he moved to the center of the room and made a remarkable announcement: "I think most of you are leftists of one sort or another and you think I am a National Socialist. But what does it matter? In a few months we will be allies."

His assumption about our political complexion was dead wrong—no Communist would even give me the time of day since I had left the *New Masses* more than two years before.* And just as wrong was the assumption that all American Communists would become pro-Nazi with the signing of a Russian-German pact instead of either going into a political deepfreeze or leaving the party in loud disgust. But his prophecy of the coming alliance was no Münchhausen fantasy, or even a wild guess. I was told a few years later that the Baron was an agent whose charm was at the disposal of Herr Goebbels for softening the antagonism of American anti-Nazi editors.

The thunderclap came on August 22. The day before,

---

* The new "democratic" constitution of the proponents of twentieth-century Americanism provided that "no party member shall have personal or political relationship with Trotskyites, Lovestoneites, or other known enemies of the party and the working class," with the party of course determining who belonged to this group of pariahs.

Russia and Germany had signed a trade pact, but, despite some eyebrow raising in anti-Fascist circles, where German boycotts had long been the rule, no ideological change was indicated. Then came the simple, historic bulletin, via Tass, the Soviet news agency, that was to end the Popular Front for good and reduce the Communist Party here and elsewhere to a state of babbling incoherence:

> After conclusion of the Soviet-German trade agreement, there arose the problem of improving the political relations between Germany and the USSR. An exchange of views on this subject which took place between the governments of Germany and the USSR established that both parties desire to relieve the tension of their political relations, to eliminate the war menace and to conclude a non-aggression pact.

The *Daily Worker,* understandably slow to react, managed to put out the doughy statement on the 23rd that "Today, the Socialist USSR, reviled, maligned and slandered, yet growing stronger and stronger every hour, is more and more heading mankind away from the abyss along the safer road of human progress and victory over the dark forces of reaction, treachery and war." When the staggering fact of the agreement became undeniable, the reassuring word was sent out from party headquarters that the text would be sure to reveal an "escape clause," by which the Russians would reserve the right to come to Poland's defense if it was invaded. Alas, the text was found to contain no such reservation, but the *Daily Worker,* recovered and ready to brazen out the storm, laid down the new line: "The pact is a smashing blow at Munich treachery. . . ." So much for the British and the French. As for the Nazis, "By compelling Germany to sign a non-aggression pact, the Soviet Union tremendously limited the direction of Nazi war aims."

A week later Hitler invaded Poland; Britain and France reluctantly declared war on Germany, and hell, long-her-

alded, had arrived on earth. After a few days of sympathiz-
ing with the struggle of the Polish people for their independence, the *Worker* got its signals straightened out and
began denouncing the oppressive Polish government instead.
On the 17th the Russians, with nothing further from their
minds than escape clauses, invaded Poland from the east,
and in short order the country was partitioned between the
erstwhile enemies. The impossible had happened, and it
took the great British cartoonist David Low to present the
picture in all its cosmic absurdity: Over the smoking ruins of
Poland, Hitler and Stalin are shown bowing to each other
from the waist, each with his military cap raised in solemn
courtesy. "The scum of the earth, I believe?" says the
Reichsführer. "The bloody assassin of the workers, I pre-
sume?" says the leader of the world proletariat.

A plausible political line is not the work of a day or two,
and pending the construction of a new pitch most Communists and fellow travelers who were willing to remain such
fell back on a simple expression of faith: "Don't worry, Stalin
knows what he's doing." That is hardly the sort of thing on
which political rallies are based as a rule, but the party
leadership, acting on the same psychological doctrine that
prescribes quickly remounting after a fall from a horse,
called a mass meeting in Madison Square Garden immediately after the sudden "socializing" of Poland. As managing
editor of the *Nation*, I sent James A. Wechsler, an engaging
and perceptive young journalist, to cover the meeting. A
member of the Young Communist League a few years before, he had had his fill of Communist ways and was by then
as emphatically opposed to the party and all its works as I
was. He was also an honest reporter and sensitive to political
nuances. Thousands may have left the party in the preceding two weeks, he reported, but those who attended the
Garden were as enthusiastic as ever. Their only trouble was
that they couldn't be sure how to react to phrases that had

Annual May Day Parade, 1936. *(UPI)*

MARX

Harpo, Zeppo, Chico, and Groucho, *Monkey Business*, 1931. *(Museum of Modern Art)*

RELAXATI

Harry Hopkins,
(Photo by Walter
enport, Culver Pi
Inc.)

Mae West in *Klondike Annie*, 1936. *(UPI*

W. C. Fields with Baby Leroy. *(UPI)*   Fred Allen. *(Wide World)*

MORE PERSONALITIES

Fiorello H. La Guardia. *(Culver Pictures, Inc.)*

Capitalist Vincent Astor at America's Cup Races. *(Wide World)*

Socialist Norman Thomas. *(Culver Pictures, Inc.)*

PANACEAS

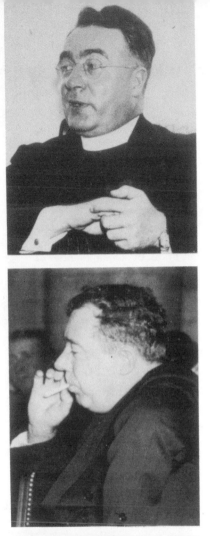

Father Coughlin of
Social Justice. (Wide World)

Huey Long of Every Man
A King, 1934. *(UPI)*

William Lemke of
the Union Party, 1936. *(UPI)*

EVANGELISTS

Dr. Frank Buchman, founder of
Moral Rearmament,
1933. *(UPI)*

Father Divine near Hudson River "Heaven," 1938. *(Wide World)*

Technocracy, Inc.'s motor corps. *(UPI)*

UTOPIAS

Dr. Francis E. Townsend of Townsend Old Age Plan, after conviction for contempt, 1938. *(Wide World)*

RADIO
STARS

Information Please: John Kieran, left; Master of Ceremonie
Clifton Fadiman, standing; and Franklin P. Adams. *(Wid
World)*

F.D.R.'s fireside chat. *(UPI)*

previously called for automatic responses. Recalling the episode much later, in *The Age of Suspicion*, he wrote:

. . . on the few occasions when Hitler's name was mentioned, it was plain that the audience did not know whether to boo or whether, in the light of recent developments, such an expression of hostility might henceforth be defined as "imperialist warmongering." Any mention of Mr. Roosevelt's name evoked the same irresolution; his reincarnation as international villain was not yet complete. Finally, however, the crowd got a real chance to jeer; the speakers began denouncing "Trotskyism" and everybody knew that, no matter what else might change, it was safe to boo.

Far more uncomfortable were the signers of one of those open letters, so fashionable in the Thirties, which ran in the *Nation* the very week that we carried news of the Nazi-Soviet pact. It was a blast in which four hundred artists and intellectuals indignantly replied to another open letter by 150 artists and intellectuals condemning all totalitarian states, Russia emphatically included. The four hundred, essaying some fine distinctions between the Soviet dictatorship and all others, denounced their opponents for sowing dissension among peace-loving countries and made the unfortunate argument that "The Soviet Union continues as always to be a consistent bulwark against war and aggression, and to support the goal of a peaceful international order." Red Army invasions of Poland, Finland, Esthonia, Latvia, and Lithuania followed in quick succession, and into the jaws of doubt rode the four hundred—at least some of them.

By the time the Russians went into Finland in December, however, a new line had been pretty well worked out for those who could take it. The fight against Fascism, which the Popular Front had so long promoted, was now an "imperialist war" after all, and no good worker need be at all concerned over whether it was won by England and France on the one side or Germany on the other. The Popular Front went out of business, but the old management clung to the premises, busily taking down such signs as "Stop Hitler" and "Fight Fascism" and putting in their place banners reading "Keep America Out of War" and "The Yanks Are Not Coming." Fascism ceased to be the great enemy, but the Soviet's "fraternal assistance" to the people of Poland, Finland, and the Baltic states was curiously defended on the ground that their military governments were "semi-Fascist."

The *Nation* did not go as far editorially in lashing out at this dismal stuff as its critics thought it should, but its editor, Freda Kirchwey, let those of us on the staff go as far as we liked under our own names. I wanted to go far on Finland, and I did:

Few enlightened persons imagined a year or so ago that there could be anything worse than fascism. Now, thanks to the men of the extreme left, we know that there is. It is semi-fascism. This is what the Red troops of the Soviet Union fought against in Poland, as soon as they discovered it had been there all the time, and it is what they are fighting now in Finland. . . . There ought to be a League Against War and Semi-Fascism. Probably there will be.

So the historic episode of the Popular Front—idealistic and cynical, noble and base, grim and hilarious—came to an end, characteristically with the Hollywood Anti-Nazi League slyly but futilely changing its name to the Hollywood League for Democratic Action.

Panaceas, Nostrums, and Cure-alls

5

Every American knows that anything broken can be fixed. He knows, too, that while he is fixing it onlookers will offer suggestions for making the repair twice as efficiently in half the time. And, finally, he knows that if he is not quickly successful someone else will show up with an ingenious new attachment or magic chemical which for a low price will absolutely get things running smoothly again. So it was that when the economy ran down in the Thirties, tinkerers, free advisers, and salesmen of shiny new parts turned out in record numbers, for it is likewise a national belief that what is true of automobiles and cement mixers is also true of economic and political "machinery." Get the bugs out and add the right contrivance, and your problem is solved.

The economic tinkerers, as we have seen, were for the most part in Washington, in charge of repairs. The free advisers were to be found in every editorial office, at countless bars, and in most barber shops. Except for the Marxists, nobody said, "Get a new machine," which is a revolutionary notion appealing mostly to Europeans. But everywhere it was a fine time for the native gadget men, the promoters of mechanical cure-alls, who accordingly contributed much to the turbulence and color of the decade.

Not least among these dealers in sovereign remedies was

the Reverend Charles Edward Coughlin, who belonged to that peculiarly Midwestern subdivision of the species sometimes known as the "funny money" men. Their special nostrum was currency reform, a preoccupation that had run like a silver stream through five decades of American history, providing a common aberration for such otherwise improbable soulmates as William Jennings Bryan and Ezra Pound.

On a Sunday afternoon in the days before the New Deal, millions of Americans regularly stopped loafing at two o'clock Eastern Standard Time to tune in on the young Canadian-Irish priest from the Shrine of the Little Flower in Royal Oak, Michigan. Of a total, though intermittent, audience estimated at thirty million people, some may have listened as they would to an organ recital, admiring the keening tenor, complete with trilled r's ("the Charrrch") and wondering at the spectacular range from high and plaintive eloquence to the low-pitched vituperation reserved for "moneychangers," those "wily servants of the murderous High Priests of Capitalism." And a few may possibly have tuned in hoping for a bit of spiritual uplift on a Sunday afternoon, though this was rarely the primary aim of the Father's airborne sermons. But the vast majority of those who regularly shared "The Golden Hour of the Little Flower" simply wanted to hear a master tub thumper lay it on to the bankers and politicians they were sure had brought the country to its low estate.

Eighty thousand ecstatic letters were the normal response, but when the father damned J. P. Morgan, Andrew Mellon, Ogden Mills, and Eugene Meyer as the "Four Horsemen of the Apocalypse," the number jumped to 600,000. And when he predicted a new war unless the nation's economy was made more Christian, by which he meant more inflationary, no fewer then 1,200,000 letters cascaded into the little post office of Royal Oak. Much of this flood was accompanied by small bills from people whose pantries were probably in short supply, and regularly on Tuesday mornings the Father personally carried to the bank some $20,000 in cash received in the Monday mail, which soon taxed the labors of his 150 clerks. No one since Bryan had so effectively combined religion, silver currency, and elocution; and Bryan, without the twin blessings of radio and Depression, did not hold a patch on Coughlin for breadth of audience.

The Father's career exemplified to perfection the American custom of turning a man into a demigod, with his knowing cooperation, and then, with his *unknowing* cooperation, discovering him to be a quack and reducing him to that dreadful privacy which is the hell of politicians. Three scenes in the life of the Radio Priest may serve to mark the stations on this traditional course, to wit:

Scene 1 ("Roosevelt or Ruin"). A cold evening late in November of 1933. Seven thousand New Yorkers are packed into the old Hippodrome, while some fifteen thousand others mill about, trying to keep warm and get as close as possible to the loudspeakers that will soon bring the magic voice to Sixth Avenue. Through a side entrance Father Coughlin advances to the stage, where an odd assortment of celebrities has been tuning up the audience. There is New York's former Governor William Sulzer, impeached; two Senators from Oklahoma, both hot for the New Deal and cold on bankers; and former Mayor John F. Hylan, known as "Red Mike," whom Al Smith in his halcyon days had eased out of City Hall and who is happy now to be among Democrats that despise the new Al, suddenly so beloved by conservative Republicans. Ironically, in view of Father Coughlin's later fancies, the chairman of the evening is Henry Morgenthau the Elder, who is introduced to the crowd as "the father of an illustrious son, the Acting Secretary of the Treasury."*

At a quarter past eight the broad-shouldered priest takes his seat on the platform, touching off a standing ovation, which is repeated a few minutes later when someone in the balcony proposes "Three cheers for Father Coughlin." At last he approaches the microphone and the audience falls silent. "Stop Roosevelt!" he begins—and his listeners are momentarily stunned. "Yes, stop him from *being* stopped!" The ornate walls of the building rock with applause and rock again as he puts the rhetorical question: "Who stopped the revolution in this country, Herbert Hoover or Franklin Roosevelt?" And catcalls fill the hall when he repeats his fixed story about Al Smith—how that one-time "Happy Warrior" stepped into the ranks of the wicked the day he paid a visit, in the company of two bishops, to the office of J. P. Morgan in quest of a loan for the Empire State Building.

But soon the speaker gets around to his favorite subject. Demanding the "100-cent and not the 165-cent dollar," he lights into the tight-money bankers—"individuals who . . . welded link by link the economic chain which has bound us to the floor of hellish poverty." And always it is the President who will free the slaves of hard money, especially the white-collar slaves: "When anyone stands in the way of President Roosevelt, and it's either Roosevelt or ruin, I've got to take a stand. This is war."

Scene 2 ("Roosevelt *and* Ruin"). Two and a half years have gone by. Father Coughlin's influence has spread to the extent that when a Philadelphia radio station asks listeners to choose between the priest and the New York Philhar-

---

* Not long after he graduated to full honors as Secretary, the illustrious son revealed Father Coughlin's sizable silver holdings, the largest in Michigan and acquired in the name of his secretary. For this and other mistakes of policy, Father Coughlin was to declare the younger Morgenthau a Communist and a foe of "gentile silver."

monic on Sunday afternoon, they choose the priest's music by 187,000 votes to 12,000. But his favorite tune has changed somewhat and his audience with it. He has cooled toward Roosevelt, whose abandonment of the gold standard was good but not good enough, and at least on alternate Sundays he is fed up with the Democrats altogether. The two major parties, he says with a delicacy not always heard on the air, "should relinquish the skeletons of their putrefying carcasses" to museums; and, turning lighter in mood, he quips that Washington is on its way to becoming "Washingtonski." But not so fast—he is "more optimistic about the final outcome of the New Deal than ever before."

The New Deal, however, is not so optimistic about Father Coughlin. The President has picked out Joseph P. Kennedy and Michigan's Governor Frank Murphy, both distinguished Catholic laymen, to try keeping him in bounds, but at the same time Hugh Johnson has been comparing him to Hitler, and coupling him with Huey Long as co-producers of a "magic financial hair tonic . . . guaranteed to grow economic whiskers on a billiard ball overnight." And Representative John O'Connor has offered to kick him up Pennsylvania Avenue with all the silver jingling in his pockets. It is a proposal with broad appeal but one that only a Catholic in good standing can afford to make.

By now even Father Coughlin's oratorical habits have undergone a change. He tips off his audiences when to come in with applause by pointing to the microphones and clapping, and he is capable at the end of a fiery peroration of glancing at his watch and in a soothing announcer's voice saying something like "This concludes our broadcast this afternoon. Father Coughlin will be on the air next Sunday through the Mutual System."

He is also having increasing difficulty with the hierarchy of his own church. Secure in the backing of his local bishop, he scorns the rebukes of Cardinal O'Connell, informing his fol-

lowers that the Cardinal has no authority outside his Boston
archdiocese and that His Eminence would do better in any
case to think about the needs of the poor and less about the
financial worries of the rich. As for himself, he claims only to
echo the great social encyclicals of Leo XIII and Pius XI.

So much for background. The immediate scene is laid in a
Cleveland meeting hall, where the devoted followers of Dr.
Francis Townsend are in convention assembled. The date is
July 16, 1936. Father Coughlin has already created, announced, and endorsed a new "Union Party," which will
support one William Lemke, a North Dakota Congressman,
for the Presidency. The hope is to gather all the dissidents
under a single tent, and to this end Coughlin has been summoned to Cleveland to prevent regular Democrats among
the Townsend leaders from swinging delegates to the support of Roosevelt. The quixotic doctor has already attacked
the President, and his lieutenant, Gerald L. K. Smith, a leftover from Huey Long's Share-Our-Wealth movement, has
whipped the delegates to a froth with revelations about the
"communistic atheist" in the White House.

Now it is Father Coughlin's turn to discuss current events
as viewed by a man of the cloth who only two years before
had pledged, "I will never change my philosophy that the
New Deal is Christ's deal." After playing for forty minutes
on his listeners' need for comfort and soothing unguents, the
Father rips off his black coat and vest, discards his clerical
collar, and, with flushed face and fists raised to heaven, in-
dicts the President of the United States as "that great be-
trayer and liar," that ally of the money-changers and champion of communism, "Franklin Double-Crossing Roosevelt."
Ten thousand elderly delegates, disposed to cranky passions,
embrace for the moment the new slogan now offered by
Father Coughlin: "Roosevelt *and* Ruin!" And, when he asks
how many will follow Dr. Townsend and himself into the
Union Party, virtually every one of them, putting aside his

box lunch of oranges and bananas, struggles up from his seat.

With three such rampant egos as Coughlin, Smith, and Townsend, harmony is not destined to last, not even for the sake of unseating Roosevelt, much less for elevating the obscure Mr. Lemke. But for the moment, reviewing the parade of their elderly admirers, the three musketeers unblushingly pose arm-in-arm for the cameras, each for one and one for each.

In a week Father Coughlin is to apologize, under pressure, for having called the President a liar, but two months later he will refer to him as "the anti-God" and "a scab President" leading "a great scab army." Protests from an Archbishop and a Monsignor, as well as a public outcry, will cause him to apologize once more, the tactics being to hold his moderates in line while inciting his fanatics. Among the most excitable of the latter group is himself, by now so carried away on the wings of his own rhetoric that he publicly pledges: "If I cannot swing at least nine million votes to Mr. Lemke, I will quit broadcasting educational talks on economics and politics."

Scene 3 ("Ruin"). Between Scenes 2 and 3 Father Coughlin's fortunes have plummeted. On election day his Union Party, far from getting nine million votes, has drawn much less than one million. But reversing his field once more, like the football player he once was, the Father has returned to the radio after six or seven weeks of observing his solemn pledge. Leaving behind him the cranky innocence of Midwestern Populism, he now glides into something crankier but less innocent, something more suggestive of the European breed of clerical fascism. What is so wonderful about majority rule, he wants to know, in which "mankind is king" and a "magic of numbers" denies "the entrance of Christ's principles into economy, business, industry, and agriculture?" Americans would do well to think of scrapping their

Congress, he suggests, and borrowing the system of the Corporate State from Mussolini's Italy.

What is more, his banker targets are no longer the Morgans, Mellons, and Rockefellers, with an occasional Kuhn-Loeb thrown in for religious balance. They are now the "international Jewish bankers," just as the Communists are now the "Communistic Jews." And naturally his following has shifted dramatically. The trade-union support has all but vanished with his bitter attacks on the C.I.O. The growing sharpness with which high Catholic Church officials have taken him to task has greatly reduced his following among those of his own faith. And among his former Jewish supporters his popularity is now only a notch or two above that of Adolf Hitler. Acknowledging the *Protocols of the Elders of Zion* to be a forgery, he nevertheless prints them in his *Social Justice* as a matter of "interest" to his readers and because, he says, even if they are not authentic, they are "factual." And his weekly now regularly carries objective news analyses straight from the Nazis' World Press Service in Berlin.

Bit by bit a following once bourgeois, peaceable, and confined to living rooms is replaced by a scabrous army of the streets. In every major city the pathetic failures, the delinquents, the poolroom toughs, and the commercial bigots are organized into platoons of twenty-five to form the quaintly titled "Christian Front." Their functions are to hawk *Social Justice* on the corners, to pick fistfights with Jewish passersby, to set up a "Christian Index" of local storekeepers, and to hold inflammatory little rallies all over town.

Technically the Front is not Father Coughlin's responsibility, and he alternately endorses it and disavows it, depending on the direction of the political winds. But it is constantly inspired by effusions from Royal Oak such as the Father's warning to his critics: "We will fight you in Franco's way if necessary."

By way of an afterword, it is a combination of his own church and a wartime government that gives Father Coughlin the last gentle jog into limbo. Subjected to review by a board appointed by his new Archbishop, his radio speeches no longer excite the frustrated or incite the moronic. In spite of countless appeals and a seedy army of Christian Fronters, the $15,000 a week necessary to keep the show on the air is not forthcoming, and Father Coughlin again fades from the radio, this time for good. His paper would linger on for a few incredibly shabby years until, shortly after Pearl Harbor, the Department of Justice would charge it with violations of the Espionage Act, the Postmaster General would bar it from the mails, and Father Coughlin himself would agree to let it go down the drain rather than put up a formal defense. By this time hardly anyone cares, and the only ones to protest, it seems, are the board members of the American Civil Liberties Union.

After the depressing Father Coughlin, it is something of a joy to look back at his raucous and colorful rival in the Demagogues' Sweepstakes, namely Huey Pierce Long, whom I remember most vividly in brown suit and pink shirt, dancing a jig in the aisle of the United States Senate. The man who called himself "the Kingfish" did not have Father Coughlin's chance to wither away in peaceful obscurity, because a young Louisiana doctor shot him down when he was still on the upcurve of his eccentric orbit. But until that very moment there were many, Huey among them, who thought he would escape any such glissade not by assassination but simply by becoming President of the United States.

If men were to be judged solely by the quality of their dreams, Huey Long would enjoy a somewhat higher niche in history than he has so far been accorded. For the Kingfish dreamed rather well—grandiosely, it is true, with some of the vindictiveness that marred all his behavior and with more than a touch of the Walter Mitty, but with a yearning, too, for a more equitable America which would be peacefully achieved and impishly administered by himself. Many a rising politico has with his inner eye fondly seen himself in the White House, but as grown men few have brashly trumpeted their vision beyond the circle of family and intimate friends. Huey Long, even after he was Governor, not only advised everyone he knew to stick with him because "I'm gonna be President someday," but in the very year of his death produced a book about that shimmering vision. Supposedly it was written by a ghost. (Huey's own language was saltier and more colorful—"I was born into politics," he once said, "a wedded man, with a storm for my bride.") But the ideas were all his and the book meant so much to him that he was reported to have talked of it as he lay dying and to have murmured his expectation that it would be a best seller.

Huey's prediction about the book was as wrong as his predictions about the Presidency, but *My First Days in the White House* did throw a vivid light on his character— adolescent longing, vengefulness, dreamy idealism, and all. No ghost would have imagined, and probably no other American politician would have committed to paper, the extraordinary passages in which "President" Long names to his Cabinet men he has scorned and who have scorned him in turn—not in order to honor them, mind you, but to humble them.

Informed that he has been offered the post of Secretary of Commerce, Herbert Hoover telephones the newly inaugurated Chief Executive: "Er-r-r-r, Mr. President—er-r-r, this is Hoover. . . . I should have been consulted. This has placed me in a very embarrassing position. . . . I am a former President of the United States, and it's a terrible step down for me to be asked to serve in your Cabinet."

To which the Long of Long's dreams responds: "Now let

me put you straight. You say you are being embarrassed because, as a former President of the United States, it would be a step down for you to serve as a Cabinet officer under another President. Just what is your position in public life today, Mr. Hoover?" When the shaken man falls back on the truth that he might "not care to be associated" with Huey Long, the suddenly stern President leaves it to his vanity and his Quaker conscience: "It is something between you and the American people. You will have to explain to them why you will not serve your country again in its hour of need."

Naturally Mr. Hoover succumbs. So does Al Smith, who had once refused to campaign for Roosevelt if Long was included among his active supporters and who was now being offered the Directorship of the Budget. Here Huey sees himself so persuasive that the dumfounded Smith is driven to murmur, "I think I've had you wrong all the time."

But the cheeky climax of the daydream is the appointment of his great predecessor and lately his arch-enemy, Franklin D. Roosevelt, to the inglorious post of Secretary of the Navy.

. . . Some minutes after ten o'clock that night I was called to the telephone.

I heard a voice:

"Hello, Kingfish! . . . What in the world do you mean by offering me a cabinet post, after all the things you have said about me as President?" he demanded.

"I only offered you a position which I thought you were qualified to fill."

"Well, I thank you for the gesture, Huey, but I can't feel that you have complimented me very much . . . it's a terrible fall from the Presidency to the Secretaryship of the Navy."

"You sound just like Hoover," I said, "but he couldn't call to mind any position he held just now."

"Well, Huey, I'll have to give this more consideration," the former President told me. . . . "Say, suppose I accept and fail to become the best Secretary? What's the penalty then?"

"In that case," I replied, "people will hold me responsible, and they may punish me for your failure."

The former President chuckled; "Well, Huey, that's almost reason enough to accept the position."

He does accept, and the reader is left to share the author's vision of Secretary Roosevelt bucking memoranda along to the White House for the approval or disapproval of the nation's Kingfish, Huey P. Long of Louisiana. Just as ethereal are the chapters in which John D. Rockefeller, Jr., accepts the chairmanship of a committee to draw up plans for carrying out the President's Share Our Wealth program, and Andrew Mellon gratefully signs on as Vice Chairman. Huey appears before Congress and smashingly answers questions from the floor and some time later attends the session of the Supreme Court when that august body hands down its decision upholding the legality of his forcible redistribution of America's wealth. As he quietly moves to leave the Court, the Chief Justice leans over to say, "Mr. President, the Court is glad to note that you have kept alive your membership at this bar."

But the most touching moment of all in this gentle fantasy of a violent man comes when he first steps to the rear of the train on a journey undertaken to find out whether the people are satisfied with what he has done. "Tell me," he says to the throng on the station platform, "what can I do for anyone? What's wrong?" And through the prolonged cheering comes at last a loud voice: "Nothing! We have just found out how bad we needed you for President all the time."

In view of the passions aroused in the breasts of "economic royalists" by Roosevelt's comparatively mild New Deal, nothing could have been more fanciful than the sweetness and light conjured up in these pages. For Huey's plan called for a drastic capital levy that would have limited any one man's wealth at first to $5 million and eventually to something between $1 and $2 million. Incomes above a million or so would be similarly confiscated, and all the fortunes thus seized and converted to cash would be redistributed so as to guarantee every family in the land a homestead worth $5,000, an annual income of at least $2,000, a radio, an automobile, low-priced foods, free education from kindergarten through college, and old-age pensions to top it off.

The details changed from time to time, but the spirit was always the same. In an accelerating staccato Huey would put it this way:

How many men ever went to a barbecue and would let one man take off the table what was intended for nine-tenths of the people to eat? The only way you'll ever be able to feed the balance of the people is to make that man come back and bring back some of the grub he ain't got no business with.

And his delighted followers would respond with the song that Huey himself wrote for them, even to deciding which syllables got eighth notes and which sixteenth:

Every man a king, every girl a queen,
For you can be a millionaire,
But there's something belonging to others,
There's enough for all people to share.
In sunny June and December too,
In the winter time and spring
There'll be peace without end,
Every neighbor a friend
With every man a king.

Would the government have to take over vast segments of the great industrial empires and issue shares? Would the confiscated wealth cover, or even begin to cover, the prescribed payments? And was the whole scheme even faintly compatible with a profit system? The "Rednecks' Robin

Hood" was above such trivia. If his plan wasn't sound eco-
nomically, it was very sound politically, and if it ever got
down to a question of application, he would gladly accept
any semblance of it as a major victory. Benjamin Stolberg,
who was still writing for the *Nation* when I went there, told
me of the perfect W. C. Fields response he got from Long
when he asked him to explain how he proposed to share the
wealth without socializing the productive process: "Never
explain, my boy, never explain! Explanation is the mother of
sectarianism."

Between cynicism and a real passion for raising up the
downtrodden, Huey Long was split down the middle. The
cleavage afforded views of what seemed like two very different creatures. For his worshipers there was the dimple-
chinned, curly-headed rustic who, in the best log cabin tradition, had come off the farm to whirl through a three-year
law course at Tulane University in eight months, a man
capable of remarkable feats of concentration and an intellectual mastery of legal and administrative detail. One might
balk a bit at the awed tribute of the Reverend Gerald L. K.
Smith, who in the days before he went rancid wrote of Long
in the *New Republic*, of all places: "He seems to be equally
at home with all subjects, such as shipping, railroads, banking, Biblical literature, psychology, merchandising, utilities,
sports, Oriental affairs, international treaties, South American affairs, world history, the Constitution of the United
States, the Napoleonic Code, construction, higher education,
flood control, cotton, lumber, sugar, rice, and alphabetical
relief agencies." But the unimpeachable Raymond Gram
Swing marveled likewise at the brilliance of a mind that
grasped the most abstruse points of law, government, and
banking and the smallest details of the business of the Port
of New Orleans. Chief Justice Taft and Justice Brandeis
praised him highly for the brilliance with which he argued
the case for giving free textbooks to the parochial schools as
well as the public schools of Louisiana.

Huey's wit and language, when they weren't vicious and profane, had an almost Mark Twain quality. Gibing at New Orleans high society, one of his favorite targets, he told a redneck audience what he had to do once when he got invited to a fashionable ball: "I went down to a pawnshop and bought a silk shirt for six dollars with a collar so high I had to climb up on a stump to spit." He dismissed Father Coughlin as "a political Kate Smith on the air." And likening himself to his hero, Frederick the Great, he explained: "He was the greatest son of a bitch who ever lived. 'You can't take Vienna, Your Majesty,' his nitwit Ambassadors said. 'The hell I can't,' said old Fred. 'My soldiers will take Vienna and my professors at Heidelberg will explain the reason why.' Hell, I've got a university down in Lou'siana that cost fifteen million dollars that can tell you why I do like I do."

Huey's foes—and this included holders of wealth who were disinclined to share it with perfect strangers, the organized Left, and a vast and easily shocked middle class—got a very different picture. They saw a man whose lust for personal power, said one observer, was "almost visibly lascivious." He wanted to be Kingfish of the United States as no one had ever wanted to be Kingfish before, and in his certainty that he would realize that ambition he had become arrogant somewhat beyond the call of his profession. Arriving in Washington a full year late to take his seat in the U.S. Senate, he immediately proceeded to treat his colleagues as he had successfully treated his legislature back home—on the principle, that is, that any one of them could be bought like a sack of potatoes, and for about the same price. In debate he regularly made monkeys of them while seeming to be making a monkey of himself, with the result that his usefulness as a legislator was nil. When he mockingly raised as a parliamentary inquiry the question of how he should vote on a bill that he was "half for and half against," Vice President Garner blandly ruled from the chair, "Get a saw and saw yourself in two; that's what you ought to do anyhow." Another Senator observed that Long "couldn't get the Lord's Prayer endorsed in this body." And Alben Barkley told him wonderingly, "You are the smartest lunatic I ever saw in my whole life."

He was vulgar, too, in a way that Americans will happily accept in a mayor or a congressman but not in a potential President. He threw food on a restaurant floor when it wasn't cooked to his taste, kept his hat on throughout an interview with President Roosevelt, and at the Sands Point Club on Long Island committed a nuisance on another guest's trouser leg when the gentleman was slow to yield Huey a place at the urinal. The last of these episodes became rather well publicized and almost undermined his standing, because the guest in question punched him enthusiastically, leaving a deep cut above the eye to advertise the conquest. Huey explained the injury in various ways, usually that he had been set upon by a waiting band of thugs, dispatched for that purpose to the men's room by Wall Street conspirators.

Besides lustful ambition and inordinate vulgarity, Long's enemies could not overlook the extraordinary vengefulness of the man. Whether or not he carried about with him a "son-of-a-bitch book," as alleged, in which he recorded all offenses against his own majesty, he made little secret of the fact that many of his official acts were motivated at least in part by revenge. When he proposed to tax Standard Oil five cents on every barrel of refined oil, he wanted the money for highways, hospitals, and free textbooks—but he also wanted to pay off Standard Oil for having once denied its pipelines to a small company in which he then had an interest, thus keeping him from becoming a millionaire. When he poured millions into making the state university an impressive institution, he wanted to strike a blow for public education—but he also wanted to strike a blow at Tulane and Loyola, both of which had slighted him. Campaign grudges were paid off when he managed to remove the entire city administration of Alexandria, where he had once been egged, and when he took over the local government of Baton Rouge, which had rashly voted against him.

The views of friend and foe alike were just, and since Huey was both brilliant and vulgar, socially idealistic and politically cynical, devoted to the underdog and voracious for power, he left behind him, like many another dictator, a record compounded of material achievement and the plain rottenness of tyranny. As Dr. Jekyll he lifted the educational system of Louisiana out of the swamps with free schoolbooks, buses, night classes for grown illiterates, and a vastly improved state university whose free college of medicine was among the best in the country. He laid down some six thousand miles of highway (which occasionally failed to link up with towns controlled by his political enemies) and built toll-free bridges. He cut telephone and utilities rates and modernized the penal system. He taxed those who could pay and relieved those who couldn't, brought 300,000 new voters to the polls by killing the poll tax and publicly referred to the head of the Ku Klux Klan in the state as "that Imperial bastard."

But even for those who thought well of these Jekyll-like achievements, especially those who viewed them at a considerable distance from Louisiana, the villainies of Mr. Hyde weighed more heavily in the balance.* Whether he was Governor or Senator, he ran the legislature by purchase, threat, and blackmail, personally invading the chambers and committee rooms to give his directives, squelch opposition, and oversee the voting. He loaded the courts with his own judges and absorbed, through his so-called Civil Service Commission, the power to remove state, city, and parish officials at will, whether appointed or elected. He enjoyed the services of a secret police force, which made arrests and

---

* Possibly an indication of Long's insight into himself, if not into literature, he thought *Dr. Jekyll and Mr. Hyde* the greatest book ever written.

held people incommunicado until they were tried, often by his own special prosecutors and just as often on trumped-up charges. Through other subordinates he used the power to fix assessments as a handy economic weapon, harried the "lyin' press" with special taxes, used highway routes as a means of bringing recalcitrants into line, and undid his great contribution to the state university by running it, as he said, "like any other damn department." In fact he installed as president of that institution a backwoods teacher named James Monroe Smith, to whom he paid the delicate compliment: "He doesn't have a straight bone in his body." Smith's virtue as a university president was that he didn't get in Huey's way but innocently occupied himself with stealing state bonds, for which he went to prison some time after the Kingfish was interred in the front lawn of his capitol.

"Fascist" was a word that was bandied about pretty freely in the Thirties, and possibly Huey Long earned it, with his self-intoxication, his deliberately vague pitch to rural and lower-middle-class misery, his flamboyant oratory and seeming recklessness, and the limitless cynicism with which he viewed the essentials of democracy. But there is no evidence that he saw himself in any such ideological light. It seemed to me then—and still does—that he was a unique combination of backwoods Populist and Latin American *caudillo*, with a measurable whiff of the old Tammany Hall. By the time Dr. Weiss's bullet cut him down he had no doubt become a dangerous man, and the young doctor, who supposedly acted for personal reasons, may have done the country a greater service than he knew. But the real tragedy of the Kingfish lay in the deficiency described to his face by the kindly Senator Barkley: "You are clever, you are resourceful, you are a great debater; if only you had a balance wheel inside of you, like the little gadget in a piece of machinery, to keep you from doing so many crazy things, you would be a really great man."

Where Father Coughlin cried, Cheapen our money, and Huey Long said, Call in the whole pie and cut it up all over again, Dr. Francis E. Townsend, gentlest and least self-seeking of the Big Three dreamers, hawked a crankier scheme than either. Let the Treasury send a check for $200 every month to each unemployed man and woman in the United States over the age of sixty, he proposed, with the legal requirement that the money be spent in the following thirty days. Thus the aged would be supported, the economy vastly stimulated by the forced spending, and the job market left to the young. No millionaires' fortunes were threatened, for the pension fund was to come from a tax on all transactions—producer to wholesaler, wholesaler to retailer, retailer to consumer. The more people spent, the greater the fund. Here was no socialism, which the good doctor had espoused in his salad days, no capital levy, not even free silver. "Hallelujah!" cried the elderly, the middle-aged, and a good many of their Congressmen, all devoutly believing they had been shown the Northwest Passage to permanent prosperity and economic justice. Millions of Americans who had formerly dreaded the advent of their sixtieth birthday now actively looked forward to becoming, not pensioners, but "Distributor Custodians." For highflown titles no fraternal society outdid the Townsendites, whose governing board, scorning mere directors, was made up of "Citizens Maximi."

Inevitably economists and other spoilsports were not long in pointing out certain flaws in the plan. With at least eight million eligible pensioners, the dole would come to some $20 billion a year, which was close to half the national income. The bulk of this gargantuan tax, if not all of it, would be added to the price of goods as they proceeded through the stages of distribution, with the consumers, including the pensioners themselves, paying two or three times what they had paid for the same items before the Townsend salvation. If wages didn't follow prices, thousands would go hungry;

and, if they did, each increase would boost the price level still higher. An insane spiral would soon wipe out the pensions altogether and probably the rest of the economy along with them.

But the followers of the dream were not for having hope dimmed by fact. "God deliver us from further guidance by professional economists," prayed the good doctor, and his millions of followers echoed a fervent amen. As simple as his faith in his plan was their faith in him, for Francis Townsend was a homey man, born to be called "Doc." A country physician who had practiced for years in the Black Hills, he had, like so many other Midwesterners, gone late in life to California, where the natural climate was mild and the social climate eccentric. Looking out the bathroom window while shaving on a depression morning in 1933, he had been genuinely horrified at the sight of three old women rummaging in a garbage can for scraps of food, and out of his righteous wrath grew the Old Age Revolving Pension plan, with 7,000 clubs in the country and a reliably estimated membership, at its peak, of some 2.2 million citizens.

Anything but a spell-binder on the platform, Townsend kept his following by a combination of his own simple earnestness and the hope he held out to them. The angular awkwardness of his speech and manner contrasted soothingly with the wrathful rhetoric of Father Coughlin and the profane impishness of Huey Long. For people who had no thought of changing the world but just wanted to collect $200 a month, high-flown oratory was not required; they were perfectly satisfied with old Doc Townsend's reliance on "My goodness" and "Bless your souls," and they stood piously ready to cash in on the movement's early slogan, "Honor thy Father and Mother." In the glare of adulation even the simplest country doctor can acquire a touch of the messianic, and Townsend did get to comparing his mission with Lincoln's, which made it all the easier for him to see villainy in those who stood between him and his vision of a good society achieved without blood, sweat, or tears. The chief of these villains could only be President Roosevelt. Politicians on all other levels could, and shamefully did, cadge votes by praising the Townsend fantasy while logically passing the buck to the national Administration, but there it had to stop. Publicly Roosevelt voiced no opinion of the movement, but he left no doubt where he stood. When Dr. Townsend sought an appointment at the White House, he was invited to see Madam Perkins instead, a suggestion that his *Townsend Weekly* viewed as "an insult that the masses of the people should resent," a sign that "We have aristocracy in the White House—not democracy."

Much more drastic was the President's apparent sanctioning of a Congressional investigation, which could only have been undertaken on the initiative of his leaders in the House. Few doubted that the hearings were at least in part politically motivated, and they included the kind of badgering and innuendo that reinforced such suspicions. Dr. Townsend emerged personally clean, although the clubs may have been surprised to learn that he was drawing $250 a week plus expenses when they had had reason to think his salary was $100. But many of his impoverished followers were jolted to learn that Robert E. Clements, his co-founder and high-powered organizer, had legally though disingenuously netted $79,000 in two and a half years of operations. Worse still, there was evidence of racketeering on the local levels, possible misuse of the mails, and infiltration of the leadership by characters of less than savory reputation. One had traveled through the country dressed as a monk named "Father Sylvester," lecturing and collecting money; a regional manager turned out to have been a Ku Klux Klan organizer; and another regional official had a past that included indictments for a variety of gaudy offenses, including pimping. Stung by what he regarded as an "inquisition," Dr. Town-

send walked out of the hearing room, and was cited for contempt of Congress.*

As if the Congressional steamroller were not misfortune
enough, poor Dr. Townsend, leaving the committee room in
a daze, fell into the waiting arms of the Reverend Gerald L.
K. Smith, a fate he did not deserve. According to Townsend,
Smith let loose a rebel yell as "an inward force caused him to
leap to my side and risk possible jail sentence for contempt."
The "inward force," it later developed, was Smith's recognition that Townsend had a going organization and juicy mail-
ing lists, which were just what he had been looking for ever
since Huey Long's political henchmen had euchered him out
of the scraps remaining from Share-Our-Wealth. At any rate,
in what must have been one of the weirdest emotional
sprees of the decade, the two swore to each other to stand
together until "the common people of this country take over
the government of the United States."

From that point Dr. Townsend slid down the steep descent. When Gomer Smith, his vice-president, tried to save
the movement from the bigoted likes of Father Coughlin
and Gerald Smith, the irate doctor talked of getting a "divorce" from Gomer. And when that Cherokee from Oklahoma went on to hail Roosevelt as a "church-going, Bible-
reading, God-fearing man" and "golden-hearted patriot,"
Townsend overruled his Citizens Maximi and ousted Gomer
for his "impudence." He had already broken with Clements,
whose organizing talents had built up the movement, and
now splits and fissures developed up and down the line. The
Lemke debacle in November shook the wobbly structure to
its foundations, but even before that event the Rev. Gerald

---

* The charge was kept on ice during the 1936 campaign to avoid the
accusation of political persecution, but in 1937 the doctor was convicted and
sentenced to a year in jail. President Roosevelt, possibly feeling a little
contemptuous of Congress himself—he had just lost his fight on Capitol Hill
to reform the Supreme Court—pardoned the old doctor before the prison
doors closed in on him, an act much to his credit.

Smith, possibly seeing the cracks in the wall, had announced plans for heading a new nationalist movement which would "seize the government." Dr. Townsend, declaring himself "against fascism," decided not to stand with him after all, oath or no oath.

What was left of the Townsend movement after 1936 was still a fairly big business, but as a political force it was doomed. The new Social Security Act, though no match for it in glamour, was at least a reality and what it left standing of the doctor's structure was pretty well wiped out by succeeding years of defense prosperity and wartime demands for labor, even elderly labor. As for the good man himself, he was still busy in 1948 promoting his plan, but this time, having tried Socialists, Democrats, Republicans, and pro-Fascists, he was for Henry A. Wallace and his Progressive Party—which may not have been too far-fetched, after all, because, reverting to the beliefs of his youth, the doctor was now for nationalizing the mines, banks, and railroads. Erratic he was, and more than a bit of a crank, but he did make the world's most youth-centered people move from a pained toleration of "old folks" to at least a political respect for the votes of "senior citizens."

Happily, the Big Three were not alone in the salvation business; for Huey, who was admittedly entertaining, was too dangerous to be comfortably enjoyed and, whatever one thought of Father Coughlin and Dr. Townsend, no one professed to find them personally amusing. Some of their rivals, on the other hand, added considerably to the color of the times, posed no political threat to the democratic order, and might even be said to have stimulated public thought.

The earliest and most grandiose by far of the new Utopias was that of the Technocrats. It was quite possible to make the industrial society bloom forever, avoiding completely the booms and busts that had caused all our misery, said

Howard Scott, a young engineer who took time out of his
floor-waxing business to dabble in Veblenist economics. All
that was necessary to balance production and consumption
permanently and automatically was to convert the price system from dollars and cents to one of ergs and joules, that is,
to units of energy. With corresponding currency issued in
the same denominations, a perfect harmony would be preserved, depressions and unemployment would be impossible,
and such full use could be made of machinery that a living
standard ten times as great as that of 1929 could be had on
the basis of a four-hour day and a four-day week. Naturally,
of course, the new system would have to be run by engineers
in place of industrialists and by technicians in place of politicians.

In spite of Al Smith's sour note that in Washington we had
just *had* government by engineers, Technocracy caught the
public fancy and was for a year or so the biggest thing since
mah-jongg. Books and articles poured out on the subject, but
when the dazzle wore off and the jargon was penetrated,
people seemed to feel that it left unanswered several large
and bothersome questions: Could all the types of energy
that went into an item really be calculated and apportioned?
If so, wouldn't a pound of cheese be more highly rated than,
say, a concert ticket representing only a fractional interest in
the energy expended on a performance by Yehudi Menuhin?
Wouldn't the elimination of politicians take a bit of doing,
and why would the owners of industry turn their plants over
to engineers any more readily than they would to committees of workingmen? With the intrusion of such questions,
the movement subsided, eventually retreating to Southern
California, which was even then the boneyard of abandoned
social doctrines. Nevertheless, only a freshly conceived and
native paradise, especially one run by engineers, could have
won so quick and respectful a hearing for dropping the
profit system. In plain envy a Socialist acquaintance of mine

complained: "Socialists have been saying 95 percent of what the Technocrats say, and saying it better, but the American public has gone on believing that socialism has something to do with free love, anarchy, and dividing up all the world's wealth equally among workers and loafers."

At the opposite pole from the Utopia of these machine-minded men were the dream worlds of the Southern Agrarians and the Distributists. The Agrarians were for undoing as much of the industrial revolution as possible and getting back to the land, especially the plantation land of the ante-bellum South. They would have stopped short of slavery, but that was as realistic as they got. The Distributists seemed to favor undoing not only the industrial revolution but the Russian, American, and French revolutions as well. They were for medievalism, complete with monarch, guilds, and submissive peasantry. For achieving this goal the required tactics seemed to be confined to writing articles for a few esoteric reviews, with occasional forays into the letter columns of the *New Republic,* and when these somehow did not seem to be producing a medieval world, Seward Collins, the leading Distributist, took up fascism instead. A writer and editor, he tried for a while to keep a line between his fascism and that of the man in the gutter, entertaining wealthy potential Fascists at the Lotos Club and making it clear that his anti-Semitism was not of the vulgar Goebbels variety but derived directly from the writings of Hilaire Belloc. But like Lawrence Dennis, the deep thinker of American fascism, he found out in time that elegant Fascists— even elegant medievalists for that matter—were in short supply and he had sadly to settle for the support of the usual louts until, at the end of the decade, he was dispatched to Lake Geneva, Wisconsin, to help the America First Committee put out *Scribner's Commentator,* the perverted shade of the old *Scribner's.*

Dennis himself was a dark and chilling specimen, given to

dispensing the theory of fascism from the Harvard Club but capable of reminding a listener that "the easiest way to unite and animate large numbers . . . for action is to exploit the dynamic forces of hate and fear." A one-time Foreign Service officer in Central America, he had learned to despise the ways of free enterprise as much as those of free politics and longed for "some form of state capitalism." Russia might almost as well have furnished the model as Germany or Italy, but he coolly calculated that fascism had a better chance than communism here and was in fact developing nicely, with the New Deal showing the way. By the middle of the decade, however, Roosevelt had bogged down in a "planless revolution" and only someone like Huey Long, he felt, could straighten it out. As for himself, he was "much too intellectual to be a good demagogue," but Long would "need a Goebbels." When Dr. Weiss's bullet took Long from the scene, Dennis was left to a frustrating search in the middens of American politics, a lonely Goebbels looking for a Hitler.

On the religious front Dr. Frank Buchman was offering Moral Rearmament, which proposed to remake a tawdry world by helping the individual to remake himself, to develop through group confessionals his capacity for "absolute honesty, purity, unselfishness and love." Social critics among the clergy derided Moral Rearmament, also known as the Oxford Group, for being no more than "evening dress evangelism." It dealt in personal peccadillos, they argued, while leaving untouched the sinfulness of a social order on which most of Dr. Buchman's upper-crust followers continued to depend for their comfortable existence. Asked why he and his co-workers always traveled on luxurious ocean liners and stayed at the best hotels, the "soul surgeon," as he was sometimes billed, unhesitatingly offered the counter-question: "Why not? Isn't God a millionaire?"

Nevertheless, people went in substantial numbers to Oxford Group "house parties," where in well-appointed drawing rooms they confessed to each other their respective sins of pride, temper, unkindliness, and sexual irregularities, combining release from feelings of guilt with a certain amount of entertainment. Indeed, in his earlier days an emphasis on the erotic at these confessionals, possibly encouraging youthful braggadocio on the part of the students, had got Dr. Buchman banished from the grounds at Princeton. But by the mid-Thirties a social note had clearly crept in. Occasionally in the "quiet times" that followed the revelations, local union leaders were known to have come to a softer attitude about management, and management men about unions. Louis B. Mayer, the movie chieftain, George Eastman of Kodak, and David Dubinsky of the International Ladies' Garment Workers were all reported to have spoken well of this unorthodox aid to collective bargaining.

For a different type of religious experience, likewise a product of the times, one could drop in at one of the numerous "heavens" which Father Divine had generously scattered around for the refreshment of his "angels." At these establishments free dinners of stewed chicken, fish, ham, green vegetables, cake, and ice cream were available to respectful visitors as well as to the angels, who literally regarded the little, coffee-complexioned, benevolent-looking man as God. "The real God," said an article of the faith, "is the God that feeds us." Guests were expected only to clap hands during the chanting, which broke out intermittently during the meal, perhaps drop something in the collection basket, though nobody watched, and say the ritualistic "Thank you, Father" for each dish that came their way, though Father may have been present only in the spirit.

Once in a while the divine one would show up in the flesh, which in the summer would be covered by a soft blue shirt and a sparklingly fresh suit of light-colored flannel. He was extravagantly admired in a relaxed and informal way, especially by the ladies, and after a good deal of chanting and

dancing he would make a brief talk. I never heard one of
these speeches, but Langston Hughes, in a 1966 column in
the New York *Post,* reported the text of one as follows:

Sisters and Brothers, I want you to eat and eat and eat, and
dine and dine and dine. And when you have eaten and eaten and
eaten, and dined and dined and dined, I want you to get up
and give your places to others that they might eat and eat and eat,
and dine and dine and dine. Peace! It's truly wonderful!

For years New York was full of maids with wonderful
"angelic" names like Quiet Love, Merry Light, and Joyous
Faith, who never failed to greet you on meeting and parting
with that attractive message—"Peace, it's wonderful!" Of all
the world savers of the era, none was more pleasantly be-
nevolent or ran a more innocent Utopia than Father Divine,
proudly proclaimed by his angelic hosts as "Dean of the
Universe."

Of the remaining utopians, many sold variants of Dr.
Townsend's popular nostrum, notably among them the
promoters of "Ham and Eggs Every Thursday." This proposal to have the state pay $30 a week to all who would
retire at the age of *fifty* was such political dynamite that,
with endorsements from both A.F. of L. and C.I.O., it
elected a United States Senator and came within an ace of
becoming law in California—even though the frightened
San Francisco Stock Exchange had served notice that if Ham
and Eggs won, it would move to Reno.

The same state had been the scene of similar near-hysteria
early in the decade when Upton Sinclair, running for Governor, offered the voters his plan to End Poverty in California. EPIC was basically a scheme to establish, with state
funds, small cooperative enterprises on idle land and in idle
plants. These would prove such powerful arguments for
practical socialism, Sinclair thought, that the doctrine of
production for use would at last come into its own, spread-

ing from town to town and state to state. Shrewd and experienced Socialists like Norman Thomas thought the notion absurd, a throwback to the ill-fated utopian colonies of the nineteenth century, but Southern Californians came to it fresh and their enthusiasm threw the state's businessmen, especially the moving-picture moguls, into spasms. Millions of dollars were spent to blacken, or rather redden, Sinclair's name, with public-relations experts getting their first full-scale workout in political campaigning. In the end Sinclair was done in as much by his own party, President Roosevelt included, as by his opponents but, primarily a writer, he found solace in getting to work on a new book. Having launched the campaign with a dreamy volume entitled *I, Governor of California—And How I Ended Poverty: A True Story of the Future*, he proceeded to write one called *I, Candidate for Governor—And How I Got Licked*.

Needless to say, the Administration established none of the Utopias promoted by this spectacular assortment of dreamers. It neither nationalized the banks nor erected a silver calf for public worship. It put no limit to any man's fortune in order to make any other man a king. It set up no revolving pension scheme and doled out neither ham nor eggs on Thursdays. It continued to issue dollars and cents rather than joules and ergs and made no effort to turn over the country either to gentleman farmers out of a Jeffersonian Virginia or to feudal gentry out of a Plantagenet England. It established no cooperative villages and did not interest itself visibly in personal sin or the cultivation of Green Pastures with dinner.

Yet somehow, in that mysteriously vapory way in which the democratic system bumbles along, all these objectives, or almost all, found a reflection in Mr. Roosevelt's New Deal. Gold did lose its magic and debtors' burdens were eased, which was the idea. What with toughly progressive income taxes, collective bargaining, and minimum-wage laws, the distribution of wealth in the country did get a good shaking up. Full employment and a rationalized economy became at least respectable goals of government, even if engineers were not put in charge. Old-age pensions did become a reality and could thereafter only grow in magnitude. And government-organized cooperatives did electrify the farms, though they operated no villages. If nothing official was done about private sin, economic sin was at least for a time rendered unfashionable, and many found their pastures a little greener as a result of all the pottering in Washington. As for moving the country toward medievalism, it cannot honestly be argued that any progress was made, but otherwise it is fair to say that in all the raucous outcry of the Thirties no voice was wholly lost.

The Dire Threat
of Alf Landon

6

In keeping with the unconventional nature of the decade, as well as the vagaries of American politics, Alfred M. Landon owed his chance at the Presidency to Dr. John R. Brinkley, a medicine man who specialized in goat glands for the rejuvenation of elderly Kansans. Barred from practice for quackery and hotly pursued by the Federal Trade Commission, Brinkley was moved to run for Governor as an Independent in 1932 and 1934, no doubt with the idea of avenging himself on those who had interrupted his career.* So deeply did he cut into the Democratic vote that Landon was twice sent to the Kansas executive mansion in years when everywhere else in the country Republicans were being buried under Democratic landslides.

So it was that when Republican leaders went through the land in search of a candidate who might regain the White

* Besides performing the "Brinkley Compound Operation," a graft from the testes of Toggenberg goats performed for a flat $750, Dr. Brinkley prescribed freely over the radio. Take "Brinkley No. 7" or "Brinkley No. 9," he would advise, whereupon the patients would report to certain designated drugstores to get their castor oil, aspirin, and the like, on all of which the radio doctor got his cut. In time Brinkley became rich enough to own his bank, to contribute a park to his home town, and to hunger for political power. In the 1932 election for Governor he ran up the astonishing vote of 244,607.

House for them in 1936, their divining rods pointed inevitably to the modest man in Topeka. And they were no more bothered by his innocent obscurity than are Tibetan monks when they discover by signs and wonders the infant who is destined to be their new Dalai Lama.

Landon did, to be sure, have claims to the nomination besides his two Brinkley-aided election victories, but in the perspective of thirty years they seem hardly more impressive than they did to most of the electorate at the time. For the run-of-the-mill Republicans his great attraction was that in happy contrast to the big spenders in Washington he had for four years held Kansas to a balanced budget. Few of them knew that the state's constitution forbade spending in excess of revenues. Fewer still knew that 70 percent of the state's relief funds came from the Federal Government and that down to the month of his nomination the Kansas of Governor Landon had drawn some $200 million in New Deal bounty. Practically no one knew, until Secretary of the Interior Ickes made it public in the campaign, that Landon had visited him in Washington to ask for a PWA grant of $35 million to finance a state-owned natural gas pipeline and had even suggested a state-owned telephone system, to be similarly financed. All that *was* generally known, and all that mattered to those who cared about such things, was that while That Man in Washington had been pouring out the nation's wealth, this man in Topeka had been tidily balancing his budget. They called him "The Kansas Coolidge," a tag he was perspicacious enough to discourage. He knew it might help him to a Republican nomination, only to kill him in a national election.

For the ferocious anti–New Dealers anyone pitted against Roosevelt would have done, Beelzebub included. But Landon offered the possibility of appealing to moderate, even liberal, Republicans as well. He had come of political age in the era of the first Roosevelt and, like his father, had been carried away by the spirit of the Bull Moose. That spirit may have had more to do with clean government than with economic change, but it was in the liberal tradition, and it lasted with Landon strongly enough to elicit his vote for the Progressive Party ticket of La Follette and Wheeler in 1924. On such things as civil liberties and the League of Nations, too, he held civilized views and was all in all a far cry from the monster of toryism which many of us Popular Fronters and New Dealers believed him to be at the time, almost as an article of political faith.

As a Presidential candidate, he had few other assets than these and with one exception they were either too unexciting to count for much or were offset by corresponding deficiencies. In personality, for instance, he was pleasant and friendly, with a warmth and a liking for people that one missed in Hoover, despite the latter's record of humanitarian good works abroad, and that could hardly even be imagined in connection with Coolidge. Landon's was the manner of the small-town professional man who had made good and who felt secure enough in local esteem to wear a battered four-year-old hat and leather jacket, to work in his shirt sleeves, and in general "never to look as if there were any starch about him." His engaging smile, his candor, his informality, even his campaign trick of borrowing a cigarette from a stranger on the street—all had a certain appeal. Even stern opponents softened their attacks with remarks like, "I hate to say this, because I really like the man." Most people who met him did.

But in hard and exciting times the combination of blandness and hominess has limited value, especially when it is pitted against a combination of self-confidence and vast charm. For public purposes the Landon personality was pleasant but faint. One did not get a feeling of anything bad about him, in spite of his having been nicknamed "Foxy" when he was still in college and in spite of his having made a modest fortune as an independent oil producer. ("An honest and scrupulous man in the oil business is so rare as to rank as a museum piece," said the suspicious Harold Ickes.) But the aura of mildness that he radiated made so shadowy an impression that even after the campaign was well under way I heard a Republican politician wind up a speech with a peroration that went: "If you want to return to liberty that is real . . . to those tenets of self-initiative that have made this country great" etc., etc., "then vote for—vote for—Good Lord, I guess I've forgotten the man's name!" Happily someone in the audience, not I, remembered and helped him out.

Yet, as far as the nomination was concerned, Landon had one asset that was undeniable: there was so little alternative. Of his few rivals as late as the spring of election year, only Colonel Frank Knox, publisher of the Chicago *Daily News*, was openly in pursuit of the nonimation. And aside from pinning down the favorite-son vote of Illinois, Knox had only a handful of delegates lined up at convention time, plus underground reports that Hoover, still the party's titular chief, preferred his political truculence to the mildness of Alf Landon. Senator Arthur Vandenberg of Michigan would gladly have run for President, but since he really was foxy he suspected that 1936 was not the right time nor Roosevelt the right opponent. Senator William E. Borah of Idaho actually declared for the nomination and ran, not badly, in a few primaries. But he was an anomaly in the party, a man who would have outdone the New Dealers in hewing away at wicked bankers and corporate power. He was prickly and independent, too. In a sketch written at the time by the astute Elmer Davis a character asked rhetorically, "Ever find anybody that could agree with Borah?" and answered himself, "Not if Borah knew it. He'd be so stricken with shame at discovering that his isolation had been disturbed by an intruder that he'd go out and change his ideas immediately to regain his beloved privacy."

All Borah had in his favor, ironically, was an unfailing party regularity, at least in Presidential elections. In practice he was not so much a lone wolf as a lone porcupine. Where Landon and Knox had both been Bull Moosers in 1912 and Knox had tried all his life to sound like T.R. himself, Borah had gloomily and grumpily plodded along with William Howard Taft, not to mention Harding, Coolidge, and Hoover. Formal party loyalty was not nearly enough, however, and by the time the convention met, Borah's candidacy was no more than a personal hankering.

Privately Herbert Hoover was known to harbor hopes that the party would draft him, but publicly he gave no pre-convention hint of this human desire for vindication, rightly sensing that an open pursuit of the nomination would be both unseemly and impolitic. Even Republican leaders to whom he was still "The Chief" felt that, although he had been unfairly saddled with blame for the Depression, there was no sense in deliberately rousing up the remembrance of things past—such as Hoovervilles. His only chance lay in taking the delegates by storm, and few Americans pictured him taking anything that way.

Little did those of us who divided the politicians of the moment into "progressive" sheep and Republican goats imagine that one of the most vociferous of the New Dealers, though he had once been a Republican, secretly thought of himself as a GOP Presidential possibility. In the privacy of his diary, which was not to see publication until seventeen years later, Harold Ickes confided his regret that he had not resigned in 1935, when he was approached (he does not say by whom) with the advice that if he left the Cabinet "there was a good chance" of his being nominated for President on the Republican ticket. After all, he had been a Republican, of the Bull Moose variety, before his days as a New Dealer. However, he would probably not have been nominated anyhow because he "would not have made the terms necessary to secure the support" he'd have needed.

But on third thought, "if I *had* been nominated, in all probability I could have won in November" against Roosevelt, who was too much "up in the clouds" to get himself re-elected. In fairness to "Honest Harold," he soon descended from his own cloud and served as Roosevelt's most bellicose campaigner against the challenge of the party he had half dreamed of leading against his chief.

As so often since those days, the Republican delegates who met in Cleveland on June 9 were torn between emotional desire and political expediency. For at least two years they had been engaged—in country-club locker rooms, in Pullman cars, and at Rotary luncheons—in hot-eyed excoriation of the New Deal and all its works. Their hearts belonged to Herbert Hoover, the Wronged Man, the Scapegoat, the Martyr to Circumstance. But they were not on that account prepared to give him their standard once again and go down to inevitable defeat. Landon, on the other hand, though clearly touched with the sordid spirit of the times, might conceivably win—and the chance was enough. Analysts could have made something of the fact that even those who promoted his candidacy wistfully advertised their man on the streets of Cleveland with a covered wagon drawn by four oxen. In fact, reporters did comment that here they were, talking about lifting the Grand Old Party out of the horse-and-buggy days, and using an oxcart as an emblem. To add to the confusing symbolism, the party met in a public auditorium that had just been renovated in time for the gathering by that corrosive tool of the enemy, the WPA.

The Republicans assembled in a mood of anxiety and concern which left less than the usual margin for frolic. Between renditions of "Onward, Christian Soldiers" and the "Song of Love" from *Blossom Time,* the band played Landon's theme song, which was "O Susanna." The melody was gay but the words were grim. From widely distributed sheets, whose cover depicted a bearded pioneer strumming his banjo, a caroling barefoot boy, and a train of covered

wagons in the background, they haltingly chanted a new
version:

> If Roos-e-velt would have his way
> We'd all be in his grip,
> And soon he'd change the Ship of State
> To his Dictatorship.
> He'd make Il Duce and Hitler green
> With envy in their eye—
> American traditions we would
> Have to kiss goodbye.

But they did come in lustily with the chorus:

> Landon, Oh Landon
> Will lead to Victory—
> With the dear old Constitution
> And it's good enough for me.

At Landon headquarters delegates could find entertainment of sorts in blown-up photographs illustrating the candidate's life and ancestry: the house where he was born,
Landon in oil-stained clothes, squatting on the ground;
Landon before a battery of microphones; his mother in a
receding bustle; and other such tidbits of Americana. But to
even the friendliest delegates this sort of thing can convey
only a minimum of excitement. Bruce Barton sensed that the
convention was off to a slow start and in need of his public-
relations skill. His proposal for livening the affair was to
invite the oldest member of the party to come up on the
platform and tell why he was a Republican. There may have
been a spark in the idea, very relatively speaking, but when
he was told that the oldest member of the party on hand was
John D. Rockefeller he had to agree that he had been hasty.
At one point the widow of Benjamin Harrison, who had carried the party to triumph in 1888, was brought to the
podium to give the crowd a thrill, but she displayed what a
reporter described as "an air of boredom and distraction."
The platform had no more consistency than such docu-

ments normally have, but in several ways it fixed the line Republican Presidential candidates would take for close to thirty years. Until Barry Goldwater disastrously took another tack in 1964 that line was, in Mencken's words, essentially a promise "to bring on Utopia at an inside price." William Allen White, a Landon delegate and an influential member of the platform committee, was as effective as anyone in compounding this early "me-too" formula:

> Who in the world thinks "it is wrong to give federal assistance"? . . . Where the Republican plan differs from the Democratic practice is in our promise that this federal aid shall be administered by the states, counties, and cities . . . following local knowledge and wisdom. [Otherwise you] build up a great political machine centered in Washington and pay for it with waste and extravagance. . . . It's sensible if you are a Democrat but mad as a hoot owl if you are a taxpayer.

What the platform lacked in specific targets (it did attack the Social Security Act as "unworkable") it more than made up in free-swinging rhetoric. "America is in peril," it began. "The welfare of American men and women and the future of our youth are at stake. We dedicate ourselves to the preservation of their political liberty, their individual opportunity, and their character as free citizens, which today for the first time are threatened by government itself." And it introduced a catch phrase that was to run through the convention— "For three long years . . ." Turned into a kind of chanted prelude to all recitations of New Deal wrongdoing, the phrase was thoroughly worked by the keynote speaker, Senator Frederick Steiwer of Oregon, who used it to punctuate his indictment of the Administration.*

---

* Steiwer had to overcome certain inhibitions in attacking specific New Deal measures due to the fact that, like many another Republican Congressman, he had voted for them. He chose to explain in a parenthetic aside that he had been deceived by the nefarious design to convert what he thought would be temporary legislation "into permanent policy." However, the Democrats, especially Jim Farley, were able to point out gleefully that

The delegates, feeling no less guilty than the keynoter for what they were about to do, let off a little steam with a quickly composed song they found on their seats. Sung to the tune of "Three Blind Mice," it went, lugubriously:

>   Three long years,
>   Three long years,
>   Full of grief and tears,
>   Full of grief and tears.
>
>   Roosevelt gave us to understand
>   If we would lend him a helping hand,
>   He'd lead us into the Promised Land
>   For three long years!

But

>   When we got to the Promised Land,
>   We found it nothing but shifting sand
>   And he left us stripped like Sally Rand
>   For three long years!

It was thought to have real possibilities as a campaign song, but what with national income up $23 billion since 1932, unemployment down from fifteen million to around seven, and farm incomes up sharply, it somehow failed to catch on.

The closest the convention came to taking fire, and the only time when Landon's nomination seemed less than certain, was surprisingly the hour set aside for Herbert Hoover's Return. I have since witnessed at several Republican conventions this same phenomenon of delegates politely and with calculated enthusiasm endorsing their foreordained candidate, while reserving their real warmth, their love, their admiration for a proved conservative of the old school

---

he had supported not only the NRA, the AAA, and the Civilian Conservation Corps, but likewise such obviously permanent measures as the banking reforms, the Tennessee Valley Authority, and the National Labor Relations Act.

whom they will not nominate because he wouldn't have a prayer in November. No wonder they went berserk at last when emotion triumphed over prudence in 1964.

At any rate there was no mistaking the fervor with which they greeted Herbert Hoover's display of pent-up evangelism. Even before he had spoken a word, the delegates gave a fifteen-minute ovation to their former chief, who looked less tired and beaten than when he had appeared before them four years earlier. This was his great chance, for vindication at the least and possibly for restoration, and he took full advantage of the opportunity. "To some people," he told the convention, the New Deal appeared to be only "a strange interlude in American history . . . sheer opportunism . . . a muddle of a spoils system, of emotional economics, of reckless adventure, of unctuous claims to a monopoly of human sympathy, of greed for power, of a desire for popular acclaim." But that, he explained, was "the most charitable view." To others—and he himself seemed to share both views—"it appears to be a cold-blooded attempt by starry-eyed boys to infect the American people by a mixture of European ideas, flavored with a native predilection to get something for nothing." Comparing the New Deal with the "March of socialism and dictatorships" in Europe, he told his deeply stirred audience that "For the first time in the history of America we have heard the gospel of class hatred preached from the White House," and wound up with a call for a "holy crusade for liberty which shall determine the future and the perpetuity of a nation of free men."

Emotionally this was the high point of the convention. The New York *Times* described the effect of Hoover's words as a "wild and uncontrollable burst of frenzy." Men waved hats and women wept and both chanted "We want Hoover" while the band played "The Battle Hymn of the Republic" and the ex-President smiled wistfully, waving from time to time at the churning crowd below the rostrum. Yet the galleries were silent, and some observers thought the bands were officially directed to carry on whenever the demonstration showed signs of sagging. Whether or not the speech was a conscious bid for the nomination it is impossible to say. But, even while the demonstration continued, Hoover waited in the wings, and, returning to New York that night, he gave reporters reason to think that he did not count himself out of the running. To newsmen who boarded the train at Albany he pointed to news stories in the early editions about the shouts of "We want Hoover!" that had so touched him. "I wonder," he asked, "if that phrase went out over the radio?" And, when he was told that it had, he beamed with pleasure.

But Landon's managers, John D. M. Hamilton and Roy Roberts, a pair of wily Kansans, had no intention of letting matters get out of hand. They had arranged the invitation to Hoover and seen to it that he left Cleveland in a glow. Meanwhile, they had quietly lined up the Pennsylvania and New York delegations and had everything well pinned down for their man's nomination. Inevitably there had been talk of a "Stop Landon" movement, but it amounted to no more than such movements generally do, the supposed conspirators always being more suspiciously concerned with stopping each other than with stopping the front runner, who might win after all, in spite of their efforts, and remember them unkindly in his days of glory.

So it was that, when the balloting began, Arizona yielded to Kansas, John Hamilton formally put his man's name before the convention, Vandenberg and Knox made seconding speeches, and the auditorium burst into a mass of sunflowers, waving to the tune, inevitably, of "O, Susanna." Alfred M. Landon was nominated on the first ballot, and the historically minded recalled Daniel Webster's remark when the Whigs chose Zachary Taylor—that henceforth no man could feel safe from being nominated for the Presidency.

Vandenberg could have had the Vice Presidential nomination for the asking, but he did not think enough of the job to ask and Hamilton, the new party boss, was known to favor Knox. It was a choice which in retrospect had a fair measure of irony, because four years later Hamilton, who was still Republican National Chairman, was to have the job of reading Knox out of the party for accepting a post in the Roosevelt Cabinet.

If the Republican convention was predictable and just a little grim, the Democratic convention was even more predictable but as *gemütlich* as a family reunion. Politically there were no problems, and as Jim Farley said, "We could have completed our work in one day and gone home." But he didn't say it at the time, because no city would hear of a one-day Presidential convention, which would hardly pay the hotels, restaurants, and taxi drivers for the trouble expended on the delegates. Vaudeville and speeches could fill out the week's time, and they did. A stableful of donkeys were loosed on Philadelphia and hay mowers manned by local farmers paraded through the town purportedly to cut the alfalfa and timothy that Hoover had once predicted would grow in the streets of our cities. Old Guard Republicans looked out bleakly from the window of the Union League Club, which throughout convention week bore on its façade a sign reading, "Landon and Knox—1936—Love of Country Leads."

Inside the auditorium the obliging and happy Democratic boss found a way to achieve two purposes—to keep the convention going five days and to satisfy the dozens of requests from loyal partisans eager to get their tribute to the President on record. In an oratorical marathon which observers hoped would stand as a record for all time, speeches seconding Roosevelt's nomination were made by fifty-seven "gr-e-a-t Americans," each rating a fulsome introduction in his own right. The process, starting at one in the afternoon and going exactly around the clock, was cited as "one of the greatest bores of its kind in American history."

For intermittent relief, the convention featured some entertaining defections. There was the moment, for example, when Senator Ellison D. Smith of South Carolina, outraged at the party's first invocation by a Negro preacher, loudly stomped out of the hall and the preacher interrupted himself to explain understandingly that "Brother Smith needs more prayer."

A more sensational walk, though in the end no more important, was that of Al Smith and his Liberty League fellows, among them Bainbridge Colby, who had once headed the Wilson Cabinet and was now convinced that Roosevelt meant to nullify the Constitution; former Senator James A. Reed, the irascible Missourian, and Joseph B. Ely, ex-Governor of Massachusetts. The names were impressive, but politically their owners no longer were. They had long since identified themselves with the most bitter opponents of the Administration and were now regarded as more Republican than Democrat. If there was lingering doubt on this score, their ultimatum to the convention dispelled it. To prevent the United States from being turned into "a dictatorship on the European model or an Asiatic absolutism," they urged the delegates to repudiate Roosevelt and choose a "genuine Democrat." Otherwise, they warned, "patriotic voters of all parties will know unhesitatingly to what standard they must rally."

The sense of the convention was variously and irreverently expressed. Senator Clark of Missouri observed that if the rebellious ones were appointed as a committee to pick the "genuine Democrat" required, "they would be deadlocked for all time because each one of them would vote for himself." Farley said simply, "This convention *will* nominate a genuine Democrat—Franklin D. Roosevelt." And the reaction of Senator Alben Barkley, the temporary chairman, was even simpler: he hadn't received the ultimatum, he said, and therefore couldn't read it to the convention. "If Postmaster General Farley had handled it properly," Smith noted with heavy sarcasm, "it would have reached the proper hands and been read."

What more than made up for the inanities of the convention was the stunning acceptance speech of the nominee— "the greatest political speech I have ever heard," said Harold Ickes, and many shared his view. More than a hundred thousand Democrats packed into Franklin Field felt well rewarded for hours of waiting in the rain when the President, under a suddenly cleared moonlit sky, compared the fight of an earlier generation of Americans against the political royalists of England with the fight of contemporary Americans against their own "economic royalists." In the most human and engaging terms he conceded at once that "Governments can err, Presidents do make mistakes." And then, all but inviting them to contrast his mistakes with his predecessor's: "But the immortal Dante tells us that divine justice weighs the sins of the cold-blooded and the sins of the warm-hearted in different scales. Better the occasional faults of a Government that lives in a spirit of charity than the consistent omissions of a Government frozen in the ice of its own indifference." And, as few who were grown men and women in the Thirties are likely to forget, he went on: "There is a mysterious cycle in human events. To some generations much is given. Of others much is expected. This generation has a rendezvous with destiny."

Poor Alf. Against that heady brew what he had to offer was small beer. Without a script he tended to fumble, and when he had one he read badly, with a high-pitched nasal twang and no sense of timing. As Mencken well reported, "If it was possible, by any device, however tortured, to stress the wrong word in a sentence, he invariably stressed it. If the text called for a howl of moral indignation he always

'TAMP, STAMP, G.O.P. IS MARCHING

TIONAL REPUBLICAN COUNCIL · HOTEL McALPIN · NEW YORK

ATIONAL REPUBLICAN COUNCIL · HOTEL McALPIN · NEW YORK

Milwaukee *Leader*, Jan. 16, 1936

Proposed ammunition for the 1936 GOP campaign, these stamps were challenged by the Post Office.

Batchelor, *Sunday News*, Oct. 11, 193[

Time to Take Him Off

Evans, Columbus *Dispatch*, Oct. 14, 1936

Two Gems for Today

Prize Bunk	Pure Poppycock
The Literary Digest poll.	Father Coughlin's prediction that the election would be thrown into the house.

Milwaukee *Leader*, Nov. 4, 1936

ROOSEVELT RIDDLES

Answers to Questions the Voters Are Asking.

By RUSSELL MOORE.

365

Q. How much will the taxpayers lose from the Government cotton loans?

A. No one knows. The Commodity Credit Corporation advanced 12 cents a pound on 4,500,800 bales of 1934 cotton. This cotton has been selling from 1 to 1½ cents a pound less than the loan. Carrying charges and interest have made this cotton cost the Government about 14 cents a pound.

366

Q. Who pays all taxes in the end?

A. The man who works to produce things.

367

Q. How many times does a man pay taxes during the day?

A. It is estimated that the average citizen pays 922 different taxes in twenty-four hours.

368

Q. What will be the cost of the WPA sightseeing guide for which the wife of the publicity director of the Soviet embassy is field supervisor?

A. The WPA allotment is $1,500,000.

369

Q. Is it true that the Roosevelt administration is costing the American people $13,000 per minute?

A. Yes, according to Senator Byrd, the Democrat, Virginia.

370

Q. What part of his wages does an unskilled worker pay in taxes?

A. It is estimated that one-fifth of his pay goes for hidden taxes.

More Questions and Answers Tomorrow.
Copyright, 1936.

New York *Sun*, Sept. 25, 1936

"GONE WITH THE LANDSLIDE"

Page, Louisville *Courier-Journal*, Nov., 1936

New York *Sun*, Sept. 25, 1936

The Nation, Sept. 2, 1939

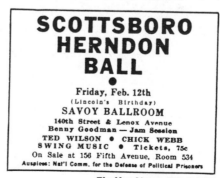
The New Masses, Feb. 9, 1937

LOST

LADY

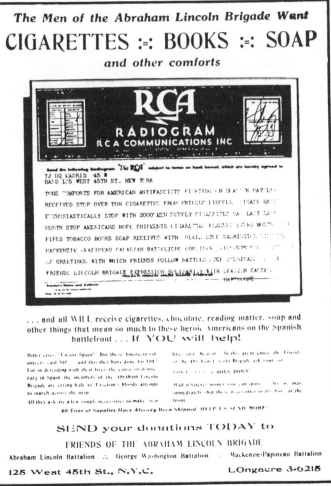
[163

Batchelor, *Daily News*, Sept. 13, 1938

Storm Clouds in the East

Seibel, Richmond *Times-Dispatch*, Feb. 24, 1938

U.S. Must Keep Out
of Europe's War

WE can keep out of war if we want to.
Europe could keep out of war if it
wanted to.

There is no situation in Europe which could
not have been solved by the peaceful discussions
which the President urged.

But the traditional hatreds and jealousies and
the long established warlike habits of Europe
made war inevitable there.

But war is in no sense inevitable here.

We have not the established warlike habits.
We have not the racial hatreds, the international jealousies.

We have not the greed for power and added
territory.

And if we follow the injunctions of Washington, we will not have the partisanship which might
lead us into war.

IF the President wants to keep us out of war—
as it is evident from his broadcast that he does
—if the Congress acts intelligently to keep us out
of war, if the people continue their desire, so often
expressed, to keep out of European conflicts, there
is no reason why we should become involved in
this European catastrophe.

When it is over, Europe will be prostrated,
of course.

The people will be exhausted and impoverished.

A large part of what we considered civilization, but what is apparently only an empty shell,
will have been destroyed over there.

But here in America peace and prosperity
will prevail, the best benefits of civilization will
have been retained, and the United States in her
full strength can stand forth to lead and aid the
world back to such peace and happiness as these
warring peoples are then capable of securing and
enjoying.

AMERICA has a great opportunity, a great
mission, which it can only fulfill if it keeps
out of war, and if it keeps its resources, its institutions, its democratic principles intact, and fully
available for its own benefit, and for the reconstruction of the world.

WILLIAM RANDOLPH HEARST.

New York *Journal American*
Sept. 4, 1939

CONFUSING TO THEIR FOLLOWERS

COMRADE HITLER!

HEIL STALIN!

LITTLE BONUS PRO-NAZIS ETC.

Ray, Kansas City *Star*, Aug., 1939

Seemed Like a Good Idea—Once

Duffy, Baltimore *Sun*, Aug., 1939

AMERICAN NATIONAL · SOCIALIST PARTY

Propaganda Analysis, Vol. II, No. 4, Institute for Propaganda Analysis, Jan. 1, 1939

The Nation, Sept. 2, 1939

The New Masses,
Dec. 15, 1936

New York *Times*, Sept. 1, 1939

dropped his voice, and if a sepulchral whisper was in order he raised it." One of his occasional locutions when he was thinking on his feet was *he don't*, and his opponent's name he invariably pronounced in three syllables, as *Ruse-a-velt*. All this in spite of the fact that for some months he had been taking lessons from an English actor named Hawkes who was then directing a radio program called *Molly of the Movies*.

Inevitably, when the Governor replied to the President's Franklin Field address, in a delayed acceptance speech, the contrast was measurable, and jokes about Landon's platform performances soon became a staple of the campaign. A New York broker who had publicly pledged to move to Canada with all his worldly goods if Roosevelt was re-elected was said to have been badgered by a dozen moving companies the day after Landon's acceptance speech, all seeking his business. Another story with which we Landon baiters regaled ourselves was that the Kansan had lost two of his most important scheduled speeches, but they were located and rushed to him by special messengers dispatched by the Democratic National Committee.

Such was the dilemma of the Republicans, torn between a love of economy and a shrewd recognition of the New Deal's popularity, that their campaign was all but paralyzed with contradictions. Landon was on record in favor of government relief and could only talk about decentralizing it. He had to come out against the AAA but at the same time he was for higher farm prices, crop controls, and cash benefits. He was for land-conservation programs and opposed only to their being carried out with WPA funds. In short, he was for most of the New Deal, but he wanted it with a balanced budget and without any perceptible enlargement of Federal powers. He would of course keep the Rendezvous but he hoped to keep Destiny down to a reasonable cost.

While the candidate took this relatively high road, there

was no reason why his lieutenants should not travel at lower altitudes, and they did. Knox, seeing himself as a scrapper in the old T.R. tradition, stripped off his inhibitions and waded in against the "alien and un-American elements" that had seized the Democratic Party and "written into law wholly or in part the twelve principal planks of the Socialistic platform." It was a "grand sight," he said, "to see Jim Farley embracing socialism." And he hammered away at the notion that if Roosevelt was re-elected nobody's savings account would be safe, a doubtful strategy which served only to remind people of bank accounts they had lost in the days of Republican rule.

John D. M. Hamilton, the ginger-haired Chairman of the Republican National Committee, specialized in dire warnings about the Social Security Act, which would put an end to American freedom, forcing every workingman and woman in the country to wear a numbered metal tag around his neck (the New York *Sun* even displayed photographs). But, as the gap widened between Hamilton and Landon, and it did, the Chairman seemed to grow flustered. Always something of a cliché monger, he provided the *New Yorker* with one of its mixed metaphor items by charging the Democrats with trying "to throw a dust cloud when they know their ship is sinking."

The strangest albatross that Landon had to shake off, however, was the Liberty League, whose Bourbon approach to the campaign was so remote from the prevailing temper that Herbert Hoover, no less, called it "one of the humors of the times." At dinners resplendent with mink, emeralds, and du Ponts, the upholders of liberty presented so ludicrous a contrast to the New Deal that Vice President Garner thought his party need not have spent a cent or made a single speech. Roosevelt himself later paid his appreciative respects to these helpful opponents who had attributed to him "the worst features of Ivan the Terrible, Machiavelli, Judas

Iscariot, Henry VIII, Charlotte Corday, and Jesse James."

Landon deserved a better supporting cast, and he likewise deserved a more merciful opposition. The truth is that, far from being the "stooge of Hearst and the Liberty League," as the elegant phrase of the Left had it, he was a thoroughly decent candidate, forthright in such matters as civil liberties —he opposed loyalty oaths twenty years before the liberals of the post-McCarthy era—and, at least in the beginning, he was good-tempered and moderate. Indeed, at the top level the campaign got off to a most gentlemanly start. For weeks Roosevelt made his warmest enthusiasts exceedingly nervous by loftily ignoring the Republican challenge altogether and Landon made sweetly reasonable speeches, wholly lacking in the acid that usually pervades this art form. When they met at a Governors' conference in Des Moines to discuss the drought, the exchange was a study in corny good humor. "Let me tell you, Alf Landon, if you succeed me in the White House, you ought to get a boat and try out the Potomac River for fishing," said the President. "Thanks, I'll remember that," said the Governor. After which they laughed, immoderately it would seem, over a joke about "WPA rat poison—We don't guarantee it to kill rats, but it'll make them so damned lazy you can catch 'em." Parting, they promised to visit each other after the election, and F.D.R. coyly called over his shoulder, "And don't work too hard, Governor."

Naturally this sort of thing could not last; it would be a little "un-American" for any Presidential campaign. Given the bitterness of conservatives in 1936 and the corresponding militance of the liberals, the minorities, and the trade unions, there was not a chance that such mildness would survive a month of campaigning.

On this score the press played a major, if none too attractive, part. In New York we could read in Hearst's *American* that while Earl Browder was the "titular nominee" of the

Communist Party, "The real candidate—the unofficial candidate of the Comintern—is Franklin D. Roosevelt." The
Sun featured a daily attack on some "boondoggle" of the
Administration, like the nonsensical dam at Boulder, Colorado, and once ran an advertisement of unbelievable vitriol.
"A vote for Roosevelt in 1936 is a vote for bloodshed in
1937," it read, going on to describe the Roosevelt Administration as the "Washington reptile house," and winding up in
an incendiary blaze: "The time may come when defense is
imminent; that time when we must fight for our very homes.
If such time comes . . . then it would seem that the best
philosophy under such a condition would be: NEVER WOUND
A SNAKE, BUT KILL IT."

Business owners added their own fuel in the form of helpful little slips tucked into their employees' pay envelopes.
Sometimes these warned that if Roosevelt should win there
might not be a job for the recipient after November. Sometimes they explained that under the "New Deal" law the
employer regretfully had to deduct one percent of the em-
ployee's pay, that the latter might or might not someday get
it back, and that the one percent might eventually go up to
four. "There is NO guarantee. Decide before November 3—
Election Day—whether or not you wish to take these
chances."

In this warmed-up atmosphere Landon, too, shucked off
his easygoing ways and began to slug. There could be "no
half-way house," he told a Maine audience, between "free
competitive enterprise" and the New Deal. "Franklin D.
Roosevelt proposes to destroy the right to elect your own
representatives," ran his message to Albuquerque, "to talk
politics on street corners, to march in political parades, to attend the church of your faith, to be tried by jury, and to own
property." And in Baltimore he pulled out the rest of the
stops: "The profit motive is to be eliminated. Business as
we know it is to disappear. . . . It is the essence of the New
Deal that the Constitution must go."

Almost to the very end of the campaign Roosevelt stood aloof, only occasionally bothering even to toy with his mismatched opponent. True, when the Hearst press accused him of being the Comintern's choice, he had Steve Early issue a statement not merely disavowing any support from the Communists, but blasting "a certain notorious newspaper owner" for the very suggestion. For the most part, however, he felt no need for either wrath or concern. Except in Harvard Square, where the sons and spiritual sons of his college chums booed him for betraying his class, he was everywhere greeted by vast and adoring crowds. Like "a bishop come to make his quadrennial diocesan call," as one observer described his campaign, he "reported on the excellent state of health enjoyed throughout this vast diocese, particularly as compared with the miserable state that had prevailed before he took high office."

Like millions of other parishioners, I remember him looking out on a crowd of upturned faces and then saying, with a broad grin, "You look much better than you did four years ago." Sometimes he would contrast the year with 1932, briefly reviewing the improvements, and then innocently put the question of whether his audience wished to return to those abysmal pre-Roosevelt days. They never did—and they had a good time telling him so. Accurately, though with perhaps a touch of envy, Norman Thomas observed that "All Roosevelt has to say is 'Remember Hoover,' and the voter cries: 'Papa, save me.'" And yet, as the President told Ickes, there was something terrible, too, about those crowds of admirers, because their relationship to him was so highly charged with emotion. "He saved my home," one would shout as he passed by. Or "He gave me a job." Or just, "God bless you, Mr. President."

From Roosevelt's campaign finale at Madison Square Garden it was evident, however, that some of the opposition barbs had hurt—not politically, but personally. Incensed at Republican insinuations that reserve funds for Social Security might be diverted to some other purpose, he suggested that "only desperate men with their backs to the wall would descend so far below the level of decent citizenship." The New Deal had been forced from the start to struggle against "business and financial monopoly, speculation, reckless banking, class antagonism, sectionalism. . . ." The crowd waited eagerly for him to drive in the harpoon at last, and he did not disappoint them. "Never before in all our history have these forces been so united against one candidate as they stand today. They are unanimous in their hate for me— and I welcome their hatred." That would have been enough, but the President was now aroused, perhaps too aroused. "I should like to have it said of my first Administration that in it the forces of selfishness and of lust for power met their match. I should like to have it said of my second Administration that in it these forces met their master." The crowd went delirious, but the sting in the President's words would embitter the opposition for years to come.

For those whose political thought ran in channels even less orthodox than the New Deal there were the candidates of the Socialist and Communist parties, and for the downright erratic there was William Lemke, Representative from North Dakota and the chosen man of the new Union Party. With his glass eye, pocked face, cloth cap, and literal manner, he was hardly a spellbinder. His was the radicalism of the Populists—anti-capital, anti-urban, anti-Wall Street, anti-chain store, and somewhat nationalistic—having in short a bit more in common with National Socialism than with the Marxist variety. It was no great strain, accordingly, for him to accept a campaign merger with such other radicals of the right as Father Coughlin and the unsavory Gerald L. K. Smith or with so quixotic a character as Dr. Townsend.

For their part, these masters of delusion welcomed the alliance, at least for the moment, because of Lemke's long and recognized record of trying to do what no one has ever succeeded in doing, that is, to make farmers secure, happy, and politically appreciative. Although a practicing lawyer in Fargo, he came from the farm and belonged to every agricultural organization in the West. A leader in the Nonpartisan League, he believed in cheap money as the debtors' salvation, and it was the New Deal's failure to go far enough in stopping foreclosures that turned him against Roosevelt.

Lemke was nominated on a platform to end "economic slavery" under the emblem of an encircled triangle, the equal sides of which stood, predictably, for agriculture, labor, and industry. The newborn party favored Congressional control over money and credit, the guarantee of a living annual wage, the assurance of a fair profit to farmers, and a foreign policy that would avoid foreign entanglements. In the circumstances the last of these planks meant doing nothing whatever to upset or annoy the new tyrants of Europe, which appealed to the Germanic sentiments of much of the Middle West.

The combination of the indebted, the elderly, the Populist, and the isolationist should have totaled a highly respectable third-party vote—more than the 4.8 million rolled up by La Follette in 1924 if less than the 9 million promised by Father Coughlin. Interviewed by reporters in New York, the judicious Reverend Smith gave it as his considered opinion that 20 million was a fair figure for Lemke and that all that stood between him and certain victory was the "thieving, bribing tactics of the Farley machine." His own guarantee to deliver some six million followers of the late Huey Long was somewhat dampened when Long's secretary, Earl Christenberry, suggested over the radio that Smith's activity was prompted by the "call of the almighty dollar." It would not be the first time Smith had attempted to betray Huey's ideal and "prostitute it to his own benefit," he observed, recalling that on the very morning that Smith preached Long's eloquent funeral oration he had sidled over to Christenberry to propose that they get together and run the movement. "With eight million members at ten cents apiece each month," Smith is said to have mused as he warmed up for his tribute, "think what that will bring in for us." As the campaign approached its climax, if the 1936 campaign can be said to have had one, it became rather plain that the indebted and the elderly, if not the Populist and the isolationist, had more to hope for from Roosevelt than from Lemke, and the Union Party quickly came undone. Like Townsend, the dolorous-looking Lemke disavowed Smith when that clerical gentleman began to talk about seizing the government, and Smith in turn ignored the Congressman. Indeed, the remarkable thing about Lemke's campaign was that anyone with so large a prefabricated following could have made so small a dent on the national consciousness. The names of most minor-party candidates are forgotten in the months following Election Day, but Lemke's was virtually forgotten by October. Toward the end of the ordeal Father Coughlin took to making whole speeches without once mentioning his candidate, and Lemke returned the compliment.

The same powerful magnate that drew potential voters from the Union Party acted even more disastrously on the Marxists. Norman Thomas, then having his second fling at Presidential campaigning, conducted a traveling seminar in politics, the gist of which was that the major parties were dead or dying and only socialism could save the country—"the issue is revolutionary." The Communists, on the other hand, by now wholly under the spell of the Popular Front strategy, were for Earl Browder only nominally and for the most tactical reasons. They wanted Roosevelt to beat Landon, but, fully aware that their insignificant vote would not affect the result in any case, they felt that by backing Browder officially they could retain a certain advantage. Ideologically they would not have to bear the burden some time in the future of having supported a bourgeois candidate, and they thought there was at least a chance that their ostensible independence would give them a little leverage in bringing pressure on an Administration that could not take them for granted. Not least, they must have been aware that their open support would be an embarrassment.

The strategy made sense, but, as so often happened, its exercise entailed a degree of nonsense. Thus the *New Masses*, for which I was then writing, was as hotly incensed at the Hearst allegation that Roosevelt was supported by Communists as if it thought that to be the greatest possible insult. ". . . the President might well have been galled," it wrote, "at the malicious attempts of Hearst to link his New Deal with the Communist Party." The *Daily Worker* was even more irate: "They are the weapons of a desperate man, . . . by such a method, there is not a man in America who could not be convicted of murder, rape, or any other crime." The language was odd, but the point was clear. They didn't want the "greater evil" to gain an advantage from the fact that the Communists hoped the "lesser evil" would win. Their whole campaign, accordingly, was left-handed rather than left-wing. The only passion I recall was that of a party speaker addressing a meeting of the League of Women Shoppers. "We must take the women out from Lemke," he shouted, "And put them under Browder."

Looking back at that campaign of thirty years ago, it seems to me now that one of its several strange characteristics was the extreme capacity for self-delusion that it revealed. All Presidential contests show the phenomenon, but 1936 exceeded the normal bounds by a substantial degree, and it showed up in unlikely persons. A year or so before the election H. L. Mencken, incautious but usually astute, was certain that any Republican could throw Roosevelt: "Is it really a fact that you can't beat something with nothing? There are days when I find myself doubting it. . . . It is my suspicion that the More Abundant Life may be just as dead, by the Tuesday following the first Monday of November, 1936, as the Anti-Saloon League was in the late Summer of 1928—just as dead, and just as offensive to the nostrils of the plain people." And much later, in midsummer of '36 he still thought the chances very good that "the Rooseveltian Rendezvous with Destiny will turn out, in November, to be a rendezvous with a bouncer."

Landon himself was persuaded that victory lay ahead, and so were his lieutenants, but for the candidate and his entourage that is the usual thing. Without such self-hypnosis it is doubtful that they could get through the grueling business of a campaign. What helped greatly in Landon's case was the parallel self-delusion of so much of the press. Paul Block, in spite of Landon's refusal to let him hitch his private car to the Republican campaign train, made an extremely rash statement for a publisher. Just seven weeks before Election Day he proclaimed, "I have never felt more certain of anything in my life than the defeat of President Roosevelt. By mid-October people will wonder why they ever had any doubt about it." High taxes and increased cost of living, he thought, would do the trick. William Randolph Hearst went just as far. Leaving for Europe early in August, he told reporters: "The race will not be close at all. Landon will be overwhelmingly elected and I'll stake my reputation as a prophet on it."

And of course there was the historic gaffe that cost the life of the *Literary Digest*. On the eve of Election Day its primitive poll indicated that Landon would win with more than three hundred electoral votes. It had sent out some ten million straw ballots, but its technique was more laborious than scientific. All of the ballots had gone to names culled from telephone directories and automobile registries in a year when millions of Americans could afford neither telephones nor cars—and were overwhelmingly for Roosevelt. The result was that in 1937 the chastened *Digest* felt compelled to

merge with the *Review of Reviews* and, even more desperate, to take liquor advertising. But nothing could save it,
except possibly to have made James A. Farley its new editor.
The night before Election Day Farley had dispatched to
the President at Hyde Park a book containing reports from
party leaders and summarizing the campaign picture in each
of the forty-eight states. "After looking them all over carefully and discounting everything that has been given in
these reports," he wrote, "I am still definitely of the opinion
that you will carry every state but two—Maine and Vermont." The day after the victory Roosevelt complimented
him on "the most uncanny prediction in the history of the
country."

It looked for a time as though the Republican Party might
go the way of the *Literary Digest*, and for much the same
reason. Addressing itself to people with telephones, automobiles, and even yachts, it had overlooked the tens of millions
shortly to be described by the President in his Second Inaugural—the "one-third of a nation ill-housed, ill-clad, ill-
nourished," but not, like two-thirds of the press, ill-advised.

What was worse, those who had hated the President before the election hated him even more enthusiastically when
it was over. Dorothy Thompson, the emphatic columnist,
who had been as mildly for Landon as she could be mildly
for anything, wrote to Robert Sherwood of how her fellow
Republicans moved her for the first time to side with Roosevelt. To an overwhelmingly pro-Landon group gathered on
election night in the Iridium Room of the Hotel St. Regis,
she had sportingly proposed a toast to the President of the
United States. Two or three Democrats in the room stood
up, of course, but the orchestra, which had stopped for a
moment, immediately struck up a tune and with averted
eyes the unhappy Republicans danced. They may not have
felt like dancing, but anything was better than drinking to
Franklin D. Roosevelt.

WPA, Willing Patron of the Arts

7

In the history of the world few depression governments can have given housewives free piano lessons. Fewer still can have put thousands of artists to work reproducing ancestral designs of ships' figureheads and coffeepots. And before the 1930's probably none had given stage people an annual wage, even a modest one, to put on free marionette shows and the works of Christopher Marlowe. But the New Deal did all of these, and in addition paid ninety dollars a month to stranded reporters, unpublished novelists, skilled researchers, and an indeterminate number of bohemian hangers-on to turn out some 250 volumes of first-rate Americana.

It has been pointed out *ad nauseam* that the Arts Projects, as these operations of the Works Progress Administration were known, spawned no Mozarts or Da Vincis. Neither, it may be conceded, did they produce lasting works of drama or fiction. What they did do was to see many a talent through exceedingly thin days and to expose to those talents millions of Americans who would otherwise have remained forever innocent of anything like their charms. In this sponsored introduction of struggling artist to untapped audience the projects at the very least served to destroy in four years certain American myths that had been a century in the aging: that painting had to be European to have merit and required wealth to be appreciated; that all concerts except those by the town band were in the nature of good works to which dutiful ladies dragged long-suffering husbands; and that outside of four or five cities the American people required no theatre at all and if offered any would demand *East Lynne*, *Charlie's Aunt*, and *The Girl of the Limberlost*. At most, the projects set off what some of our critics call rhapsodically, and some sneeringly, the cultural explosion.

Granted that statistics are no key to quality, they *can* point to a highly stimulated interest in music, painting, and plays, if not quite to a Renaissance. By the end of the decade close to seventy art centers were flourishing in communities many of whose public-school art teachers had never before beheld a professional canvas. Some sixty thousand Americans had taken painting lessons from government-paid artists, and public offices and lobbies across the land boasted murals and fresh paintings where once their tenants had made do with old prints, chromos, and blank walls of penal gray. Audiences estimated to total 100 million people had heard some 150,000 free concert programs, most of them by three dozen newly created symphony orchestras, which featured more native composition in two years than professional ensembles had offered in the preceding decade. And a half-million Americans a month had enrolled in free music classes, forty thousand in New York City alone.

A visiting English critic, a breed not notably charitable on the subject of American culture, was staggered. "Accidentally WPA has dug up an extraordinary amount of talent," said Ford Madox Ford. "Art in America is being given its chance and there has been nothing like it since before the Reformation." Even if it was not that good, it was good enough to frighten many Congressmen, and on one of the several occasions when the lawmakers threatened to stop the music, Lewis Mumford wrote in protest to President Roosevelt. In somewhat more measured terms than Mr. Ford had

used, he recalled Emerson's comment on a proposed shipment of pianos to the frontier towns of the West: "The more
piano, the less wolf!" And he went on to point out that "The
discovery of art as a vital factor in contemporary American
culture was not, of course, the original intention of the WPA
art projects. But the fact is that the discovery has now been
made; and it would be blind, perhaps even perverse, to ignore its implications."

Certainly a Renaissance was not what Harry Hopkins and
his aides had in mind when the Arts Projects were conceived. What interested them was the hope of evolving a
whole new concept of government relief. In three years the
country had come a long way from the Hoover view that
direct aid to the victims of flood or earthquake was right and
proper but not to the victims of man-made economics. For a
time the dole was the answer, then work of any kind for any
purpose. And now, here was Harry Hopkins telling Aubrey
Williams on the way to the racetrack that the country had
had enough of demoralizing leaf raking. The time had come
for "maintaining the morale and skills" of the unemployed
by paying them to perform the work they could do best until
a rejuvenated private enterprise was ready to rehire them. It
was all very well for the Public Works Administration to go
on with its building, but the newly conceived Works
Progress Administration would serve human beings. This
was to be no mere switching of initials. WPA funds would be
spent on people, not things, and what they were to do would
be determined solely by what they *could* do, not by what the
community might lack in the way of parking lots or sewage
disposal plants. Let the PWA build to satisfy public need
and to prime the pump of industry. For its part, the WPA
would not build a hospital even if one was wanted unless a
town happened to have a pool of idle construction men looking for work. But, if the same town had a group of jobless
musicians, the new agency would launch an orchestra with

pleasure. As Williams put it later, "We don't think a good musician should be asked to turn second-rate laborer in order that a sewer may be laid for relative permanency rather than a concert given for the momentary pleasure of our people."

Carrying the idea further, WPA proposed to make do with *all* the jobless artists who might come to it for help, rather than concentrate on the truly gifted, who would presumably be the least in need. For years government agencies had hired the best artists, or those it considered such, to do murals and sculpture for its buildings, but now the problem was to employ not just the best, but also the merely good—in practice even the mediocre and sometimes the downright inferior, who also had to eat. An enormous supply of just adequate talent existed in the country and an even more enormous potential audience of unsophisticated tastes. WPA would bring them together, at the same time preserving the talent, such as it was, from sterility and elevating the spirit of the country at a moment when it most needed elevating. This concept of employing the inferior with the good and both in large quantities would profoundly affect the nature of the projects.

Of all Americans engaged in the arts midway in the decade, the worst off by far were show people. Writers, musicians, painters, and sculptors are almost as likely to need help in good times as in bad. They are loners. Professional show people, on the other hand, are dependent on the availability of capital—gobs of it—and for a business already hard hit even before the crash by the "talkies," the high cost of theatre rentals, and stage-union wage scales, there were in the mid-Thirties not many gobs of capital to be had. Throughout the country stock companies had all but disappeared, vaudeville was a wistful memory, some forty thousand show people were destitute, and even the Shuberts had just emerged from the hands of receivers. So it was that, of all the good works of the WPA, the Federal Theatre Project had the greatest opportunity, made the biggest splash, and left the most vivid memories of the decade.

People who were lucky enough to have caught the *Swing Mikado* will remember it well even if they can't tell you a thing about Harry Hopkins. The scene was transposed from a Victorian English caricature of Japan to a Harlem caricature of Tahiti. The Emperor wore a top hat and pheasant feathers, and Koko, disporting himself in a loincloth, wielded a straight-edge razor for a snickersnee. The most memorable aspect of the show, however, was neither sets nor costumes, but a wild and infectious rhythm. The Three Little Maids from School started off as coyly as Gilbert could have wished, but by the time they got to describing themselves as "all unwary" they were swinging it against a chorus line of jitterbugs doing the Suzie-Q. And the "Flowers That Bloom in the Spring" wound up in a smashing chorus in which jungle youths and dusky maidens with flowers in their hair shagged all over the palm-decked stage while tom-toms pounded out a beat that must have had Sir Arthur Sullivan trucking in the Elysian Fields. It cost fifty-five cents to see the show, I think (many of the WPA shows were free), and it sent the critics into delirium. My own recollection is that it was improved upon by the *Hot Mikado* which it inspired Mike Todd to produce commercially. A hit of the World's Fair of 1939, the Todd show owed its all to the imagination of the WPA theatre.

To appreciate the fantastic range of Federal drama one might contrast its unshackled *Mikado* with the sensitive and risky production of T. S. Eliot's *Murder in the Cathedral*. Here was a play that had run in a small London theatre and become recognized as the most important drama in verse to be done in at least a generation. But Broadway considered it "difficult" and only, dubiously commercial. Put on by the WPA, with Harry Irvine as the Archbishop—he had been discarded by commercial managers because a tremor of the hands had persuaded them he was too old—it was received with honors by the critics and played to forty thousand people. In *Newsweek*, George Jean Nathan, no friend of the New Deal, was driven to observe: "If the Federal Theatre Project can put on something like *Murder in the Cathedral* better for fifty-five cents than a professional manager subsequently proves he can for $3.30, then—much as it pains us to say it—the hell with the professional managers."

One of the great charms of the Federal Theatre was that it really covered the country. WPA shows were not just for the likes of New York, Chicago, and San Francisco. They were also for Tacoma (Washington), Reading (Pennsylvania), and Timberline Lodge (Oregon), not to mention Gary (Indiana), Peoria (Illinois), and Red Bank, (New Jersey). They brought theatre to towns in the United States that had not seen live actors since minstrel shows and Chautauquas went out of fashion. And they were received with something close to ecstasy. One of the motorized units, which took portable theatres to remote mountain towns, prairie villages, and backwoods settlements, played a one-night stand in Valley, Nebraska, to such effect that the mayor wrote to Hallie Flanagan, the national director, to ask whether the cast would come to live in Valley and give shows indefinitely. Mrs. Flanagan herself was so carried away by the warmth with which a mobile troupe was received on the "turpentine circuit" in rural Florida that she wrote for the *Federal Theatre Magazine* a long free-verse tribute, in the fashion of the day, which began:

> We played Ohumpka and they came in by oxcart.
> They came in with lanterns to see *Twelfth Night.*
> An old man barefoot, helping children from an oxcart,
> Said, "They may be pretty young to understand it
> But I want they should be able to say
> They've seen Shakespeare—
> I did once, when I was a kid."

The very ubiquity of the Federal Theatre made possible its greatest coup. As if competing with the movies, it opened Sinclair Lewis's *It Can't Happen Here* in eighteen cities across the country on the same night and in many more as the weeks went on, with additional Yiddish productions in New York and Los Angeles, a Negro production in Seattle, and a Spanish version in Tampa, Florida. Before it had run its course some 275,000 Americans had seen it in one of its several versions. For one of the most effective aspects of the venture, and a great advantage over the movies, was that each production had an indigenous character, appropriate to the message that fascism *can* happen anywhere. In place of the New England setting of the book, the play was variously set against a dairy farm background for Midwestern audiences, in a local Harlem for a Seattle Negro theatre, and in a Jewish urban area for one of the New York productions, with Doremus Jessup as editor of a Yiddish newspaper.

Even the regular New York version, comparatively sophisticated, was less subtle than the Lewis novel, which was far from subtle to start with, and when the author was called on for a curtain speech he candidly told the audience, "I have been making a speech since 8:45." The critics thought so too. Nathan called the play "anything but a satisfactory example of drama" and Brooks Atkinson thought it "careless, slipshod theater work." But in the emotionally charged atmosphere of the time it was political lightning. Making his debut as an actor, Lewis himself played the role of Jessup in a summer-stock production, and after the first-night audience had called him back for a number of curtain calls he made a short talk in which he modestly credited his novel and play with having helped to forestall the coming of fascism to America.

Inevitably there were cries of propaganda—columns of pro and con argument filled the papers for weeks before opening night—but since fascism was generally in bad odor, only the far Right got really exercised about *It Can't Happen Here.* Other productions, however, came under more general fire, and if the attacks were often unwarranted, they were sometimes at least understandable, especially those directed at the Living Newspaper.

Sponsored by the Newspaper Guild and combining the reportorial techniques of daily journalism with the staccato urgency of radio documentaries and the tricks of the stage, this brand-new form was ideal for the Theatre Project. It could employ scores of mediocre actors who otherwise reported daily and were paid but who couldn't possibly be absorbed by small-cast plays requiring real talent. Moreover, the Living Newspapers called for fresh material that cost very little and they made up in ingenious lighting and staging what the WPA could not afford in sets and costumes. In the nature of their auspices, however, and their subject matter, they generally outdid the New Deal in liberal outlook, and while their emphasis on the social and the economic was wholly defensible, it is true that the hand was inclined to be heavy.

As good an example as any was *Power,* which dealt with that classical theme of the theatre, the consumer in search of cheap electricity. Soon after the curtain rises, Thomas A. Edison is seen holding aloft his newly invented electric bulb while a bevy of businessmen reach up to grab it, clearly with the idea of getting in on a good thing. In a later scene the spotlight falls on a utilities tycoon, who with the aid of lighting effects is shown in a double role, so that he can explain to himself for the audience's benefit what a holding company is. Having expounded on this corporate mystery with the aid of a pyramid of colored boxes, he proceeds to sell himself worthless stock in some of the subsidiary companies at a handsome profit.

In another scene a father patiently explains to his little girl why the government can't make electricity because gov-

ernment is not efficient enough, and the child, who for one of
her years seems in retrospect to have been morbidly interested in the subject, asks why, then, the government is able
to operate the Post Office. (In those days the Post Office was
at least efficient enough to make two deliveries a day.) Skip-
ping about the stage, the spot picks up, among others, a
goateed old farmer who is being prevailed upon by his bon-
neted wife to "raise holy blazes" until the company agrees to
bring current to their farm; Senator George Norris, who
shows up intermittently to advocate public ownership; and,
for a first-act curtain, a procession of workmen carrying
lanterns against the backdrop of a waterfall at Norris Dam.
They sing the "TVA" song, beginning:

> My name is William Edwards,
> I live down Cove Creek way;
> I'm working on the project
> They call the T.V.A. . . . .

Toward the end of the show nine masks appear above a high
desk, before which lawyers are heard arguing while a chorus
asks in unison, "What will the Supreme Court do? What will
the Supreme Court do?"

Of course it was propaganda, but, as Harry Hopkins was
reported to have remarked to the cast backstage on opening
night, "Well, I say what of it? . . . The big power companies
have spent millions on propaganda for the utilities. It's
about time that the consumer had a mouthpiece. I say more
plays like *Power* and more power to you."

What *Power* attempted for the consumer, *One-Third of a
Nation* tried for the slum dweller and *Triple-A Plowed
Under* for the farmer. Like all the Living Newspapers, they
were extravagantly praised and unfairly condemned. The
only one that seemed to escape all criticism was Arnold
Sundgaard's *Spirochete.* Even the Chicago *Tribune* praised
this fine documentary as "a valuable contribution to anti-

syphilis propaganda," an endorsement that caused some New Dealers, the jest went, to reconsider their opposition to venereal disease.

So vast was the Theatre Project's undertaking, so varied and regional its repertoire, that critics had only to be selective to find evidence for whatever they wanted to prove. Southerners could damn *Battle Hymn,* a eulogy of John Brown by Michael Blankfort and Michael Gold, the latter an outstanding Communist luminary of the decade. Northerners could look askance at *Jefferson Davis,* sponsored by the Daughters of the Confederacy and summarized by Burns Mantle as a "sympathetic recital of decisive moments in the life of the President of the Confederacy through which the attitude of the South . . . is defended and the political intrigues that destroyed faith in Jefferson Davis are exposed." Even *Prologue to Glory,* a moving play about the young Lincoln, was faulted by Representative J. Parnell Thomas, who was to succeed Martin Dies as chairman of the House Committee on Un-American Activities. By portraying the youthful Lincoln as battling with politicians, he said, the work served as "a propaganda play to prove that all politicians are crooked." It was a prophetically sensitive point perhaps with Congressman Thomas, who was fated to rest from his public labors in a Federal jail for having been one of those politicians who really were crooked.

With these charges of propaganda we were all familiar, but only those who were close to the Theatre Project knew of its many other troubles. Censorship was less of a problem than might have been expected but, subtle or overt, it was there and had to be taken into account. The very first Living Newspaper, dealing with Italy's rape of Ethiopia, was canceled when the Administration declined to allow its subsidized theatre to portray Mussolini on stage. Elmer Rice, who headed the Theatre Project in New York, pointed out that the stage Mussolini merely delivered a speech that the real one had actually made. But Washington officials may reasonably have felt that the more truthful the representation, the more discreditably it reflected on Il Duce, with whom we still maintained technically friendly relations. When Rice declined to change the script, his resignation, offered in an earlier acerb exchange with Washington, was swiftly accepted and neither he nor Mussolini had any further part in the operation of the Federal Theatre.

There were not many such instances of censorship but those that occurred usually got explosive publicity. When the project chiefs in Washington frowned on Marc Blitzstein's *The Cradle Will Rock*, a class-conscious opus to say the least, young Orson Welles, in charge of the production, walked out a half-hour before curtain time, taking audience, cast, and props along with him to an empty commercial theatre, where he went into business for himself. And *Lysistrata* was closed down by the Washington State WPA administrator after the Mayor of Seattle reported getting two complaints about what the press described as Aristophanes' "spicy show."

Local administrators, making full use of their regional autonomy, often chose productions with less of an eye to art than to local sentiment. Louisiana turned down *It Can't Happen Here* out of respect for its late dictator Huey Long. Local Jewish protests were enough to queer *The Merchant of Venice* in a New England town. And in Los Angeles a show was allowed to go on only after the cast was relieved of a chorus boy who had run for Congress as a Communist candidate, an act that then only came under the mild heading of "undue political activity."

In spite of an anti-bureaucratic spirit at the top, the WPA *was* a bureau and red tape was almost as much of a nuisance to the Theatre Project as it has been to government agencies and armies since Neanderthal times. Rulings and recommendations had to go up and down a chain of command, and supplies and money were notoriously slow to come in. Since theatre openings were not taken as seriously as troop movements, help more often failed to arrive in time. So it was that local citizens were sometimes asked to advance funds so the show could go on, or the supervisor in charge had to satisfy creditors out of his own insubstantial pocket. On one more than normally trying occasion doors on the set were still without hinges an hour before curtain time, and the company carpenter had to remove some from dressing-room doors to satisfy the more urgent need onstage.

Such frustrations were minor, however, compared with the strain of dealing with the Project's basic dilemma. In the nature of things the most talented performers and the most successful shows were the quickest to be picked up by the commercial theatre—a step which a government relief agency was bound to encourage. Yet the more talent it lost and the more it had to rely on has-beens and fledglings, the less success it could hope to enjoy. The Project's very triumphs were its undoing. Yet at no time could the casting problem have been anything like as acute as the Project's severest critics suggested. George Jean Nathan described the great majority of the younger people as "spongers and grafters and no more deserving of charity from this particular source than they were deserving of Civil War pensions or Congressional dispensations of pâté de foie gras." But if that was even close to the truth it is unlikely that George Bernard Shaw and Eugene O'Neill would have allowed the Project to put on their plays. Shaw was always a fanatic about either high production standards or money, and WPA royalties represented nothing to speak of in the way of money.

All the same, it is true that in casting a show a director had to consider the pool of unused labor that was always on tap. It included large numbers of elderly ingenues, bicycle riders who had performed before the crowned heads of pre–World War I Europe, tap dancers, and youngsters who had possibly played major roles in performances of *H.M.S. Pinafore* put on by the graduating classes of their hometown high schools. There was a sprinkling of major talent too, of course—among others Rex Ingram, Canada Lee, and Howard Da Silva were alumni of the WPA Theatre—and the law allowed the Project to bring in non-relief people to the extent of 10 percent of its personnel. But, by and large, directors did lean toward the fresh and untried talent, especially for the dance, and old-timers understandably took the selection grimly. They also resented the hordes of non-show people who did the clerical work and other such chores and always identified themselves as part of the Theatre Project —"show people." Some of the old pros went to the length of forming a Veterans League against these "scabs."

Many Congressmen had from the start been articulately unhappy about all the arts projects and about the Federal Theatre more than any other. Provincials among them, like provincials for centuries, looked on the theatre as sinful in any case, and Southerners were further incensed by the commingling of white and Negro actors in those pre-integration days, though regional directors dutifully kept that from happening on Southern stages.

In December, 1938, the Dies Committee unintentionally provided entertainment for the literate in a by now familiar scene, but it was entertainment that was to prove costly. In an unguarded moment Mrs. Flanagan spoke on the witness stand of "a certain Marlowesque madness," and immediately Representative Starnes of Alabama, scenting game, broke in: "You are quoting from this Marlowe. Is he a Communist?" Knowing better than to share the laughter that broke out in the hearing room, Mrs. Flanagan said simply that she had referred to Christopher Marlowe, but Starnes plunged on. "Tell us who Marlowe is, so we can get the proper references, because that is all we want to do." To which Mrs.

Flanagan replied, "Put in the record that he was the greatest dramatist in the period of Shakespeare, immediately preceding Shakespeare."

The guffaws at the hearing, and in the country at large, probably did nothing to endear the Federal Theatre to members of a House subcommittee on WPA appropriations which held hearings the following month. In any case, the Theatre Project was allowed to die, and few were taken in by the gabble about economy. All the arts projects together cost less than one percent of the whole WPA appropriation, and the Theatre had actually returned money to the Treasury via the box office. What angered its Congressional critics was "propaganda" and nothing else. In vain did Mrs. Flanagan cite statistics to show that all Congressional criticisms, even if valid (a fantastic assumption), related to fewer than 10 percent of the productions and only a third of these originated with the Federal Theatre. But the knives were out. "Salacious tripe," said Representative Dirksen. According to Representative Woodrum, casts included "fish peddlers" and "garment workers" rather than actors. Senator Reynolds, charging immoral Russian propaganda, cited *Up in Mabel's Room,* which had not up to then been thought to contain any ideas at all or even a spirit uncongenial to the run of Congressmen.

It was farce on Capitol Hill, but tragedy elsewhere. At the WPA theatre in New York they wound up with *Sing for Your Supper,* which included a scene in which Papa is borne in on the shoulders of celebrating neighbors. He has landed a job, and the players, as though there were no tomorrow for them to worry about, spiritedly belted out their lines:

> Ain't it lucky, ain't it swell
> I ran all the way home to tell
> I'm so happy it's just like ringing a bell—
> Papa's Got a Job!

The next day they were all out of work, with nothing to console them but President Roosevelt's indignation. "This singles out a special group of professional people for a denial of work in their profession. It is discrimination of the worst type . . . an entering wedge of legislation against a specific class in the community."

It had been an exciting experiment—from Orson Welles's Julius Caesar in a blue business suit to Pinocchio, who after thrilling countless children in schools and hospitals was interred in a pine box that bore the inscription: "Born December 23, 1938; Killed by Act of Congress, June 30, 1939." And it left in the country a yearning for the theatre it had not known before.

Three other WPA sallies into the realms of art left more tangible monuments than the Federal Theatre. About the Music Project I know little beyond the story of a violinist in a WPA orchestra in Florida who apologized to the audience on behalf of his colleagues and himself for the quality of their concert. Their hands were still stiff, he explained, from their previous relief job, which was working on a road gang.

The lasting work that the Music Project did was to dig out and record the real folk music of America—the songs of the Southern mountaineers, the Indian-flavored songs of early Oklahoma, the Cajun songs of Louisiana, and the African-inspired songs of the Mississippi bayous. Units of the Project recorded for the first time the early music of Mexico, the Texas plains, and California, some of it harking back to the time of the conquistadors. American Bartoks came into a mine that could be worked for generations.

On the Art Project, as the specifically painters' and sculptors' unit was confusingly called, nobody pretended that the quota of genius was high, although it did nurture such future greats as De Kooning, Bohrod, Shahn, and Pollock.

Spurning the notion of art as a "matter of rare occasional masterpieces," Holger Cahill, the Project director, proceeded on the principle that "it is not the solitary genius but a sound general movement which maintains art as a vital functioning part of any cultural scheme." It was just as well, because all that was needed to sign on with the Project was a certification by the local relief authorities and a simple test to establish some link, however tenuous, to the world of art.

Considering the varied talents it had to work with, some minimal, the Art Project sensibly made no attempt to seat everyone before an easel. Of the four to five thousand Federally enrolled artists, far fewer than half were ever engaged in painting pictures or sculpturing or doing murals. Many taught free classes, some made photographs of old and decaying American houses as part of the historic cultural record with which all the Projects were concerned, and others worked on posters and stage sets for the Federal Theatre.

But the Art Project's real monument, and in itself an ample justification for its existence, was the Index of American Design. For this magnificent work, still widely used, some four hundred people who did not have to be geniuses reproduced in oil and water color the native art with which Americans, from early settlers to late Victorians, had decorated their homes, their possessions, and their persons. Here appeared in all their brightness the scarlet tulips that enlivened the coffeepots and barn doors of the Pennsylvania Dutch, the embroidered chair-seat covers of seventeenth-century Massachusetts, gayer than the Puritan myth ever suggested, and the wonderful carved figureheads that led the old square-riggers into Salem and New Bedford harbors. Here were the patterns of antique quilts and samplers and weathervanes; designs blown in glass and designs wrought in iron, flower-embroidered dancing slippers and flower-

embroidered suspenders from Spanish California, and elabo-
rately carved paneling from the upper berths of early Pullman cars. It took this massive work, with its seven thousand
skillful illustrations, to convince many Americans that we
had a native art at all, but once the discovery was made
"early American" came into its own and it has not waned
since.

Like the Federal actors, the Federal artists had occasional
trouble with would-be Congressional censors and were as
often accused of propaganda. On the trivial side there was,
for example, the frustration of a Capitol Hill emissary who
arrived in New York to investigate rumors of the local unit's
unwarranted preoccupation with nudes. Seizing a packet of
the models' photographs, he retired to Washington to study
the evidence, only to find that without exception the ladies
pictured were singularly unattractive, apparently chosen for
a mural depicting a witches' Sabbath or one of the lower
levels of the Inferno. The matter was dropped.

The only opportunity for propaganda came in the painting of murals for public buildings, and there *was* evidence
that from time to time the opportunity was seized. In sweep-
ing social and historical scenes, common to this art form, the
influence of Mexican revolutionaries like Rivera, Siqueiros,
and Orozco was strong, particularly among artists who
found themselves on relief. Heroic workers with bulging
muscles, weather-beaten peasants of natural nobility, and
ladies with the feminine grace of Madame Defarge were
common in these massive wall decorations of post offices and
courthouse lobbies—and they were accepted without much
objection. But once in a while a more overt touch of class
angling was introduced. I was told of one such case in
which a tiny, almost imperceptible, figure of a child could
be seen, if one looked closely, being ground under the foot of
"Justice." And it is a fact that Swarthmore College felt
obliged to close up a room in which no fewer than six

clenched fists were detected in a WPA mural. After a mild uproar the room was reopened with three of the fists removed—a fair compromise for the times.

With monotonous regularity in the life of the fourth of these Federal forays into the arts, it was charged that the WPA Writers' Project had little to do with writers. True, the memorable names connected with it can be counted on the fingers. Conrad Aiken, John Cheever, Richard Wright, Maxwell Bodenheim, George W. Cronyn, Edward Dahlberg, John Steinbeck, Vardis Fisher, Vincent McHugh, and Claude McKay just about complete the list, with Harry Kamp added if you have an extra finger. One severe New Deal critic claimed to have definite proof that only 21 percent of the persons employed by the Project in New York City had ever written for a living or seen a line of their own composition in print. But if even that proportion held for the 7,500 people employed by the Project, it must have taken care of close to 1,600 more or less professional writers, a service that I would regard, in a fraternal way, as highly laudable.

It was probably true, nevertheless, that what passed for a Writers' Project was essentially what Bernard DeVoto called it, "a project for research workers." Happily, good writers and skilled journalists, headed by Henry Alsberg, its first national director, were strategically placed to turn the yield of the diggers into the most colorful and illuminating series of guides a nation could ask for. A one-time newspaperman and also a director of the Provincetown Theatre, Alsberg felt that Americans might want to know more about places, people, and things in the United States than they could get from filling-station maps or Chamber of Commerce handouts. There had not been a Baedeker on America since 1909, and its timeliness in 1936 was indicated by a solemn assurance that travel on this side of the Atlantic was "as safe as in the

most civilized parts of Europe." Tourists would not need
firearms, it advised, but would do well to bring matches,
buttons, and dress gloves.

Alsberg's instinct was right, and it fitted in, moreover,
with the concept that ran through all the arts projects,
namely, that given the talent at their disposal and the controversy that creative work might entail, their best contribution would be to expose Americans for the first time to true,
detailed, and vivid Americana. The result was that the
Guides—one for each of the forty-eight states, thirty for
major cities, and twenty others for great travel arteries like
U.S. One and *The Oregon Trail*—were remarkably rich in
oddities and lore. Traditional landmarks and monuments
were well and duly treated, but in the essays and descriptive
"Tours" much was added that local boosters' clubs would
rather have seen omitted. It gave the works a salt and savor
that made them not only good reading but an indispensable
key to the national character and the national past.

Even as the Guides were coming off the press, Robert
Cantwell, a perceptive critic on the *New Republic,* noted
that alongside the conventional America it portrayed another America, inhabited by "a fanciful, impulsive, childlike,
absent-minded, capricious and ingenious people," a land in
which many prominent citizens "built big houses (usually
called somebody's folly) that promptly fell into ruins when
the owner backed inventions that didn't work."

This iconoclastic note resounded through all the Guides.
An eighteenth- or nineteenth-century fisherman of Marble-
head, Massachusetts, talking of the Puritan search for freedom of worship, is quoted with the reflection that "'Our
ancestors came not here for religion. Their main end was to
catch fish.'" For every fortune founded by foresight and
celebrated in school histories, dozens were lost through bad
guessing and worse timing, and the Guides do not neglect
them—bankers who invested in canals just before the rail-

road became a certainty, traders plunging heavily on slaves as late as 1859, and, on a more modest level, the New England farmer who contracted to board a supposedly 94-year-old fellow Yankee for the rest of his life for $120. The tenacious boarder died at 116, says the Guide, happy in the knowledge that for 22 years he had eaten for about $5 a year. Among those who guessed more shrewdly than the farmer, on the other hand, were two Maine paupers who escaped from the Bangor almshouse and, before they were apprehended the following morning, made $1,800 each by speculating in dubious timberlands.

Eccentrics abound in the Guides, their homes being pointed out along with the poets' and Presidents'. Types in the gallery are the inventor who installed a machine on his roof to capture power from the sun, and the man who plotted to rescue Napoleon from St. Helena, even building a ship for the purpose, before he learned that Bonaparte had been dead for some time. There is also Timothy Dexter of Newburyport, who, when he wasn't engaged in selling warming pans to West Indians in exchange for molasses ladles, wrote *Pickles for the Knowing Ones*. All punctuation in that work, the Guide informs us, appeared at the end in several pages of solid commas and periods under the caption "Salt and Pepper to Taste." Even the famous seem to emerge from the Guides with egregious trimmings. We learn, for example, that the great soprano Giglia Nordica, née Lillian Norton of Backus Corner, Maine, was in the act of divorcing her first husband when he sailed off in a balloon, never to be seen again, and that she herself died in Java as the result of exposure suffered in a shipwreck off Thursday Island.

As Cantwell pointed out, discussions of local architecture gave considerable space to secret rooms, hidden stairways, and false halls, which seem to have been one of the odder preoccupations of early American builders. And when these sober forebears of ours weren't concentrating on trapdoors

and sliding panels they seem to have busied themselves com-
posing humorous epitaphs for themselves and their relations.
Much of their frivolity finds its way into the Guides, along
with information of a more conventional and less amusing
nature. So do legends, ghost stories, and countless tales of
lovers' leaps, usually made by frustrated and romantic Indians. The Missouri Guide is especially rich in superstitious
lore, which in the Mississippi basin seems to have changed
little since the boyhood of Huckleberry Finn. For a visitor it
is pleasant, and for one writing about the area downright
useful, to know that in the Ozarks some still hold it an ill
omen to see a cross-eyed person, especially at the intersec-
tion of two pathways; believe that the initials of one's future
spouse will appear on a handkerchief left out in a wheatfield
on the night of April 30; and are convinced that a hoop
snake will put its tail in its mouth and roll toward an intended victim, even going uphill, faster than a horse can
run.

Criticism of the Writers' Project was comparatively mild.
The only valid point of any importance was the fact that the
excellence of its work—not only the Guides, but also the
"Life in America" series, ranging from *The Italians of New
York* to *Baseball in Old Chicago*—owed so much to the
handful of experts who edited them or contributed to them
from the outside. The handicaps, on the other hand, were
formidable. Besides red tape, local pressure, the constant
draining away of the best reporters, and the incompetence of
the worst, there was always the threat from Capitol Hill. No
one ever knew when Congress would cut appropriations,
condemn the work being turned out, or eliminate the Project
altogether. And this was true for Art, Music, and Theatre
Projects as well.

In the consequently jittery and tentative atmosphere,
morale, not high to begin with at a wage scale averaging $90
a month, wobbled badly. Relief investigators snooped about

to make sure that nobody had a spare dime to squirrel away,
the future was shaky, and people on the Projects talked constantly of getting a "real job." Since no increases in pay were
attainable by direct action, collective bargainers concen-
trated on being recognized as collective bargainers, on raising *rates* of pay by getting their hours reduced, and on vio-
lently protesting the periodic appearance of pink slips
announcing layoffs.

Inevitably Communists were charged with leading the
uprisings that broke out from time to time, and there is not
much doubt that by way of the Workers Alliance they had a
good hand in them. On one occasion some six hundred workers on the Art and Writers' Projects staged a sit-in for days at
the Forty-second Street offices of the agency, barricading the
administrator in his cubbyhole and cutting off all incoming
telephone calls. The only concession was that a fortunate
subordinate was allowed to leave from time to time to take
special calls at a saloon across the street. Aubrey Williams,
among the most militant of the Administration liberals, put
in a request for a police escort to get the officials out and
clear the building, but the most Mayor La Guardia would do
was to send an officer around every couple of hours to make
sure the sagging floor wouldn't collapse under the unnatural
load, which for the sake of drama included an extra comple-
ment of the maimed and the pregnant. Only when the administrator agreed to recommend cancelation of threatened
layoffs was he allowed to leave, happily reassigned to Washington.

Such excesses were no doubt a drag on the program, as
were the fulminations of Congressmen and the endless
charges of "boondoggling" by newspaper editors who somehow never thought of their own highly perishable editorials
in that light at all; who must indeed have thought that their
repetitious carping would outlast the Guides, the Index of
American Design, the native songs preserved by the Music

Project, the impact of Shakespeare on De Funiak Springs, Florida, and all the rest of the WPA's unique experiment in Federal art.

It was, take it all in all, a magnificent experiment and one that went far to bear out Gutzon Borglum's eloquent letter to Aubrey Williams when the WPA was still a gleam in the eye of Harry Hopkins: "I want to suggest to you that you make your thought of aid to the creative ones among us greater, more effective in scope. . . . You are not after masterpieces, and you should not be discouraged if you have many failures; the real success will be in the interest, the human interest, which you will awaken; and what that does to the Nation's mind. I believe that's the door through which Hopkins, you and his aides can coax the soul of America back to interest in life." It certainly coaxed it over to a somewhat *different* life.

Ostriches and Umbrellas

8

If there had been no news reports except those from abroad between 1937 and the end of the decade, only the dullards among us would have survived; anyone with the least sensitivity would have gone down under the sense of calamity, present and to come. As it was, the successive triumphs of lunacy in Europe and Asia were interspersed for us, if not drowned out, by political excitements at home, the usual broad spectrum of domestic events, personal preoccupations, and the diversions of daily living—all of which allowed a time that should have been unbelievably painful to be not only endurable but, in its own way, stimulating.

All the same, the last years of the Thirties would have been more enjoyable than they were if somehow the weekends could have been skipped. For while the British were taking a weekend in the country, as a contemporary wit observed, Hitler was taking a country in the weekend. An exaggeration, of course, but some of the most ominous events of the decade, it seemed, *were* deliberately staged on Saturdays and Sundays to catch the statesmen of the democracies off-balance. It was like shooting fish in a barrel and probably distressed the sporting English as much as anything else about the dictators.

Those weekends are vivid in my memory not only because I had the normal sensitivity of my contemporaries to the terrible moments of the time, and their fearfulness as well, but because my job compelled me to react to those events concretely and immediately. As managing editor, I had to tear up whole issues of the *Nation* which had been made up on Friday and remake them, with new material arranged for on the spur of the moment and a new cover as well, in time to go to press Monday evening. Long and feverish telephone conversations with my fellow editors, cable exchanges, and a great rejuggling of space filled out those historic holidays. Outrageous as it seems to me now, the awfulness of the news was somewhat tempered by the excitement and the feeling of success, or at any rate relief, in getting the issues out on time with the maximum of up-to-the-minute catastrophe.

Not counting Hitler's march into the Rhineland on a March Saturday of 1936—a year or so before I joined the staff of the magazine—the first of these great weekend disasters was the *Anschluss*. Piecemeal, by radio and dispatch, the story of Vienna's ordeal reached us: All day Friday rumors fly and a sense of doom is conveyed from that far-off city to Manhattan. A plebiscite on unification with Germany has been ordered by Chancellor Schuschnigg for Sunday, much to Hitler's rage because neither he nor anyone else expects the Austrians to approve the merger. Ultimatums have been served on Schuschnigg to cancel the plebiscite, but as soon as he does, the Germans, panting for the kill, demand that President Miklas replace the Chancellor with the Nazi Artur Seyss-Inquart. The President holds out for a few hours, but—as we get the news relayed to us a little later—Schuschnigg himself, with his office occupied by Hitler's agents and Nazi thugs in the street shouting for his life, gives up the ghost of the Austrian Republic.

Weekend news cables carry the story of how Schuschnigg, in the very room where his predecessor Dollfuss had been shot to death by Nazi assassins, takes to the microphone. A lilting Viennese cabaret song is interrupted by the announcer's "*Achtung, Achtung.* In a moment there will be a very important announcement." Then Chancellor Schuschnigg himself comes on: *Österreicher und Österreicherinnen,* the German Government today handed to President Miklas an ultimatum, with a time limit, ordering him to nominate as Chancellor a person designated by the German government . . . otherwise German troops would invade Austria. President Miklas has asked me to tell the people of Austria that we have yielded to force. . . . So I take my leave of the Austrian people with a German word of farewell, uttered from the depth of my heart: God protect Austria!" The Chancellor collapses, weeping.

It was hard to realize that what we were hearing and reading was the death of an ancient state, the opening of a cultivated city to the barbarian. For the moment we were caught up in the immediate drama and the sensationalism of the news. But soon the eyewitnesses would report. Correspondents like G. E. R. Gedye would tell of the doctors, lawyers, professors, artists—anyone with standing and at least one Jewish grandparent—made to scrub the gutters of the city on their hands and knees while *gemütlich* Viennese looked on and laughed. And soon a trickle of Austrian refugees appeared in New York to join the German and Italian exiles already here, some inevitably with stories that jarred the complacency of those Americans who still thought the National Socialists were just another political party, though a bit eccentric.

A number of the more articulate escapees fortunately found their way to the *Nation's* offices. Franz Hoellering, a journalist of ability and charm, joined the staff, many advised us and contributed to the magazine, and others chilled us with accounts of the takeover. I recall particularly the stories of Anton Kuh, a lank-haired, hollow-cheeked raconteur, who wrote a three-part series called "Escape from the Mousetrap." Kuh told of the fate of Egon Friedell, a famous

Viennese wit and critic, who lived on the top floor of a house which also sheltered a young lady then enjoying the attentions of two SS men. Arriving at the house one evening shortly after the *Anschluss,* the two Nazis rang Friedell's bell by mistake, and when "the Bernard Shaw of Vienna" caught a glimpse of their black Elite Guard uniforms, he turned around, walked through his apartment, and plunged through the window to his death.

In spite of their harrowing experiences, the refugees brought besides their talent, which was often great, and their material possessions, which as a rule were not, a new kind of humor. Their stories were political weapons, pathetically frail for the enemy they dealt with but in a small way comforting. Newcomers were pumped for the latest underground anecdotes as an index of the opposition's morale, if not its strength. Among the tales making the rounds, a popular one told of four friends gathered around a café table in Berlin. One drew a deep sigh. The second wagged his head despondently from side to side. The third uttered a low moan. Whereupon the fourth flew off the handle: "For Heaven's sake, when will you people learn not to discuss politics in public?"

Another favorite concerned an Italian who had been dragged off a park bench by a Fascist secret policeman for having loudly condemned Mussolini as an evil clown and his government as a collection of thugs. When a companion protested to the officer that the man was obviously not a political enemy but an unfortunate imbecile, the policeman turned on him scornfully: "Oh, sure. Then how is it he knows exactly what's going on?"

A chain letter making the rounds on Washington Heights, which had become a Mecca for the luckier of Hitler's victims, went something like this: "A Nazi with heart disease must not use digitalis, discovered by the Jew Ludwig Traube. If he has a toothache, a Nazi will not use cocaine or he will be utilizing the work of a Jew, Solomon Stricker. . . .

If he has diabetes he must not use insulin, the discovery of a Jew, Mikowsky." And so on, through Pyramidon for headaches, Salvarsan for syphilis, and psychoanalysis for what clearly was the most prevalent of all Nazi afflictions. The accuracy of the information may have left something to be desired, but in view of Jewish contributions to German medicine the point was well taken.

On the surface America did honor to the refugees, and well it might. It is not every decade that a country inherits, full-blown, the cultural wealth of a continent—writers like Mann and Zweig, social scientists and scholars like Salvemini, Borgese, Ascoli, Sternberg, and Heiden; painters like Grosz, Léger, and Chagall; musicians like Serkin, Walter, Weill, and Schnabel; and scientific giants like Fermi and Einstein. But gratitude was tempered by rivalry, generosity by concern over domestic unemployment, and appreciation by prejudice. Genius was generally made welcome, but no computer will ever calculate how much talent, skill, and simple human worth were lost to the country because of bureaucratic timidity and the callous delaying tactics of consuls who did not subscribe to the sentiments inscribed on the Statue of Liberty.

Even genius did not have plain sailing. Professor Einstein, who had abandoned his pure pacifism to urge a democratic front against fascism, was under constant attack from the lower orders of intelligence. I include in this number the simple-minded professor at City College who wanted to know what Einstein had discovered that could compare, for example, with the invention of the chair. Also the pest who kept writing letters to the editor of the *Nation* explaining that "Einstein's theories of relativity and space-time are based upon imagination and crooked mathematics . . . the products of an insane mind." And, not least, the editor of a Brooklyn diocesan organ who carried on a long and inflammatory campaign for Einstein's deportation.

Soon after the *Anschluss* we received a cable from Robert

Dell, an English correspondent we shared with the *Manchester Guardian* and one of the very best in the business. An impressive-looking old man by now, with a noble white mustache, Dell, who was not one to linger over accomplished crimes, was courageously sounding the alarm at the next point of danger. Czechoslovakia was not Austria, he wrote, and was fully prepared to fight, naturally in the expectation that her sworn allies would stand behind her. "If England and France and Russia all warned Hitler that any attack on Czechoslovakia would mean war with all of them, Czechoslovakia would be saved without war." There was still hope for Europe even if *alt Wien* had gone down into darkness, and with that hope we all went into a labored breathing spell.

The spell lasted six months, during which Hitler and his friends had to share the front pages with content of a milder sort. Roosevelt launched an ill-fated campaign in the primaries to purge hostile Democratic Congressmen, especially those who had opposed his plan to reorganize the Supreme Court. Howard Hughes flew around the world, by way of Siberia, in three days, nineteen hours, and eight minutes; and "Wrong-Way" Corrigan, denied a permit for transatlantic air travel, flew from Brooklyn to Dublin anyhow, claiming with a grin that he thought he was headed for California all the time. Joe Louis, the Brown Bomber, knocked out Max Schmeling seconds after the opening gong of the first round, sending him back to Berlin to teach boxing to other members of the master race.

Another batch of Russian revolutionary heroes were shot for treason, including the chief of the dread GPU who had found so much treason in others, and Prosecutor Vishinsky explained: "We cannot leave such people alive. They can do such things in America, where Al Capone remains alive, but not here." And, with the recession of 1937-38 beginning to fade, most Americans went on vacation, many of them no doubt whistling the hit tunes of the year as they drove off. The world being in the sinister shape it was, the songs could hardly have been more innocent—"A-Tisket, A-Tasket" and "Whistle While You Work," as well as something called "Flat Foot Floogie with the Floy Floy."

More than half of September in that last full year of "peace" was given over to the next spasm on the German agenda, known as the Munich Crisis. On Monday, September 12, we heard Adolf Hitler over the radio as the first in a cast of characters that was to include Prime Minister Neville Chamberlain, French Premier Edouard Daladier, Benito Mussolini, Czech President Eduard Beneš, and above all, H. V. Kaltenborn, who was to give us a masterly running account of history in progress and so bring radio news broadcasting to full flower.

To hear the Führer we gathered in gloom and trepidation in the *Nation's* tiny library. After a week of billingsgate from such Wagnerian figures as Goering and Goebbels, the latter known in refugee circles as Wotan's Mickey Mouse, Hitler himself was to address the Nazi Party Congress in Nuremberg, and the world was to have the privilege of sharing in the frenzy.

Listening to Adolf Hitler, one had the feeling of a world at the mercy of a lunatic. In a voice of rasping hysteria, he screamed and his followers screamed back in return. Reading of this wild man and his cohorts was one thing, but hearing the *Sieg Heils* and *Heil Hitlers* of the mob in your office in downtown Manhattan was almost terrifying. For the message itself we had to wait for Kaltenborn to come on with a quick translation: "The misery of the Sudeten Germans is without end. They [the Czechs] want to annihilate them. . . . And I say that if these tortured creatures cannot obtain rights and assistance by themselves, they can obtain both from us." (Cries of "*Sieg Heil, Sieg Heil, Sieg Heil!*")

Glued to the radio for more than two weeks, Americans of

all ranks and stations followed these developments with growing horror and fascination—and with an intimate knowledge they had rarely acquired in the past about any public affair but the choicest murder cases. We heard the Prime Minister, depicted in a thousand cartoons with furled umbrella and angular Adam's apple, announce as he left London for Berchtesgaden, "I am going to see the German Chancellor because the situation seems to me one in which discussions between him and me may have a useful consequence, and the Führer's reply to my suggestion encourages me to hope that my visit to him will not be without results."

We heard Hitler's fatal terms for Czechoslovakia almost as soon as the stricken Beneš did and avidly followed Mr. Chamberlain's peregrinations back to London, to Godesberg, back to London again, to Munich—always with his umbrella and the fate of the Czechs tucked under his arm. Leaving England on the last of these missions, exhausted but still fatuously hoping for peace through blackmail, he spoke into a microphone: "When I come back I hope I may be able to say, as Hotspur says in Henry IV, 'Out of this nettle, danger, we plucked this flower, safety.'"

The fateful meeting at Munich was efficiently broadcast, NBC bringing the final betrayal of Czechoslovakia to Americans within minutes of the signing. Two Czechs were permitted to wait in an adjoining room as "observers" and got the results at the same time we did. Hitler was to get practically all he had demanded, with phony plebiscites that would never be held, and he could send his troops goosestepping across the Czech border on October 1 as planned, so that he might make the kind of show his swelling ego required. Of the rump state the Czechs would have left, its fortifications gone and its industry decimated, Britain and France undertook to guarantee the new boundaries. By the end of the year President Beneš was safely installed at the University of Chicago as a lecturer on democratic institu-

CANDIDATE

Alfred M. Landon of Kansas with daughter and guide, Continental Divide, 1936. *(Wide World)*

Landon with sunflower, La Salle, Colorado, 1936. *(UPI)*

"It's Not Cricket to Picket," song from ILGWU show *Pins and Needles*, 1939. *(Standard Studios)*

LABOR AT PLAY

Intermission at sitdown strike, Flint, Michigan, 1937. *(UPI)*

Tobacco Road, on Broadway. *(UPI)*

HITS

The Swing Mikado, WPA Theatre Project, New Yorker Theatre, 1939. *(UPI)*

Prohibitionists pledging to go on with the fight, 1933. *(Wide World*

CRUSADERS

Veterans of Lincoln Brigade, New York, 1938. *(UPI)*

r: Joe Louis defeats member of Master
, Max Schmeling, Yankee Stadium, June
938. *(UPI)*

RACE

tim: one of the seven Scottsboro boys
aiting trial, Decatur, Alabama, jail. *(UPI)*

Workers' Bookshop, New York City, 1934. *(UPI)*

LEFT

Under two flags: the American flag and the Red flag, May Day Parade, 1937. *(UPI)*

rman-American Bund rally at Madison Square Garden, February 20, 1939. *(UPI)*

Armed citizen prepared for men from Mars, Grover's Mills, N.J., after Orson Welles' broadcast, October 30, 1938. *(UPI)*

INVADERS

Adolf Hitler, Hermann Goering, Benito Mussolini at signing of Munich Pact, September, 1938. *(UPI)*

Joseph Stalin and Joachim Von Ribbentrop shaking hands after Nazi-Soviet Treaty, Moscow, August, 1939. *(UPI)*

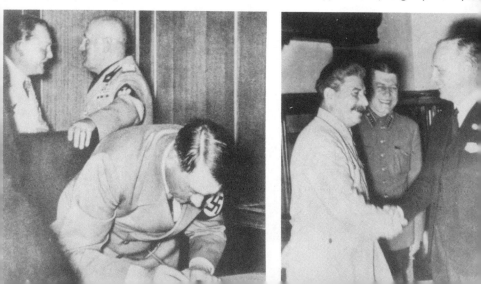

tions. Meeting him at a reception, I thought he looked like
an intelligent but not sprightly professor of statistics, eager
to get down to business and with no inclination whatever to
philosophize about what the democratic institutions of England had done to him.

Neville Chamberlain, once described by Lloyd George as
"a good town clerk of Birmingham in a lean year," returned
to London and innumerable renditions of "For He's a Jolly
Good Fellow." To admiring crowds he said, "I believe it is
peace in our time." Winston Churchill could hardly get
Commons to listen to his dissenting opinion that Britain and
the whole civilized world had sustained "a total, unmiti-
gated defeat." The British Broadcasting Company did not
carry his protest at all, but we heard him in the United
States, and millions of Americans thought exactly as he
did.

On the other hand, millions of Americans did not. On the
climactic day of Munich both President Roosevelt and
Mayor La Guardia, like many other officials around the
world, urged people to go to their churches and synagogues
to pray for peace. But, once the terrible tension was broken,
many had second thoughts as to whether peace was to be
had by throwing small countries, one by one, to the wolves.
As for the *Nation,* the cover of the first issue with a detailed
review of the crisis carried the prophetic bannerhead, "A
Peace to End Peace."

Until Munich only a minority of Americans felt that war
was inevitable between the Axis powers and that loose ag-
gregation of states which by some were called "the democracies," by others the "so-called democracies," and by still
others the "peace-loving states"—which they were in the
sense that each loved peace for itself, whatever might happen to its neighbor. An even smaller minority thought that if
such a war did break out the United States should have a
part in it, for we were the most peace-loving people of all

and looked with disdain on "foreign entanglements." It took
the abject failure of Munich and the recurrent crises of 1939
to slow down the powerful current of isolationism that had
always run through the country. It took the attack on Pearl
Harbor, two years after the outbreak of war, to make a dent
in the solid third of the population that up to that very
moment believed the defeat of the Axis was less important to
Americans than preserving a technical neutrality.

The isolationist current was fed from many streams, and
those of us who were charged with being warmongers did
not always find it easy to make fair distinctions. There was
first the kind of provincialism that many Americans felt had
been ordained for them by Nature and endorsed by History.
Nature had blessed us with two great oceans deliberately in
order to separate us from Decadent Europe on the one side
and the Mysterious East on the other. . . . The Founding
Fathers had warned us against "entanglements" and "permanent alliances." . . . Wars benefited only the bankers on
the East Coast, who were not the best Americans, but it
did not benefit the farmers, who were. . . . We thought we
were "making the world safe for democracy" in 1917 and
look at it now.

This was essentially the isolationism of the Midwest,
nurtured, exaggerated, and inflamed day after day by Colonel Robert McCormick's Chicago *Tribune* but none the less
genuine for all that. Oscar Ameringer, a rural Socialist editor
in the Populist tradition and as simon-pure Midwest as Mc-
Cormick ever was, put it rather differently:

. . . we are so busy rustling shirts for our own backs that we can't
afford to do much tearing of them over the woes of the Croats,
Slovenes, Finns, Letts, and Lapps, concerning which the *Nation*
is so constantly het up. It isn't that we are callous about the fate
of our European brethren. It's just that we can't take on so much
territory and that we are in touch with these affairs anyway
through the capitalist press, whose editors are tickled to keep us

looking toward the Atlantic Ocean while they pick our pockets on the home front and millions of Americans go hungry.

Intensifying the suspicion of Croats, Slovenes, *et al.* were national loyalties which suggested ironically that ancestral attitudes were not as easily abandoned even by isolationists as they supposed. Irish-Americans were not at all appalled to see a British Prime Minister do a bit of groveling, though they would no doubt have preferred to see him grovel in Dublin rather than Munich. Thousands of Midwesterners of German descent who were not at all pro-Nazi were none the less pleased to see the ancient Fatherland spread out a bit and were certainly of no mind to check its progress with their own comfortable bodies. And Americans whose Scandinavian relatives had made a science of standing aloof even in the midst of Europe were similarly disposed to keep their distance over here.

Naturally these attitudes were not peculiar to the Midwest, but they ran strongest there and produced the highest concentration of isolationism where it counted most—in the Congress of the United States. It was there that a Missourian even as late as 1941 could rise from his seat and say, "It was Great Britain and France who declared war upon the German Reich after being clearly forewarned by Colonel Lindbergh that it would be utterly impossible for them to compete with Germany's air force. . . ." It was Montana's Senator Wheeler who could warn, "Do not let yourself forget that war means dictatorship and the end of civil rights, that war means the end of all liberty for all times, for your generation and for generations to come."

Wheeler went to the extent of echoing Father Coughlin's interest in "international bankers," who always turned out to be the Rothschilds, the Warburgs, and, with some relish, "the Sassoons of the Orient." After one such oration I asked him why he did not include the Rockefellers, the Morgans, and the Aldriches of the Occident, all more powerful by far than those he mentioned, just as international in their dealings, and, by chance, quite Aryan. Unclamping his jaws to release the long cigar which was his hallmark, he told me that he had himself written in the very names I mentioned—unaccountably his speech writer had originally omitted them—but when he came to read the sentence in public he could see at a glance that it was too long. Having to omit something, he naturally skipped what he had interpolated between the lines. His pained grin indicated that he hoped for indulgence rather than belief.

Exploiting these strong native sentiments in every conceivable way were the small but nasty bands of committed Fascists, well-heeled Axis agents, professional anti-Semites, and other sympathizers with the New Order. They actively wanted for the United States the enlightenment that had already come to Italy, Germany, Austria, Spain, Rumania, Hungary, and even Brazil, where the green-shirted Integralistas of General Vargas were bringing Fascist primitivism to the very borders of the civilized jungle, comparatively speaking. Besides the Coughlin devotees, to whom respects have been paid in an earlier chapter, we had our own crackpots in shirted color. The Khaki Shirts, led by "General" Art J. Smith, were planning to march on Washington, as Mussolini had marched on Rome, but after a police raid on their armory in Philadelphia the General vanished with a good part of the profits the organization had made on shirts and boots. Ultimately Smith went to jail for six years, not for the killing he had made in men's ready-to-wear clothing but for perjury in connection with the literal killing of a heckler at one of his rallies.

Somewhat weirder were the Silver Shirts of William Dudley Pelley, a fiction writer successful enough at least to have made *Who's Who*. What was not a fiction, he insisted, was that he had died and gone to heaven for seven minutes sometime in 1928. After that experience he was in daily contact with an oracle who predicted the rise of Hitler and directed him to form the Silver Shirts, as "the cream, the head and flower of our Protestant Christian manhood." The cream, etc., turned out to be a good deal like the Ku Klux Klan in silvery shirts instead of plain white sheets, and its chief head and flower went to the Federal penitentiary for sedition during World War II, a prediction the oracle had neglected to report.

No doubt there would have been other shirt movements if the colors had not been pretty well pre-empted.* But there were literally hundreds of conventionally-shirted fantasy groups, each with only a handful of members but enough money to put out isolationist, pro-Fascist, and usually racist propaganda by the ton. And for low comedy there was always the bull-necked Fritz Kuhn and his German-American Bund.

At a Bund rally in Madison Square Garden in 1939 a giant figure of George Washington dwarfed the stage, which was decked out with huge swastikas and jammed with booted and uniformed Bundsmen, all giving each other the Nazi salute, singing "The Star-Spangled Banner" in a Katzenjammer accent, and denouncing their favorite villain, "Franklin D. Rosenfeld." Dorothy Thompson found it all so funny in a grisly way that she laughed loudly when the Bundists were at their most solemnly asinine and in the ensuing hullabaloo had to be escorted from the premises by the police.

But the Thompson laughter was more a demonstration, as she later admitted, than a sign of amusement. At the time it was hard to be amused by the antics of these "patriots"—

* Besides the black of the Italian and British Fascists, the brown of the Nazis, and the domestic khaki and silver, blue was the shirt color favored by Irish Fascists and green, as already noted, by the Brazilians. For obvious reasons red was not considered suitable, yellow would have invited easy gibes, and few crackpots, even, could have been induced to go around in purple or orange shirts.

even by the one who maintained that Pope Pius had been
raised to the throne of St. Peter not by the College of Cardi-
nals, but by international Jewish bankers who held a fifteen-
million-dollar mortgage on the Vatican.

Just as opposed to any suggestion of "foreign adventures"
but infinitely remote from these surrealist figures in character were the pacifists and Socialists of varying shades. Profoundly opposed to war itself, even a war against fascism,
these were people who were as pure in motive as the pro-
Fascists were devious, as dedicated to principle as the simple isolationists were to self-interest, and as confident in
their judgment as those of us who thought the threat of
fascism had to be met head-on.

Their most effective spokesman was Norman Thomas, and
he argued, first, that the Fascist menace was not a military
one—"The combined might of the non-Fascist nations of
Europe is overwhelmingly superior to Mussolini or Hitler,
with the Mikado thrown in for good measure. Three prima
donnas don't make a chorus." Point Two in the discourse was
that "the minute America enters war democracy will yield to
the totalitarian state necessary for totalitarian war. . . ." And,
finally, "there is no inevitable necessity that will drive the
United States into such a war."

The argument was rooted in the widespread conviction of
the decade that all wars were started by munitions makers,
"merchants of death," and had inevitably to produce conditions worse than those they were waged to correct. It was
plausible enough, but through organizations like the America First Committee it gradually brought some of these high-
minded people to the point of joint operations with individuals they would normally have met only in nightmares.
Norman Thomas himself was one evening to appear on a
platform in Madison Square Garden before an audience
packed to the galleries with massed Bundists and Cough-
linites, all taking advantage of every opportunity to give the

straight-arm Nazi salute to Colonel Charles A. Lindbergh. Lacking a press credential I sat a few rows behind Joe Mc-Williams, the Führer of Yorkville, who smiled and waved an American flag as John T. Flynn, the chairman of the evening, denounced him in the hope of salvaging the Committee's respectability and for his pains was drowned out by the booing of the mob. Technically the episode occurred a little after the Thirties had passed into history, but it was an inevitable sequel to what had been going on for some time.

The collective security camp—"warmongers" was the word used by our opponents—similarly attracted supporters many of us would gladly have foresworn. There was about the Communists an embarrassing implausibility even when they were right in an immediate sense about the dire need to check the aggressors. When the American gunboat *Panay* was sunk in the Yangtze River by Japanese bombers, the tone of the Communist Party press recalled that of the Hearst newspapers over the sinking of the *Maine*. In a public debate Earl Browder—he had once declared, "The only way to fight war is to begin by fighting the war-makers in our own land"—conjured up a picture of Japan about to crash through our Pacific defenses and seize "the rich and beautiful lands of California." In the light of the bombs that fell on Pearl Harbor three years later, the Communists, flamboyant as they were, appeared to have been on firmer ground than the isolationists. By then, however, they had forfeited all possible credit for foresight, having put in a year and a half as the most vociferous isolationists following the German-Russian period of happy accommodation. But even in the Thirties they were for a few months an embarrassment to the advocates of peace at any price, as they had been for so long to the champions of collective security.

This citing of bedfellows was one of the major political pastimes of the day, and it was carried so far that in parlor discussions of foreign policy right or wrong often seemed to matter less than who was on your side. Even within the family of the *Nation*'s readers and contributors the game was played. Pacifists, Socialists, and isolationists wrote in, singly and collectively, to condemn the magazine's stand and deplore its ideological association with the Standard Oil Company, the House of Morgan, and those drumbeaters of war Harold Ickes and Fiorello La Guardia. Oswald Garrison Villard, who had his own page but no longer controlled the magazine's policies, took this same view and was shocked, in turn, when Heywood Broun, still on the editorial board, served notice that he would not back the "curious alliance" of Villard and Father Coughlin.

For a warmonger, as President Roosevelt was classified in the Chicago *Tribune,* Dr. Goebbels' *Völkischer Beobachter,* and, often enough, the *Congressional Record,* he was certainly a slow starter. To be sure, the country was, from the beginning of his Administration, in an extremely withdrawn mood. An early Gallup poll taken in 1935 indicated that some 75 percent of the voters actually wanted Congress to agree to hold a national plebiscite before ever again declaring a war. No President could favor so potentially fatal a delaying action as that, and Roosevelt managed to get the proposed resolution killed off in Congress, but beyond that his actions until 1937 were hardly calculated to disturb the dreams of would-be world conquerors. He not only signed the Neutrality Act of 1935, which forbade the sale of munitions to any nation engaged in war, but saw to it that the law applied to civil wars as well as international.

What was worse, our neutrality in those mid-decade years not only seemed to work in favor of one side, but always of the *wrong* side. Nothing prevented our sending munitions to Japan because she had sensibly neglected to declare a formal war on China, preferring to bomb it into the New Order for East Asia informally and as an act of friendship. The Neutrality Act helped Italy against Ethiopia, because the Italians started out with far more of everything than the Ethiopians and could get more if they wanted it. And Hitler had already made it clear that he preferred having his way by threatening war rather than making it.

It was not until the fall of 1937, after Ethiopia, after the Axis intervention in Spain, after Hitler's march into the demilitarized Rhineland, and after the Führer's first attempt to snatch Austria, that the President made his famous "quarantine" speech. To those of us who had long waited for the word, it was a speech that still reverberates:

. . . the hopes for peace thus raised have of late given way to a haunting fear of calamity. The present reign of terror and international lawlessness began a few years ago . . .

If those things come to pass in other parts of the world, let no one imagine that America will escape. . . . When an epidemic of physical disease starts to spread, the community approves and joins in a quarantine of the patients in order to protect the health of the community against the spread of the disease.

What went over big at the *Nation* was not so well received by the country as a whole. The President was shrilly attacked as a jingo, and away from the Atlantic seaboard opinion polls continued to show powerful sentiment against any policy likely to involve the country in the turbulence of Europe and Asia. The "scientific" techniques of Dr. Gallup had acquired such prestige after showing up the crudity of the *Literary Digest* Presidential poll in 1936 that great interest attached to its findings in the field of foreign policy. Not least of these was that 66 percent of those asked thought the country that could least be trusted to keep its word was Germany (only 7 percent picked Russia), but when asked which system they preferred if forced to choose between fascism and communism, they divided cleanly down the middle, 50 percent for each.

It took the aftermath of Munich to do what even Roose-

218]   Just Around the Corner

velt's eloquence was powerless to do, that is, to shake the
country loose from its isolationist moorings. It was not the
hamstringing of Czechoslovakia in 1938 that finally convinced most Americans of Hitler's insatiable appetite; it was
his compulsive devouring of what was still left of that country in 1939, in spite of all his pledges to Neville Chamberlain
that he wanted no Czechs in his pure German Reich.

Considering the anticlimactic nature of the Czech finale,
its repercussions were widespread and emotional. True,
Neville Chamberlain's first reaction was simply that Mr.
Hitler's behavior "was hardly in the spirit of Munich," but
this was generally put down to British understatement and
the stiff upper lip. For the first time Hitler had swallowed up
a wholly foreign people. In the New York *Times* appeared
the first of that endless series of comparative maps, three or
four in a strip, showing that the Germany of Today, in black,
was not only greater than the Germany of Versailles but
greater than the Kaiser's Germany of 1914.

In Washington the viscous prose of diplomatic protest
poured forth like lava: "This government . . . cannot refrain
from making known this country's condemnation of the acts
which have resulted in the temporary extinguishment of the
liberties of a free and independent people with whom . . . the
people of the United States have maintained especially close
and friendly relations," etc., etc. In both Senate and House
the isolationists were for the moment struck dumb. But only
for the moment. In a few weeks Senator Robert Reynolds of
North Carolina, one of the most raucous of the Congressional
group christened by Rex Stout the "Illustrious Dunderheads,"
was excusing the seizure of Czechoslovakia as an exhibition
of the frontier spirit such as animated our own pioneers.

More significant, Mr. Chamberlain, harried and chivvied
by his own partisans, went to his home city of Birmingham
and confessed his doubts. "Is this the last attack upon a
small state or is it to be followed by others? Is this in fact a

step in the direction of an attempt to dominate the world by force?" And then, for the first time and feebly anticipating Winston Churchill, he warned that "no greater mistake could be made than to suppose that because it believes war to be a senseless and cruel thing, this nation has so lost its fiber that it will not take part to the utmost of its power in resisting such a challenge if it ever were made."

But the string was not yet quite played out. Toward the end of the month Hitler casually took the East Prussian port of Memel from Lithuania and stepped up a running attack on Poland, painfully reminiscent of his long pre-Munich attentions to Czechoslovakia. And Mussolini, seemingly in response to a secret suggestion from Roosevelt that he take the initiative for peace, took Albania instead, since countries now seemed open to that sort of diplomacy. The biting story of the week in refugee circles, always happy to play off one dictator against another, was that Il Duce telephoned Hitler to tell him of his triumph. "Did you say Albania?" Hitler is supposed to have asked in amazement. "Yes, Adolf, and we have crushed all resistance," Mussolini proudly replied. "Idiot!" screamed the Führer. "I distinctly said Rumania!"

The British Labour Party's Intellectual-in-Chief, Harold Laski, who used to come to the *Nation* office for an occasional staff lunch when he was in the country, made a straightforward estimate of the prospects: "Europe is like an artichoke. The Nazis are eating it leaf by leaf. France and Britain are the heart of the artichoke, to be eaten later."

The percentage of Americans who thought we should sell war materials to Britain and France if war broke out rose from 52 to 66 percent in a single month, but Congress still refused to repeal the Neutrality Act. Senator Borah had assured his colleagues that "There's not going to be any war this year." Invited to drop in at the State Department and read the ominous cables pouring in from all over Europe, the Senator from Idaho told Secretary Hull there was no need.

"I have sources of information in Europe that I regard as more reliable than those of the State Department." Repeal of the Act, which might have discouraged the Axis powers from starting a war, had to wait until they had already started it, after which it was passed very promptly.

In the summer of 1939 many of us—nearly thirty million, they said—forgot about Memel and Poland and went out to Flushing to have a look at the World's Fair, directed by that natural exhibitionist Grover Whalen. Except for Germany, most of the countries of the world were represented, including the former Republic of Czechoslovakia, but there was little else under the shadow of the Trylon and Perisphere to recall the grimmer facts of life. The general idea was, Isn't science wonderful? Especially applied science, which was going to make the World of Tomorrow, if any, a delight to the housewife, the automobile driver, and the consumer of technological goodies. The General Motors exhibit showed how the United States would have the traffic problem solved by 1960 with rebuilt cities and gleaming new highways. It would all be paid for with Federal funds, General Motors being prepared to concede the bureaucrats in Washington a share in American enterprise after all. But the best feature about the World of Tomorrow was to be the ingenious new housing, in glass bricks, plywood, cinder blocks, and the like —all equipped with electric refrigerators, gleaming metal kitchens, dishwashers, and the new Disposall, a scientific breakthrough on the garbage front.

A gigantic figure of a worker, very much like the ones in WPA murals, held a great Red Star high above the Soviet pavilion, and inside the building a dozen inscriptions told the visitor all about Russia's new social order, different and better than any that had gone before. But the exhibits, hardly distinguishable from our own, seemed intended to convince Americans that the new Russia was just like the United States, with skyscrapers, democratic politics, noisy industrial cities, garbage, and all.

Not even these prospective glories, plus the cheery piping of "The Sidewalks of New York" from dozens of little blue-and-orange Fair trains, were quite enough, however, to block out all thought of what might really be in store for the World of Tomorrow. You could still mix your anxiety with hope, but you had to work at it. A visiting Member of Parliament rather tidily summed up the wishful-dreamy state of mind prevailing that summer. "We shall not be able to enjoy ourselves again until Franco's widow tells Stalin on his deathbed that Hitler has been assassinated at Mussolini's funeral."

From such pleasant but remote fantasies we were all rudely snatched on the 24th of August. On that day the unbelievable, hinted at and whispered about for several months but nowhere taken seriously, became an accomplished fact. Russia and Germany had joined hands, as though fire and flood should come to terms for the purpose of doing joint mischief.

Rationalizations by American apologists for the Soviet Union, some of them set forth in an earlier chapter, were prompt if far-fetched. The Munich men, they said, had hoped to drive Germany into a war against Russia and then sit back and enjoy watching the two totalitarian giants smash each other to bits. Russia had merely turned the tables on them. When the *Nation* scoffed at such dialectics, rebukes and denunciations were quick in coming, by no means all of them from Communists or professional cynics. A Boston man of the cloth, patiently explaining that Stalin was fighting for the life of his regime, concluded: "I would suggest that you leave the morals of the situation to us parsons and concentrate yourselves upon the realities in terms of *Realpolitik*."

For hard-shell Communists, of course, concentrating on such realities was a way of life. The war against fascism was to be left to "warmongers" until such time as the Nazis should turn on their Eastern confreres and so reawaken their anti-fascism. Then the line would change again, just as swiftly. If I may anticipate that event for the sake of illustration, a strongly pro-Communist official of the Newspaper Guild, one of the few then remaining and destined to be ousted soon afterward, told us in May of 1941 that our union would "never be tied to the coattails of that warmonger Franklin D. Roosevelt, but will stand foursquare behind our great leader John L. Lewis." Rising to address us again in July, following the German double-cross, he announced with no visible embarrassment, "This union will never be tied to the coattails of that isolationist John L. Lewis, but will stand foursquare behind our great fighting leader Franklin D. Roosevelt."

But, for all their arguments, even the apologists—at least the ones I knew—were for the moment as appalled as anyone else at the details which soon leaked out about the jolly get-together of Foreign Minister von Ribbentrop and Foreign Minister Molotov in Moscow. When word of the signing was flashed back to Berlin, Hitler was reported by an eyewitness to have joyfully beaten at the walls with his fists —in contrast to biting the carpet, which he did when enraged—and to have hailed Herr von Ribbentrop as "a second Bismarck." For his part, Joseph Stalin proposed a toast to the Nazi emissary. "I know how much the German nation owes to its Führer," said the leader of world anti-fascism. "I should like to drink to his health."

In less than a week, as everyone knows, the dismemberment of Poland began, with Germany and Russia amicably carving out fair shares. The new Bismarck had explained to his Führer that if the British and French had failed to fight for Czechoslovakia when they would have had Russia with them, they would certainly not fight for Poland with the Russians against them. And his Führer, who wanted very much to believe him, did so. But on Sunday morning of a mild Labor Day weekend, at a time when few of us would

normally be awake, we got word from London of Ribbentrop's fatal error, one that would eventually lead him to the
gallows. Said the British Prime Minister, the man who
thought he had bought "peace in our time":

I have to tell you now . . . that this country is at war with
Germany. . . .
Now may God bless you all and may He defend the right. For
it is evil things that we shall be fighting against—brute force, bad
faith, injustice, oppression, and persecution. And against them I
am certain that the right will prevail.

President Roosevelt went on the air that evening, and he
was realistic. "This nation will remain a neutral nation, but I
cannot ask that every American remain neutral in thought as
well," he said. "Even a neutral has a right to take account of
facts. Even a neutral cannot be asked to close his mind or his
conscience." The American neutral did not. A Gallup poll
soon after the war began showed 84 percent pulling for an
Allied victory, 14 percent with no opinion, and only 2 percent avowedly hoping for a Nazi victory.

Most of us assumed that somehow we would be drawn in
before the war was over, and I recall walking in my several
customary haunts, trying to envision them in an air raid:
lower Fifth Avenue, where the *Nation* then had its offices;
Riverside Drive, which we could see from the window of our
apartment across from International House; and the quiet
little Jersey coast town where we had a summer place built
by my wife's father in the Nineties, the house where I had
listened to Mr. Chamberlain declare the war that Senator
Borah knew would not occur.

This dolorous musing did not last long, because the war,
at least for the remainder of the Thirties, was strictly in the
East. Poland was carved up in a month, the Baltic states fell
swiftly to the Russians, and before the year was out Stalin
was fighting "semi-fascism" in Finland. But in the West a

strange quiet had settled down. It was the period of the
Phony War, the Bore War, the *Sitzkrieg,* and many wondered whether England and France intended to fight after
all or merely wait for a settlement.

In the peculiar calm that enveloped the world in those last
days of the decade war once again seemed remote. Officially
it had come, but except for the poor Poles and the Finns it
was not yet a reality. With London and Paris still un-
scratched, it became harder and harder to conjure up a picture of New York in ruins or submarines off the Jersey coast.
Even after hostilities had become much hotter than they
were then, the State Department was to turn down a passport request for Eastern Europe by one of our correspondents on the mild ground of "the disturbed international situation."

Real war would come soon enough, in the spring, but for
what was left of the Thirties one could admire the autumn
foliage in New England, listen to the World Series, which
Joe DiMaggio and some other Yankees took from the Cin-
cinnati Reds in four straight games, or read *The Grapes of
Wrath,* the Pulitzer prizewinner for the year. Or one could
engage in the prevailing speculation about who would be
elected President in 1940, hardly anyone imagining even
then that it would be the man who had already stamped his
name on an era of American history.

Notes and Jottings

9

It is all very well for historians to bring order out of the day-to-day chaos of the past and for artists to impose a pattern on existence. Being neither historian nor artist, however, but only a chronicler of sorts, I have no qualms about passing along at this point some disparate and variegated fragments of the Thirties that have not yet turned up in this selective record. The thought is that, flashed at random and with small regard for continuity, these bits and pieces may carry a contemporary flavor that is sometimes lost when the heavy batteries of sociological hindsight are trained on human affairs. They are offered merely as rambling impressions of the sort that people like to dredge up when they mildly challenge their contemporaries to remember when. . . .

It was poor form to telephone a friend on Tuesday evening between half past eight and nine, because that was the time reserved for *Information Please*, the quiz show for sophisticates. The two regulars on the panel were F.P.A. (Franklin P. Adams), with a face like a basset hound's, a delight in words, and a mind that was a storehouse of quotations; and John Kieran, a naturalist, sports reporter, and amiable encyclopedia, who reeled off Latin verse with the twang of a Manhattan taxi driver. To the panel—there were always a couple of guest experts—Clifton Fadiman, the urbane master of ceremonies, put such questions as "A woman divorced her husband as a librocubicularist. What was the exact nature of her charge?" If Kieran had not correctly replied, "A chap who reads in bed," a cash register would have sounded over the merriment and the submitter of the question would have received ten dollars plus a twenty-four-volume set of the *Encyclopaedia Britannica*. Far-out puns were always in order, and so were far-out guests, including Mayor La Guardia, Georgia's Governor Arnall, who knew more poetry than F.P.A., and Wendell Willkie— all to their considerable political advantage.

Among the other pleasures of radio, when it wasn't dropping world crises into one's living room, the most enjoyable was Fred Allen's *Town Hall Tonight*, forerunner of his even more distinguished *Allen's Alley*. Endowed with names that would have done Sinclair Lewis credit—Balzac McGee, Beau Bernstein, Falvey Nishball—his characters brought a little welcome acid to airwaves otherwise clogged with soap like *Young Dr. Malone*, juveniles like *Jack Armstrong, All-American Boy*, and mild deceits like *Major Bowes' Amateur Hour*, which pretended to save unprofessional blooms from wasting their sweetness on the desert air but in reality exploited lowly professionals at even lowlier rates of pay. Typical of the Allen scripts, most of them written by himself but some with the assistance of a newcomer named Herman Wouk, was one that Allen has enshrined in his *Treadmill to Oblivion*. In a spoof of the way-out theatre that must have been prophetic, producer Dawson Bells is interviewed:

BELLS: To me the theatre is merely a test tube. In it I brew all human emotions.
ALLEN: You are not interested in the audience, Mr. Bells?
BELLS: The audience means nothing. The theatre means nothing. The play means nothing.

ALLEN: Only you.
BELLS: Yes, I mean something: . . . You saw my play *Crash?*
ALLEN: No. I—
BELLS: The curtain goes up. A bass drum is center stage. The drum is a symbol. On the drum is a cymbal. The cymbal is a symbol. The audience ponders. A termite smacks his lips. Curtain! You see the work I am doing.

Radio had for me two other major claims to gratitude. It put Arturo Toscanini on the air, with the understanding that, like the President of the United States, he and his NBC Symphony Orchestra were not to be cut off, no matter how much they ran overtime. And it gave us long winter Saturday afternoons of opera direct from the Metropolitan, with commentary by Deems Taylor between the acts. Fairly enough, the Met was saved from bankruptcy by the contributions of grateful auditors in the living rooms of Steubenville and Omaha when the pampered patrons of its Golden Horseshoe, tired of appeals, were ready to let it vanish into the good old days.

The magazine for would-be insiders, for a few months at least, was *Ken.* Fostered by the owners of *Esquire,* it was conceived as a glamorous cross between the *Nation* and *Life,* combining crusades with pictures, supplanting the butcher paper of liberal journalism with glossy newsprint, and providing crusaders with expense-account living hitherto known only to the servants of Henry Luce and the *Reader's Digest.* Under the editorship of Jay Allen, *Ken* was guaranteed to tell the truth about everything, but plans, as aft, went agley. A good foreign correspondent and a crusader, Allen was thought to be taking his mission too literally and was eased out before the first issue appeared. The story was that advertisers had served notice on the publisher that if *Ken* pursued its avowed policy of taking things apart they could see no reason for cooperating; in fact they might

228]   *Just Around the Corner*

pull advertising out of *Esquire* as well. So, when a short-
story writer allowed one of his characters to take his whis-
key with water, a foul blow at the makers of soda, the word
went out to "lay off the commodities." *Ken* disappeared, but
Esquire, which stuck by its calendar girls for another decade
or so, lived happily ever after.

The fiction most peculiar to the decade was the proletarian novel. At its worst this was a Horatio Alger story gone
astray. The struggling youth discovers, after chapters of oppression, that The Boss—the very one who in *Sink or Swim*
would have told him, "Son, I like the cut of your jib, report
to the factory gate at six"—is a Capitalist Exploiter and
probably a Fascist. The young man organizes the factory,
getting beaten up in the process, leads a successful strike,
and, clenched fist raised aloft, marches off with the Boss's
daughter into the dawn of a classless society.

No proletarian novel was quite as fatuous as that, I suppose, but a number of them came close. Characters were
given to musing in the language of stump speeches. Here is
one, in Leane Zugsmith's *A Time to Remember*, in the act of
thinking to herself: "We've seen the propertied elements of
the city join together in a union to fight us because we belong to a union. . . . The police and the courts and the city
officials are the servants of the Chamber of Commerce and
the Board of Trade. . . . We know that these few weeks of
opposition have cost Diamond's more, with their five-dollar-
a-day guards and their bribes to corrupt public officers, than
it would cost them to meet our wage demands for six
months. There was a time when we would have said it didn't
make sense; but we know the sense of it now." And there is
the man in *Marching! Marching!* who tells a fellow worker
at a meeting: "And now that the bosses and politicians is
running the country like money kings, we got to take it away
from 'em to run it for us people again. We've put kings under

the earth before. We did it in 1776 and we'll damn well do it again!"

Actually not many of these formula operas were turned out. The market wasn't there. Louis Adamic, after intensive traveling and interviewing, concluded that the people about whom, and presumably *for* whom, proletarian literature was written scarcely knew it existed and were therefore profoundly uninfluenced by its message. Most of them read pulp magazines, if anything, and the more literate among them shared the taste of most Americans of the decade for reading that had absolutely nothing to do with the United States of the 1930's. The biggest-selling novels of the decade had to do with some hungry Chinese peasants with warm hearts, flat feet, and strong family feeling (*The Good Earth*), a swashbuckler of a far-off day (*Anthony Adverse*), and the magnolia-scented South of Scarlett O'Hara (*Gone With the Wind*).

The last-named work ran more than a thousand pages and sold almost as many copies as the Bible even in that decade of tight budgets. Nor was it alone in testifying to the attraction of escape literature. Historical novels like *Northwest Passage* and *Drums Along the Mohawk* did extremely well, and the huge success of self-improvement books showed that, depression or no depression, Americans still thought they could get ahead if only they had the right formula. Professor Walter B. Pitkin assured them that, even if they had lost time in the onward and upward march, they need not despair because *Life Begins at Forty*. Dorothea Brande, likewise profitably, told them to *Wake Up and Live*. And, above all, Dale Carnegie advised them *How to Win Friends and Influence People*, thereby financially setting himself up for life.

The books that I thought really did honor to the decade were an entirely different matter. You could hardly open a volume by any of the current masters without knowing that you were about to plunge deeply into contemporary miseries, economic, social, and probably political. Dos Passos' monumental trilogy would take you on a staggering tear through the whole era of disillusionment that culminated in the Thirties, leaving the American success myth in shreds and providing no comfort at all about the foreseeable future. Faulkner, Wolfe, and Caldwell would give you the South in aspects, respectively, of Gothic decay, lyric excitement, and tragicomic degeneracy. Farrell's saga of Studs Lonigan would grind you down in the mean and infinitely depressing jungle of Chicago's Irish poor. Steinbeck's *Grapes of Wrath*, balancing social outrage with human warmth, would win a sympathy beyond the power of New Deal publicists to arouse for the Okies, those displaced farmers whose jalopies, loaded with family woe, were a common sight on the Western roads. Marquand would skillfully strip the hides of Boston's fading Brahmins. And both Lewis and MacLeish would, in their extremely different ways, envision the coming of fascism. It was a good and honest body of work and sent people scurrying for *Gone With the Wind*.

Proletarian literary critics ranged from self-consciously tough spokesmen for horny-handed labor to stern censors of romanticism and pedants who applied Marxist criteria with a micrometer. The great exponent of the roughneck school was Mike Gold, who wrote of the genteel Humanists: "A word like sonovabitch and a good healthy spit in the gutter knocks these men over, but I am sure they would exchange their whole unhealthy stale lives to be able to swear resoundingly and to spit like a man." Edwin Berry Burgum, an exemplar of the no-Nature-nonsense school, rebuked Stephen Spender for writing a couplet about the dawn: "The passive position of watching the dawn is hardly fitting to the revolutionary; nor should the dawn daze like snow those who under self-discipline have known what to expect and are ready for the next move." And a happy sample of the pedant at work was the essay of one A. A. Smirnov, applying Marxism-Leninism to the works of Shakespeare, an early proletarian poet. Iago, Smirnov explained, was "the embodiment of the cynical philistine merchant of the period of primary accumulation," a thought not easily rendered in iambic pentameter. The passionate language of Romeo was an expression of Shakespeare's "struggle against feudalism." And Caliban's gutteral gibberish was intended by the Bard as nothing less than a paean of working-class protest, "a truly revolutionary song."

I can't say I ever heard anybody singing Caliban's song, but a number of presumably non-revolutionary songs of the Thirties were every bit as unintelligible, notably "The Hut Sut Song" and the aforementioned "Flat Foot Floogie." On the other hand lyrics logically born of the Depression were scattered through the decade, ranging from wistfully reflective numbers like "Life Is Just a Bowl of Cherries" and "I've Got My Love to Keep Me Warm" to those that mixed romance and economics—"I Found a Million Dollar Baby in a Five and Ten Cent Store" and "Now's the Time to Fall in Love." The reason for the "now" as Eddie Cantor pointed out, eyes rolling and hands flapping, was that "Potatoes Are Cheaper." And, above all, it was the decade when people sang, or at least listened to, "Brother, Can You Spare a Dime?" a number with which E. Y. Harburg and Jay Gorney brought a sobering note to an otherwise flippant Broadway revue.

To the music of the period, both lovely and lively, people danced steps which I can no more describe now than I could dance then. They included the Suzy-Q, the Big Apple, the Lindy Hop, the Lambeth Walk, and something called trucking, all of which were done by jitterbugs to the strains of big-name swing bands. They meant little to me then, so I will not pretend that they mean much in retrospect. I was the Thirties' equivalent for "square," which is to say I was not "in the groove."

Among the more strenuous personalities of the period was Dorothy Thompson, the equivalent of a troop of tanks in the prewar skirmishing with Adolf Hitler. When a distraught Jewish youth named Grynszpan shot a Nazi Embassy secretary in Paris, her fiery radio broadcasts brought in $30,000 of defense funds in less than a week. But her views were often as eccentric as they were spirited. Somehow she thought Walt Disney's *Fantasia,* an experiment in flowing color patterns set to bits of classical music, was a Nazi propaganda film. She could be downright maudlin about Chancellor Schuschnigg, whose regime, though anti-Nazi, was vaguely Fascist, but she would wind up an onslaught on various New Deal measures with the damning conclusion, "And if this is not fascism, then I am deaf, dumb, and blind."

Introduced on the radio by a swooning admirer as a cross between Harriet Beecher Stowe and Edith Cavell, Miss Thompson felt called upon publicly to explain that the time was not ripe for a woman to run for President. Her husband, Sinclair Lewis, sardonically registered regret on the ground that with his wife in the White House he could at least settle down and write "My Day."

The bland sociology of the First Lady's syndicated column by that name was sometimes awkward and a bit cloying even for those who most admired her, myself for one, and a happy hunting ground for those who admired her not at all. Chief among the latter group was Westbrook Pegler, whose parody of "My Day" was one of his kindlier and certainly one of his more entertaining attentions to the President's wife. It began:

Yesterday morning I took a train to New York City and sat beside a gentleman who was reading the 1937 Report of the International Recording Secretary of the World Home Economics and Children's Aptitude and Recreation Foundation of which my very good friend, Dr. Mary McTwaddle, formerly of Vassar, is the American delegate. This aroused my interest and I ventured to remark that I had once had the pleasure of entertaining a group of young people who were deeply concerned with the neglected problem of the Unmarried Father. It turned out that the gentleman himself was an unmarried father so we had a very interesting chat until he got off at Metuchen.

Had Pegler generally operated at this level of innocent merriment he would not have been one of the demons of the liberal world, but something in his glandular makeup kept whatever joviality he had, even satiric joviality, from getting through a typewriter ribbon except on the rarest occasions. Aside from the cartoon film *Snow White* (Disney's art seemed to have a heightened effect on columnists) nothing pleased him, and for the President himself his supply of vitriol was limitless, the more so perhaps because in the first months of the Administration he had been so uncharacteristically carried away that he wrote, "I am afraid I couldn't be trusted around Mr. Roosevelt. For the first time in my life in this business I might find myself squabbling for a chance to carry the champion's water bucket."

Pegler was a good twenty years atoning for that breach of principle, but it should be said that his hostilities were not much governed by ideology. His damnation of General Franco, alluded to in an earlier chapter, was matched by his attentions to all other dictators. Earlier than most he skewered Mussolini and Hitler, and concerning even the autocracy of Huey P. Long he observed that "They do not permit a house of prostitution to operate within a prescribed distance of the state university, but exempt the state Capitol from the meaning of the act."

But it was for labor unions, and especially the Newspaper Guild, of which he had been a charter member, that Pegler reserved his prime energies. When his old friend and fellow columnist Heywood Broun took the Guild into the newly formed Congress of Industrial Organizations, Pegler, who had been growing steadily more sour on the organizing of newsmen, withdrew and took to a personal skirmishing that got progressively uglier. From taunting Broun as "Old Bleeding Heart" and the "fat mahatma," which his opponent rather relished, he got around to charging him with communism and at last with employing non-union help on the little country paper Broun had started, called the *Connecticut Nutmeg*. The first of these accusations Broun took philosophically. He would wistfully say to his friends, "If people call me a Communist, I say I am not a Communist and they don't believe me because they know that if I *were* a Communist I would say I was *not* a Communist." But the second charge angered him, and relations were permanently embittered.

A formless giant of a man who enjoyed being described as "an unmade bed," Broun was that winning anomaly, an urbane crusader. His graceful prose style inspired young newsmen for a generation, and so did his wit, not to dwell on his prowess in the Thanatopsis Literary and Inside Straight Club. After leaving the old New York *World* in a row over the Sacco-Vanzetti case, he moved restlessly from post to post in a search for what he never quite defined. He went to the Scripps-Howard *Telegram,* he ran for Congress on the Socialist ticket, and he wrote, produced, and ponderously acted in a review called *Shoot the Works,* designed to provide work for stranded actors. Even on the *Nation,* which editorially saw eye to eye with him, he found no lasting satisfaction. When its owner, Maurice Wertheim, and its former editor, Oswald Garrison Villard, were reasonably al-

lowed space to dissent from the magazine's views on reform-
ing the Supreme Court, Broun naïvely declared himself "a
little sick of the *Nation's* policy of fair play" and left for
other pastures.

The best of these pastures by far was the Guild, which was
desperately needed in those years when even reporters with
twenty years' experience averaged $38 a week. But intel-
lectual and Bohemian that he was, Broun was something of
a freak even in the higher reaches of trade-union bureaucracy. What could a hard-bitten agent of the Bricklayers
think, after all, of a union president who sat up all night in
day coaches as a mark of working-class solidarity until it was
borne in on him at last that even Earl Browder took a com-
partment? But this very mixture of naïveté and sophistica-
tion was the essence of Broun's charm, and when he died, at
fifty-one, a recent and surprising convert to the Roman
Catholic Church, the funeral was a forerunner of the
ecumenical movement. St. Patrick's Cathedral held more
grieving Protestants, Jews, and agnostics under its roof on
that occasion than had ever gathered there before or have
since.

Broun's brief, though massive, invasion of the theatre in
Shoot the Works was not the decade's most notable case of
amateur stage fever. That distinction went, improbably, to
the International Ladies' Garment Workers Union, whose
cutters, pressers, and sewing-machine operators came out
of the shops to put on *Pins and Needles*. Intended merely
as a weekend activity—part of the cultural program provided by the ILGWU—Harold Rome's saucy revue, mock-
ing everything including the union itself, was destined
to run for four years, to play on Broadway, and to have a
command performance at the White House for President
Roosevelt. One of the songs, "Sunday in the Park," made the
Hit Parade, but more characteristic was the one that went:

> Sing me a song with social significance
> All other tunes are taboo . . .
>
> It must be packed with social fact
> Or I won't—love—you.*

Other gems whose titles conveyed the impishness of the production were "Doing the Reactionary," "One Big Union for Two," and "It's Better with a Union Man" ("So always be upon your guard/ Demand to see a union card"). But brilliant as the lyrics were and bright as the music was, the joy of *Pins and Needles* was the freshness of a labor movement that could take struggle in its stride and itself without pompousness.

What was regarded as class-conscious theatre was unhappily more pretentious, but at its best it brought a new and raw vitality to a stage that badly needed the injection. If you were too serious or too poor to patronize what remained of Gay Broadway, you frequented one of the little group theatres, where the cry for a better life resounded and the price was delightfully low. People who regularly attended trade-union meetings may not have been too excited by plays like *Stevedore* and Clifford Odets's famous *Waiting for Lefty*, but for frustrated revolutionaries doing well as accountants and for well-padded ladies of advanced social thought it was a vicarious thrill. Often as not, the cast burst into action from seats located around the auditorium, and the most impeccable-looking burghers, carried along on a surge of working-class rhetoric, would applaud like crazy when the climactic strike vote was taken.

What people of my financial resources saw on Broadway itself in the early years of the decade depended largely on what tickets were available at Joe Leblang's cut-rate counter in the basement of Gray's Drug Store on Forty-third Street. Top-balcony seats regularly priced at $1.10 were to be had

---

* Copyright © 1937 by Mills Music, Inc. Copyright renewed, Florence Music Company, Inc., owner of publication and allied rights for the United States and Canada.

on that bourse for 55 cents, though generally not until a few minutes before curtain time. Naturally the most successful shows rarely turned up on the board at this bargain rate until near the end of a run, and one had to have time to lie in wait for these coups. But I would not have done badly even if I had seen only those Kaufman-Hart triumphs, *You Can't Take It with You, Once in a Lifetime,* and *The Man Who Came to Dinner.* Since, on the socially conscious side, I also saw most of the works of Lillian Hellman, Sidney Kingsley, and Clifford Odets (who in due course penetrated to Broadway), and less enthusiastically the overwrought productions of Maxwell Anderson, I did very well indeed. Add to this that I saw Gershwin's two great gifts to the decade, *Porgy and Bess* and *Of Thee I Sing,* and it is evident that the best of Broadway could still be enjoyed by modest income earners, especially if travel from exurbia, baby sitters, and other such middle-class, middle-age drains still lay in the future.

The difference between $1.10 and 55 cents may seem trifling to such teen-age readers as I may have, who think nothing of spending $1.75 for a neighborhood movie, but it would buy quite a bit in the Thirties. For a half-dollar you could ride to and from work on the subway for an entire week, or get a month's newspapers, not counting Sundays, or make ten telephone calls, or buy ten chocolate bars, with or without almonds. Or you could get a satisfying, if inelegant, dinner, in a respectable restaurant, including soup and dessert.* Or, if you were a housewife, you could get three pounds of the best round steak. On the other hand, you didn't get too many half-dollars in your pay envelope. A skilled worker was lucky to draw $35 a week, and a grade-

---

* A few eating places, trading on the well-known excess of greed over capacity, would offer "All You Can Eat for Three Dollars," the price of a good five meals. At the other extreme, MacFadden soup kitchens for the hard-pressed but not quite down and out offered lunch for seven cents.

school teacher who gets $6,000 today would have been for-
tunate to make as much as $1,500.

Movies were cheap, rarely more than thirty cents in the
neighborhood theatres even at the end of the decade, and
the fare they offered, from *The Little Colonel* to *Jezebel*—
which is to say, from Shirley Temple to Bette Davis—has
been the subject of large, learned, and lushly illustrated volumes. In the circumstances I feel it is enough merely to note
the sort of film that automatically caused me to say, "Let's
go to the Rio tonight. They've got So-and-So." My So-and-
So's included:

Any picture directed by Alfred Hitchcock. In all his films,
from *The 39 Steps* to *The Lady Vanishes*, this fresh genius
would employ a particular trick, some recurring visual or
sound effect, to heighten the sinister mood—a missing finger,
a twitching eye, a few bars of music—and the game was to
spot the device early in the show.

Any picture directed by René Clair, whose three great
comedies—*Sous Les Toits de Paris, Le Million,* and *A Nous
La Liberté*—taught American film makers how to make
sound yield maximum comedy with minimum conversation.
Won over by Clair, I was likewise responsive to those other
and very different French greats, *Carnival in Flanders, The
Grand Illusion,* and *The Baker's Wife.*

The new documentaries just then coming into vogue, like
Man of Aran, Robert Flaherty's beautiful study of life on a
bleak Irish island; *Spanish Earth,* required viewing for all
good anti-Fascists; and Pare Lorentz's love-songs to America, *The River* and *The Plow That Broke the Plains.* "What
poetry!" said James Joyce of *The River*—"the epic of this
century!"

Films that I could happily see over again—*The Informer,*
the *Thin Man* series, featuring those urbanely married de-
tectives, William Powell and Myrna Loy; Molnár's *The*

Good Fairy, with the enchanting Margaret Sullavan and Frank Morgan; and those Capra-directed gems, *It Happened One Night, Mr. Deeds Goes to Town,* and *Lady for a Day.*
Just about anything with Leslie Howard, Spencer Tracy, James Stewart, Claudette Colbert, Carole Lombard, Jean Arthur, and Fred Astaire.*
Finally, in a class by themselves, were the Marx Brothers and W. C. Fields. What the Depression had left standing of the Establishment was hilariously wrecked, to the general pleasure of the country, by the combination of the glib and fraudulent Groucho, forever on the prowl for shortcuts to the easy life; the ingratiating Chico, bent on less ambitious but more immediate larceny; and Harpo, whose pristine innocence prevailed even in the act of chasing blondes through the halls and shrubbery of great estates. For it was part of the charm of these fantasies that the three happy delinquents were always to be found, as a matter of course, at the core of society. On a university campus Groucho is president, football player, and, along with Chico the Bootlegger and Harpo the Iceman, a joint pursuer of Connie the College Widow. At a fashionable Long Island estate he is guest of honor as Captain Spalding, the African explorer ("Did someone call me *Schnorrer?*"). And in the royal palace of Fredonia he is Dictator Rufus T. Firefly, as cynical as any of his contemporary dictators without being in the least sinister. And in all their pictures the action revolves around Margaret Dumont, a lady of aristocratic bearing and Junoesque build who plays their foil with mountainous dignity and an indulgence half shocked and half amused.
Like the Marxes, Fields may have served the function of puncturing a society that needed puncturing, but he was a very different order of being. He seemed one with all the characters he played, which was not hard because they were

* To the reader: Of course I have had to omit some names in these little listings. Naturally they were the best ones, and I am sorry.

all the same. You couldn't quite distinguish between the Otis J. Cribblecoblis or Larson E. Whipsnade (who managed Whipsnade's Circus Giganticus) and the W. C. Fields who was in real life a suspicious and misanthropic man, making only the most spurious concessions to the demands of society. Like Groucho's, his stratagems were transparent. "I'm going to give you my personal IOU," he would drawl to a hard-bitten gambler who had just caught him cheating, "a thing I seldom do for strangers." And when he raised his hand threateningly to Baby LeRoy in a picture and muttered, "Don't tell *me* I don't love you," one suspected that he really entertained the thought of taking a poke at the infant scene stealer. As it turned out, one was right. According to his biographer, Fields actually slipped gin into the "little nipper's" orange juice, and when production had to be held up he was heard to mutter, "Walk him around. He's no trouper. The kid's no trouper. Send him home." All the same, Fields was a giant of a comedian, and his gravelly, inflated pomposities on the screen must have helped a little to deflate the more harmful pomposities of the world.

Possibly the two most theatrical people in the United States of the Thirties were on neither stage nor screen. One was Mayor of New York City and the other was president of the C.I.O.

To many Americans John L. Lewis was Lenin and Robespierre; to many more he was Moses and Charlemagne; but to the political cartoonists of the country he was bread and butter. For half a decade it was hard to pick up the New York *Times* weekend review or a copy of *Current History* without seeing three or four caricatures of the barrel-chested man with the overhanging eyebrows, heavy jowls, and protruding jaw. In a more flattering light the same features appeared on the walls of thousands of trade unionists' homes in competition with F.D.R. and calendar prints of "The Last Supper."

But to get the flavor of John L. Lewis one had to hear him and see him in action. Loving the feel of old rhythms on his Welsh tongue, he reveled in words like "methinks" and phrases like "high wassail will prevail at the banquet tables of the mighty." Enjoying a fight, he once exulted, "They are smiting me hip and thigh, and right merrily I shall return their blows." I heard him launch a speech to an audience of crusty trade union men with the almost whispered phrase, "Twenty-five years ago, come the flowers of spring. . . ." And when he called an ex-saloonkeeper a "damnéd publican" I have no doubt he was taken aback when the man pleaded, "Why, John, I thought you were a Republican yourself."

Like an old-time actor, cooing and thundering by turn, he was capable of hamming even his great moments, and he had a number of them. When he thought Governor Frank Murphy of Michigan might yield to pressure and drive sit-down strikers from the General Motors plant, he sent word: "Tomorrow morning, I shall personally enter G.M. Plant Chevrolet No. 4. I shall order the men to disregard your order and to stand fast. I shall then walk up to the largest window in the plant, open it, divest myself of my outer raiment, remove my shirt, and bare my bosom. Then, when you order your troops to fire, mine will be the first breast that those bullets will strike."

He might well have done it, too, because his physical courage was up to it. At the American Federation of Labor convention that rejected his plea for industrial unionism, Big Bill Hutcheson made the mistake of impugning his ancestry. Though somewhat bulkier even than Lewis, the president of the carpenters' union was thereupon knocked off his feet, an honor he shared with a tunnel mule that many years earlier had similarly attempted to do injury to Mr. Lewis.

The mine leader could be discreet, too, but he had a strange idea of discretion. He demonstrated it once in an encounter before the National Labor Relations Board with former Secretary of War Patrick J. Hurley, once a miner

himself but on this occasion counsel for the mine owners. "It
is a source of pride to the United Mine Workers when one of
its sons carves for himself a place in the nation," Lewis
began. "But it is a matter of regret and shame when one of
our number betrays his brothers—for thirty pieces of silver."
Allowing time for theatrical effect but not quite enough time
for the enraged Hurley to get down the aisle, he corrected
the stenographer: ". . . 'betrays his brothers'—strike out
'thirty pieces of silver.'"

Tragically, it was Lewis's vanity that cost him his great
power in the labor movement only a year or so after the
Thirties were past. Rashly staking his future on a Willkie
victory, after falling out with Roosevelt, he promised over a
national radio hookup to step down from the leadership of
the C.I.O. if the President was re-elected. When Roosevelt
won, he was certain the proffered abdication would be lov-
ingly rejected, but it was not, and he was through. He had
given organized labor the greatest push, by far, that it had
ever had, even from Sam Gompers, bringing in as many new
union members in three years as the old American Federation of Labor had signed up in forty—and along far more
effective lines. But now the time had come to consolidate
gains, and old Blood and Thunder was allowed to step out of
the limelight. He had obviously enjoyed it and taken it as his
due. Straightening up after tying a shoelace on one occasion,
he noticed the small crowd that had gathered on the sidewalk to watch the operation. "Even the posterior of a great
man is of interest," he observed grandly.

Fiorello H. La Guardia was as appropriate a mayor for
New York in the Thirties as James J. Walker was in the
Twenties. The difference between them was the difference
between the decades. To a naïve lady impressed with the
labors of the mayorality, Jimmy had shamelessly quipped,
"Ah, yes, you can often see the lights burning in my office

long after I'm gone for the day." But for Fiorello, the Little Flower, the business of New York was a full-time twelve-year stint with no thought for anything else.

He was the pet of news photographers because on any given day they were likely to catch him at a fire, his squat and portly figure rigged out in rubber coat and helmet, or sitting as a magistrate in a West Side court so he could hold a couple of "tinhorn gamblers" for Special Sessions, or personally applying a sledgehammer to some confiscated slot machines. An excellent cook himself, he was likely at any time to pop in on the kitchen of a city institution to check up on the performance of the chefs. And woe to the municipal servant, whether clerk, police lieutenant or commissioner, who failed to acquit himself on these surprise visits with courtesy, efficiency, and dispatch.

La Guardia's loyalty to the Republican Party was tenuous, and to the Republican machine in New York, nonexistent. "I stand for the Republicanism of Abraham Lincoln," he once explained, "and let me tell you now that the average Republican leader east of the Mississippi doesn't know any more about Abraham Lincoln than Henry Ford knows about the Talmud." His own political tradition, incongruously, was Western. Though born in a New York tenement, he had spent his boyhood in the Arizona Territory, where Army Bandmaster Achille La Guardia served as chief musician at Whipple Barracks. Accordingly, the politics he drank in as a youth was that of the Populist West, of Borah, Johnson, Brookhart, and La Follette, known to the party's Eastern Tories as "Sons of the Wild Jackass."

The difference disposed him against the claims of local Republican leaders to patronage, but he had small inclination to give them any to begin with. "My first qualification for this great office," he announced, "is my monumental personal ingratitude." And he proved it by ignoring the "punks" and "clubhouse loafers" entirely, to bring in an array of talent and integrity such as few municipal governments have ever enjoyed—Adolf Berle, Robert Moses, Rexford G. Tugwell, Paul Blanshard, and Langdon Post, to name a few.

Petulant, melodramatic, and flamboyant, the Little Flower was everything that the easygoing Walker was not, and yet Beau James, always a generous man, was one day to concede that La Guardia was the best mayor the city had ever had. And that shrewd judge of government, Huey P. Long, agreed. New York was "the best blankety-blank governed city in the country," he said. "The port here is the best managed port there is, the traffic system is wonderful, and the waterworks system is the goddam marvel of the world." Fiorello was one of his favorite figures in public life, he added, but "I'd rather vote for him for President than for Mayor."

No doubt New Yorkers enjoyed the constant show put on by the roly-poly man under the black, broad-brimmed Western hat, but they knew as well as Walker and Long that there was much more going on than a show. If His Honor had trumpets blown to mark the closing of a racketeers' market in artichokes, he was only calling attention to his continued war on the "punks." If he read the comics over the radio (they came across rather badly, I thought, in the Mayor's high squeaky voice), he did it to demonstrate his awareness that a newspaper strike left a real gap in the daily life of the city. And if he alternated between calling his subordinates "Son" and "Son" plus a few other words, as he did; if he tended to fire people in the afternoon and demand their presence the next morning, he was constantly and consciously attempting to raise their standards of performance. "When I get excited and blow off like that," he explained to John Gunther with a wink, "it was all planned two days ago."

This was not always true, of course. He had more than his share of crotchets. Organ grinders had to disappear from the streets of New York because he thought their calling an offense to Italian dignity. He exploded periodically about references in the press to his physical stature, although I saw him once walk over to an unknown bystander of even lower altitude, pat him on the shoulder, and greet him patronizingly as "Shorty." And he was an implacable feudist, especially with reporters.

But he did the city an enormous amount of good and was as entertaining in his own way as Jimmy Walker had ever been. Perhaps the best story, told by his friend Ernest Cuneo, concerns the planning for his appearance at Carnegie Hall to conduct the combined bands of the Police and Sanitation departments. At City Hall for final instructions on the great day, the nervous stage manager asked the Mayor whether he wanted a spotlight played on him as he came down the aisle and up to the podium. "Hell, no!" said Fiorello. "Just treat me like Toscanini!"

Many big news stories of the Thirties have gone unmentioned in these pages—the wreck of the *Morro Castle* off Asbury Park, the explosion of the airship *Hindenburg* at Lakeview, and the tragic kidnap murder of the Lindbergh child, to name a few, strangely all in New Jersey. Memorable stories, of course, and so was the abdication of the King of England for the sake of a woman from Baltimore. But the test for inclusion here has been the extent to which an event may have colored or reflected the Thirties, and these did not do much of either, sensational as they were. But the same cannot be said of our final order of business, the fancied invasion from Mars.

Only a month had gone by since the Munich war scare had been brought into every living room by the taut, staccato voices of radio newsmen, a new and strenuous experience for people not used to such intimate involvement in global business. Now it was October 30, 1938—Halloween, practically—and here were those voices again, worried and breathlessly controlled. The CBS program had begun routinely with an announcement that listeners were about to hear a radio version of *The War of the Worlds*, a science-fiction fantasy by H. G. Wells.

The first ten minutes or so of the show were innocent, even dull, with Orson Welles, producer, director, and star, setting the stage with a quiet program of dance music interspersed with weather and "news" bulletins. The first of these flashes concerned a report of repeated explosions on the planet Mars, sighted by a Chicago observatory. Then, after more music by Ramon Raquello and his orchestra, came word of a meteorite landing in the disaster-prone state of New Jersey. Police rushed to the site, the report continued, and, in the glare of their headlights, a long cylinder opened, revealing the leathery tentacles of—Martians! The pace of the program quickened, and the audience increased. Many dial switchers, diverted from the Edgar Bergen show by a commercial, were stupefied, supposing they were hearing straight news.

By the time word came in of lethal rays and a pitched battle between Martians and militia, something close to national hysteria had set in. Telephone calls poured into police stations and newspaper offices. People rushed into the streets with wet cloths over their faces. Bus terminals were crowded with frightened New Yorkers trying to escape creatures as tall as skyscrapers (they must have expanded since leaving the cylinder) who were said to be wading across the Hudson. Riverside Drive was jammed with cars headed north, and elsewhere in the country, as far from New Jersey as Texas and California, stricken Americans were calling their friends and relatives to say farewell. The world was coming to an end. They had just heard it on the radio.

By the time the program was over and terror had given way to routine announcements and commercials, angry police were swarming into the CBS studios and now Orson Welles was as frightened as anyone in the country. What with the first exaggerated reports of suicides and panic, he had good reason.

But what of the millions who had been terrified by what they had not seen? Surely they might have stopped to wonder why the end of the world should be coming to them by courtesy of one network while the competition had to make do with Charlie McCarthy. They might have wondered how so much could be happening in so little time—the deployment of troops, the setting-up of news coverage, and the reactions of the authorities—all in a matter of minutes. The Martians' flying time, too, would have equaled the speed of light, and much else in the show required not merely suspension of logic, but a ready and sizable capacity for hysteria, waiting only to be tapped. The country had rarely looked more jittery—even when it was fighting off historic plagues of witches and Bolsheviks.

And yet it was a short-lived hysteria and harmless compared with the sort then prevailing among certain other peoples of the planet. Sociologists quickly worked up theories to account for the episode, which admittedly was fit for inclusion in *Extraordinary Popular Delusions and the Madness of Crowds*. But I think it may have been no more than an immunization provided by the kindly Fates who watch over the Republic. After leather-headed Martians, creatures like Hitler, Mussolini, and Tojo would seem less formidable. Not more attractive, mind you, but less irresistible than we had been led to think they were by those other Halloween broadcasters who called their program "The Wave of the Future."

Afterword—with Thanks

Except for short intermittent stretches I have regrettably lacked the prudence or will, or perhaps just plain good sense, to keep a journal. For the kind of book I have written, such a document would have simplified matters greatly because my memory, while serviceable, is not quite what is thought of as total recall—thirty percent recall would be closer to it. I do not regret this fact, for there is a limit to how much of the past one can carry around with him and not be a trial to all who know him. Moreover, there is such a thing as selectivity. I would regard anyone with close to a perfect memory as a man in need of editing. Nevertheless, without either such a memory or a journal, one has to fall back on the aid of others, and, having done so, I wish to acknowledge their help.

Luckily much of what went on in the Thirties was grist for the periodical mills I worked for, and quite a lot of grist either came across my editorial desk or was ground up in my own typewriter. The resulting articles have not only served as a contemporary source of information on the Thirties but, recalling to me the circumstances in which they were written, have stimulated me much as a private journal might have done. In particular I am delighted to have saved three large bound volumes of the *World Tomorrow*, now long extinct. Each time we have moved in these past thirty years my wife has urged me to sort through all this space-consuming stuff and get rid of the excess tonnage, a Herculean assignment. I am glad now to acknowledge the sloth that happily kept me from doing it. My unsolicited advice to young writers is: Don't throw anything away. If it is not always history, it may at least yield good copy.

Besides the *World Tomorrow*, periodical files that have been of great help to me are those of the *Nation*, for the reasons just suggested, and the New York *Times*, without which works of a historical nature are unthinkable and possibly illegal. Volumes of *Current History*, while far from sprightly reading, were extremely useful sources of fact. *Harper's* articles afforded thoughtful perspectives, especially Lillian Symes's piece "Blunder on the Left" in the issue of December, 1933, and Irving Kolodin's "The Government and the Arts" in that of October, 1943. On the subject of the WPA arts projects I found "Unemployed Arts" in *Fortune* for May, 1937, similarly illuminating. I am indebted to *Life*, *Time*, *Newsweek*, and the *New Yorker* for helpful, and usually colorful, bits of information, especially on the Depression and on the Presidential campaign of 1936.

Although this work reflects the Thirties as seen from my particular points of vantage, it was not my purpose to produce a personal chronicle. I have had to fortify and expand my recollections, accordingly, by consulting in addition to original sources, the works of those who have preceded me in writing of the decade. For guidance along political and social lines, I am grateful for the first three volumes of Arthur Schlesinger, Jr.'s magnificent *The Age of Roosevelt* and for *America in Midpassage* by Charles and Mary Beard. I have also enjoyed and profited from readings in Louis Adamic, *My America;* James MacGregor Burns, *Roosevelt: The Lion and the Fox;* William E. Leuchtenberg, *Franklin D. Roosevelt and the New Deal, 1932-1940;* Richard Hofstadter, *American Political Tradition;* George Seldes,

Lords of the Press; Marquis Childs, *I Write from Washington;* Robert Sherwood, *Roosevelt and Hopkins;* Harold Ickes, *The Secret Diary; The First Thousand Days;* James A. Wechsler, *The Age of Suspicion;* Eugene Lyons, *The Red Decade;* Irving Howe and Lewis Coser, *The American Communist Party;* Edmund Wilson, *The American Earthquake;* William Allen White, *Autobiography;* and John Roy Carlson, *Under Cover.*

On matters more literary, I have dipped into Daniel Aaron's *Writers on the Left, The American Writers' Congress,* edited by Henry Hart, *The Radical Novel in the United States,* by Walter B. Rideout, again the Beards' *America in Midpassage,* Robert B. Cantwell's excellent article "America and the Writers' Project" in the *New Republic* of April 28, 1939; and, above all, the WPA Guides themselves, especially those for Maine, Massachusetts, Louisiana, and Missouri.

My memories of the movies were happily jogged by Arthur Knight's *The Liveliest Art* and Richard Schickel's *The Stars,* and I offer a special word of gratitude for Hallie Flanagan's *Arena,* without which nobody can write about the WPA Theatre Project. *Drama and Commitment* by Gerald Rabkin and Burns Mantle's *Best Plays* for the years I covered were especially good and useful.

I owe thanks for special light on the demagogues of Chapter V to Raymond Gram Swing's *Forerunners of American Fascism* and Abraham Holzman's *The Townsend Movement;* on William Randolph Hearst to W. A. Swanberg's fine biography; and on Dorothy Thompson and Westbrook Pegler to Charles Fisher's *The Columnists* and Margaret Marshall's series on the columnists in the *Nation* (1938). Not least, I am happy to mention, and recommend, those fine all-purpose roundups on the Thirties: Frederick Lewis Allen, *Since Yesterday;* Dixon Wecter, *The Age of the Great Depression;* Isabel Leighton, *The Aspirin Age;* and *The*

'30s, a very good anthology edited by Don Congdon.

To all these sources I acknowledge indebtedness and appreciation. My thanks go, too, to the Houghton Library in Cambridge, Massachusetts, where the Nation's correspondence, including my own, has been given space and where I was given courteous attention, and to the New York Society Library, which I have found extremely useful and efficient. For invaluable help in the picture research for this book my thanks are due to the New York Public Library, the Lincoln Center Library for the Performing Arts, the Museum of Modern Art, the Granger Collection, the Bettman Archives, the American Jewish Committee, and Barbara Kaplan, of Harper & Row, whose patient explorations gave me so wide a choice. To my editor, Jeannette Hopkins, go my profound thanks, and to my Wife Kas, a special word of gratefulness, not merely for typing services, editorial suggestions, and an extra degree of patience, but, more important than any of these, for shared recollections.

Some Characteristic Events of the Thirties

1930

May 1. President Hoover is convinced, as he will be repeatedly, that "we have now passed the worst" of the Depression.

August 6. Joseph Force Crater, a justice of the New York Supreme Court, takes a taxi from West Fifty-fourth Street to total oblivion.

September 2. French airmen Coste and Bellonte make first and only nonstop flight from Paris to Valley Stream, Long Island, in 37 hours, 18½ minutes.

November 4. Franklin D. Roosevelt is re-elected governor of New York by such a margin that James A. Farley thinks he can't "escape becoming the next Presidential nominee of his party," to which the Governor replies: "Whatever you said, Jim, is all right with me."

December 26. Roger W. Babson, economist, locates the Depression's silver lining: "In 1929 we were living in a palace with a powder mine in the cellar. In 1931 we may feel sure that we are living in a poor house with a gold mine in the cellar."

1931

January 19. Wickersham Commission on Law Observance and Enforcement reports that Prohibition is not working. Bootleggers working overtime.

March 15. "These really are good times," says Henry Ford, "but only a few know it."

May 1. Empire State Building, tallest in the world, completed, a consolation prize to Alfred E. Smith for not being President.

September 13. Rudy Vallee introduces a song of comfort—"Life Is Just a Bowl of Cherries."

September 18. Japan formally opens a decade of treaty-breaking by occupying the city of Mukden in Manchuria.

December 7.   President Hoover declines to see the first "hunger marchers," come to Washington to demand jobs.

1932

January 28.   With Manchuria turned into the puppet state of Manchukuo, Japanese attack China proper at Shanghai, drawing from the West a resounding moral rebuke but no ban on business.

March 29.   Jack Benny moves from vaudeville to radio by way of a program presided over by one Ed Sullivan.

May 4.   Outraged by racketeering and murder, society jails Al Capone—for cheating on his income tax.

June 16.   Republican Convention renominates Herbert Hoover, but not hopefully.

July 1.   Democratic Convention nominates Franklin D. Roosevelt, described by H. L. Mencken as "the weakest candidate before it."

July 28.   General Douglas MacArthur, aided by General George Patton and Major Dwight Eisenhower, routs an unarmed "bonus army" of jobless veterans from a squatters' encampment near the Capitol. "Thank God," says President Hoover, "we still have a government that knows how to deal with a mob."

September 1. Under pressure from Governor Roosevelt, Jimmy Walker resigns as the playboy mayor of New York.

November 8.   The "weakest candidate" gets 22.8 million votes to his opponent's 15.7 million.

1933

January 4.   Farmers in Iowa warn that further attempts to foreclose on mortgages will be discouraged by lynching.

January 30.   Having assured his Army command that he had no thought of entrusting Germany to "that Austrian corporal," President Hindenburg entrusts Germany to that Austrian corporal.

February 15. A jobless anarchist, shouting, "Too many people are starving to death," shoots at President-elect Roosevelt, missing him entirely but killing the mayor of Chicago.

February 28. A Hitler decree forbids all criticism of himself.

March 4.   Franklin D. Roosevelt takes the first of four oaths.

March 27.   Condemned as aggressor for its Manchurian activities, Japan walks out of the League as an example to others.

May 18.   F.D.R. signs legislation which shocks utilities companies and delights the people of the Tennessee Valley.

May 27.   World's Fair, featuring nude fan dance by Sally Rand, celebrates "A Century of Progress" at Chicago.

June 16.   F.D.R. signs National Industrial Recovery Act as the "most important and far-reaching legislation ever enacted by the American Congress."

November 11.   A "black blizzard" sweeps over South Dakota, the first of duststorms that will blow away forty million acres of good soil and darken the sky from Texas to Canada.

November 16.   Roosevelt Administration recognizes the U.S.S.R. after Russians agree not to foment revolution in the U.S.

December 6.   Americans buy their first *legal* hard drinks in thirteen years.

1934

January 10.   Nazis chop off the head of Marinus van der Lubbe on charge of setting fire to the Reichstag, a crime later reliably attributed to Hermann Goering.

January 30.   Roosevelt takes U.S. off gold standard, to eternal dismay of fiscal conservatives.

May 28.   A French Canadian woman gives birth to five girls, bringing 3,000 visitors a day to Callander, Ontario.

July 22.   Twenty-seven FBI men ambush John Dillinger, "Public Enemy Number One," as he leaves a Chicago movie house.

July 25.   Nazi thugs murder Austrian Chancellor Dollfuss in attempt to take over country ahead of schedule.

August 2.   Hitler uses Hindenburg's death, otherwise hardly noticeable, to merge offices of President and Chancellor into that of Reichsführer.

August 7.   U.S. Court of Appeals upholds District Judge John M. Woolsey's finding that James Joyce's *Ulysses* will not endanger American morality.

September 8.   *Morro Castle* burns off Asbury Park, N.J., attracting morbid tourists.

1935

March 16.　　　Hitler restores universal military service, violating the Versailles Treaty and creating a new national holiday.

April (exact date unknown). Harvard student swallows live goldfish on a bet, starting campus fad.

June 15.　　　Babe Ruth is through as ballplayer, released by the Boston Braves, of all people.

July 5.　　　F.D.R. signs National Labor Relations Act, a green light for the greatest organizing drive in labor history.

September 10. Huey Long dies, shot two days before by a young Baton Rouge doctor.

November 9.　Rebelling against the narrow craft basis of the A.F. of L., a caucus of union chiefs headed by John L. Lewis plans the organizing committee that will become the C.I.O.

1936

March 7.　　　Hitler's army goosesteps into demilitarized Rhineland, meeting no more than a French diplomatic rebuke.

May 6.　　　Mussolini takes all of Ethiopia except Emperor Haile Selassie, who gets away on a British cruiser.

July 1.　　　Churchmen, including Pastor Niemoeller, go to prison for questioning infallibility of the Führer.

July 17.　　　Spanish army officers launch rebellion against republican government in Madrid, providing fascist dictators with a practice run for World War II.

August 2.　　America's Jesse Owens outruns fleetest track stars of "Master Race" at Berlin Olympics.

December 11. Edward VIII decides that even a British king may aspire to happiness.

December 17. A piece of wood makes its debut on network radio, bringing fame and fortune to its owner, Edgar Bergen.

1937

February 3.　In the C.I.O.'s first big triumph, General Motors officials agree to sit down with United Auto Workers, who had been sitting down by themselves in company plants for more than a month.

April 27.   First Social Security checks are sent out and promptly cashed.

May 6.   German dirigible *Hindenburg* explodes as it approaches mooring mast at Lakehurst, N.J., sending its passengers to a fiery death in midair.

June 2.   Soviet Marshal Tukhachevsky shot for allegedly conspiring with the Germans two years before Marshal Stalin does the same thing.

June 22.   Joe Louis becomes heavyweight boxing champion by knocking out Jim Braddock in the eighth round.

July 2.   Amelia Earhart and her co-pilot disappear over the Pacific, believed many years later to have been the first victims of Japan's war against the U.S.

July 22.   F.D.R. suffers his first major defeat in Congress as Senate rejects his plan for rejuvenating the Supreme Court by vote of 70 to 21.

1938

January 1.   "Swing" fanatics go berserk at New York jam session by Benny Goodman's band.

March 13.   For not having recognized his talents as a youth, Hitler avenges himself on his native Austria by incorporating it into the Third Reich.

June 25.   F.D.R. signs the first minimum wage law, making it illegal to pay people less than twenty-five cents an hour.

September 21. Hurricane on Eastern seaboard kills some six hundred people and hits Providence, R.I., with a tidal wave.

September 30. Chamberlain and Daladier make Hitler a gift of Czechoslovakia, receiving only promises in return.

1939

March 29.   With Madrid and Barcelona lost, Loyalists yield Spain to the Fascists.

April 9.   Barred by the Daughters of the American Revolution from singing at their Constitution Hall, Marian Anderson performs instead at the Lincoln Memorial before New Deal elite.

April 30.   The "World of Tomorrow" goes on display in Flushing Meadows.

June 7.   George VI becomes first reigning British monarch to set foot on U.S. soil, warmly received by escaped subjects.

June 28.   Pan-American Airways' Dixie Clipper inaugurates
                  regular passenger transatlantic air service, linking
                  Long Island and Portugal.
August 2.   Albert Einstein warns President Roosevelt that Nazi
                  scientists are working on a nuclear bomb.
August 24.   Russia and Germany sign a friendly agreement.
September 1.   World War II.

Index